D0142204

3 0473 00150823 C

DA
155
C38
1998

Carver, Martin
Sutton Hoo

112332

DATE DUE	FEB 13 2001		

LEARNING RESOURCES CENTER
MONTGOMERY COUNTY COMMUNITY COLLEGE
BLUE BELL, PENNSYLVANIA

GAYLORD M2

SUTTON HOO: Burial Ground of Kings?

The ancient burial ground at Sutton Hoo, Suffolk, with the River Deben and Melton in the background. The white house, right, belonged to Edith Pretty when she began excavations in 1938. Next to the wood, in the kink of the track, is the site of the Mound 1 ship-burial. Excavations of the most recent campaign can be seen in progress in the field to the right. Nigel Macbeth.

Martin Carver

SUTTON HOO
BURIAL GROUND OF KINGS?

PENN

University of Pennsylvania Press
Philadelphia

This book was written for my father and mother, John and Jocelyn Carver

© M. O. H. Carver 1998. All rights reserved

First published in the United Kingdom 1998 by
British Museum Press

First published in the United States of America 1998 by
University of Pennsylvania Press
4200 Pine Street
Philadelphia, Pennsylvania 19104

Library of Congress Cataloging-in-Publication Data

Carver, M. O. H.
     Sutton Hoo: burial ground of kings? / Martin Carver.
          p.   cm.
     Includes bibliographical references and index.
     ISBN 0-8122-3455-3 (cloth: alk. paper)
     1. Sutton Hoo Ship Burial (England)   2. East Anglia (England)–
Kings and rulers–Death and burial.   3. Anglo-Saxons–Kings and
rulers–Death and burial.   4. Excavations (Archaeology)–England–
Suffolk.   5. Ships, Medieval–England–Suffolk.   6. Suffolk
(England)–Antiquities.   7. Anglo-Saxons–England–Suffolk.   8. Ship
burial–England–Suffolk.   I. Title
DA155.C38   1998
936.2'646–dc21   98-16434
                                                    CIP

Designed and typeset by Jeffery Design
Printed in Great Britain by Butler & Tanner

112332

CONTENTS

ACKNOWLEDGEMENTS

The most recent project was financed and managed through the Sutton Hoo Research Trust, formed by a treaty between the Society of Antiquaries of London and the British Museum, who later invited a delegate from the Suffolk Archaeological Unit to take a seat on the Executive Committee. Its members (see below) were unfailing in their support and encouragement. The Sutton Hoo Research Trust was reinforced by a non-executive Sutton Hoo Research Committee, which brought advice from a number of quarters of the academic sector, and by the essential offices of John Knight our honorary solicitor and Martin Burchmore our auditor. Independently formed to receive and guide visitors to the site was the Sutton Hoo Society, which the Duke of Edinburgh agreed to serve as president, paying an official visit to the excavations in 1987. The Society was a generous supporter of the campaign.

The recent excavations were carried out with the encouragement of the late Robert Pretty and through the indulgence of the Tranmer family, who owned the site. A special debt of gratitude is owed to Mrs Annie Tranmer who died in 1993, and who put up with our colourful and sometimes rumbustious team, and its numerous visitors, on her skyline; also to John Miller, her Trustee, who guided Sutton Hoo's destiny with a sure and subtle hand. Elisabeth Walters and Merlin Waterson were invaluable in helping to win the owner's gift and the National Trust's acceptance of Sutton Hoo.

My partner Madeleine Hummler was the prehistorian for the most recent Sutton Hoo project, ran the field school for students from every continent who trained with us and is joint author of the final research report. This book, consciously or unconsciously, has often relied on her inspiration. Our four children were born during the campaign and we have happy memories of the kindness shown us and them by generations of volunteer diggers, guides and visitors.

Our family, our team and the site itself gained immeasurably from the friendship and diligence of Peter Berry, the excavation foreman and site caretaker. An ex-military man and retired Shell executive, Peter Berry was engaged in managing St Mary's, Woodbridge when we arrived, and it did not take him long to see that the site team and their director were new to Suffolk and in need of serious guidance. Out on site in all weathers and affable and helpful to all, Peter has probably done more to serve the Sutton Hoo site, its staff and its visitors than any other player in the drama.

The recent Sutton Hoo project was administered by Jenny Glazebrook whose diplomacy and dedication during the excavation and advice after it enabled the project to survive, and have helped make this a better book. The long-term staff who dug the site consisted of Andy Copp, Cathy Royle and the photographer Nigel Macbeth, to whom are owed the majority of the professional procedures and results on which my interpretation depends. This small permanent core was augmented seasonally by other professionals: Angela Evans, from the British Museum, worked with the site team in Mounds 2, 5, 7 and 18; Annette Roe, then of the Società Lombarda d'Archeologia, excavated Mound 17; Kathy Dowse and Linda Peacock were finds supervisors and Justin Garner-Lahire was supervisor over the eastern sector of the excavation. Supported by a workforce of fifty volunteers and trainees, these fieldworkers actually excavated the site of Sutton Hoo, while the Director made speeches, welcomed visitors, gave site tours, introduced distinguished visitors to other distinguished visitors, planned strategies, made more speeches, changed his mind and talked and talked. Members of the core staff of the Sutton Hoo team have since formed Field Archaeology Specialists Ltd at York. The project was hosted initially by the University of Birmingham and later by the Department of Archaeology, University of York, where its base remains. In the post-excavation phase I have been especially lucky in being able to draw on the knowledge, advice and judgement of Dr Helen Geake.

Analyses of the finds were undertaken by Angela Evans, Fleur Shearman and Man-Yee Liu at the British Museum; of soils by Charles French of the Macdonald Institute at Cambridge; of plant remains by Rob Scaife of the University of Southampton and Alan Hall of the University of York; of animal bones by Terry O'Connor and Julie Bond; and of human bones by Frances Lee of the University of Bradford.

The BBC commissioned a series of television films which were produced by Ray Sutcliffe, whose knowledge of archaeology and history proved as valuable as his skills as a film-maker. *The Million Pound Grave* was an updated version of a film first made about the excavation of the Mound 1 ship-burial in the 1960s; it contained invaluable interviews with many of the principals who took part, which have been liberally drawn on here. *New Beginnings* was a film on the rather severe topic of the site evaluation, which nevertheless attracted a summer audience of over 3 million. *The Last of the Pagans* and *Sea Peoples* described the discoveries made up to 1989.

Philip Rahtz, one of the country's most experienced and inspiring excavators, was a pillar of support, always interested, always positive, throughout the duration of the project. Rupert Bruce-Mitford, the great researcher of the Mound 1 treasure, who died in 1994, was a generous provider of advice and friendship. On his last visit to the site I showed him the results of the excavations of Mound 5, and the revised plan of the cemetery, which demonstrated beyond reasonable doubt its special status. 'So you see,' I was pleased to acknowledge, 'you were right all along.' 'Ah yes,' he returned, 'but I then had no right to be right. Now we have the evidence.'

In archaeology, we never arrive at 'the answer'. But our discipline is one that achieves more through co-operation than competition. The more we agree, the more we carry conviction. I am grateful to all those named here, and to Madeleine Hummler, Annette Roe, Jenny Glazebrook, Helen Geake, Rosemary Hoppitt, Faith Ferromes, Peter Berry, Philip Rahtz, Angela Evans, Angus Wainwright, Merlin Waterson and Freddie Carver who read and commented on earlier drafts. My thanks also to Carolyn Jones of British Museum Press for much good advice and considerate management.

Members of the Sutton Hoo Research Trust

Sir David Attenborough CBE [BM]
Prof. C.N.L. Brooke PSA [SoA]
J. Cherry FSA [BM]
Prof. B.W. Cunliffe CBE FBA PSA [SoA]
Prof. J.D. Evans PSA [SoA]
S. Jervis PSA [SoA]

Dr I.H. Longworth FSA [BM]
Dr D.W. Phillipson TSA [SoA]
Prof. P.A. Rahtz FSA [SoA]
R.M. Robbins CBE PSA [SoA]
K. Wade [Suffolk County Council]
Mrs L. Webster FSA [BM]
Dr M.G. Welch [SoA]
Dr S.E. West FSA [Suffolk County Council]
Sir David Wilson FBA FSA [BM]

BM = British Museum
SoA = Society of Antiquaries of London

Non-members

Prof. M.O.H. Carver FSA FSA (Scot)
MIFA, Director of Research and
    Company Secretary
John Knight, Honorary Solicitor
Martin Burchmore, for the auditors
Kingston Smith

All members of the Sutton Hoo Research
Trust were also members of the Sutton Hoo
Research Committee.

**Additional Members of the Sutton Hoo
Research Committee**

Dr Paul Ashbee FSA
Martin Biddle FBA FSA
Dr S.G. Bowman
Rupert Bruce-Mitford FBA FSA
    [consultant]
Dr C.M. Hills FSA
J.G. Hurst FBA FSA
Prof. H. Loyn FBA FSA
Lt Cmdr D. Pretty RN
E.V. Wright MBE FSA

Sutton Hoo Society

PRESIDENTS
HRH the Duke of Edinburgh
The Duke of Grafton KG

CHAIRS
Mac Miles, Robert Simper,
Dr Rosemary Hoppitt

ILLUSTRATIONS

All photographs credited 'British Museum'
are © The British Museum.

Unless otherwise credited, drawings are by
Annette Roe.

SHSB I, II etc refers to the volumes of the
original Sutton Hoo publication by
R. Bruce-Mitford; see page 178.

INTRODUCING SUTTON HOO

The traveller to Sutton Hoo must make two kinds of journey: one in reality and one in the imagination. The destination of the real journey is a small group of grassy mounds lying beside the River Deben in south-east England. The imaginative journey visits a world of warrior-kings, large open boats, jewelled weapons, ritual killing and the politics of independence. To both kinds of journey, this book is offered as a guide.

Those heading for the site in a car can easily miss it, as the A12 hurries them north-east from Ipswich through the open farmland of Suffolk. They should by-pass Woodbridge, turn off to Melton, and drive straight down to Wilford Bridge, the first fordable crossing point of the tidal Deben. Beyond the bridge, the visitor turns right along the B1083 towards Bawdsey, Shottisham, Staverton Thicks and Rendlesham Forest. Here are the flat lands of the Sandlings, interlaced by thin lines of pine trees, and the occasional patch of heath. In 300 yards (275 m) is the turning to Sutton Hoo (now Tranmer) House, which heads back to the scarp overlooking the River Deben, with views of Woodbridge and Melton beyond; and there, tucked into the lee of a plantation of conifers, are the humps and bumps that cover so much English history.

Coming by train offers sufficient leisure to read up a bit of that history on the way, and the train journey from Ipswich is especially picturesque. It runs by marsh and sedge and water's edge, and generates the same kind of excited anticipation as child-hood holidays spent in the remote countryside. Alighting at Melton station, some will want to take a taxi, but the reasonably fit can enjoy a two-mile walk to the mounds. The route crosses Wilford Bridge, and then turns right along a track through the woods that border the river. After the woods come water-meadows, now protected from the extremities of tide by a flood-bank. The vista is rich with that rarest of modern pleasures – silence. A rabbit hurries away down the turf, a pheasant clatters out of the bracken, but nothing much is louder than the noise of one's feet on the soft sand track. The meadows, woods and turf, the promontories carrying clumps of pine – all this riverside land seems eternal, immutable. But people, then as now, were restless exploiters, always unsatisfied about how to farm and how to live. Each new idea has left its mark on the countryside, resulting in a new field boundary or the shift of a settlement. In years of extremity, the unsuccessful abandoned their farms to seek their fortune elsewhere; and in years of opportunity, new methods of agriculture and ways of living were brought by incomers from the sea.

For the ancient approach to Sutton Hoo, used from before Anglo-Saxon times far back into prehistory, is up the river. The estuaries of Suffolk are a short journey across the North Sea from the mouth of the Rhine, Europe's arterial shipway, and constitute the front door, not just to East Anglia, but to the island of Britain. Three river-mouths lie adjacent; the most southerly leads along the Orwell to Ipswich, one of the earliest known ports to be established by the English at a time contemporary with the Sutton Hoo burial ground (in the seventh century AD). The northerly leads up the Alde to Aldeburgh and Snape. And the one in the centre leads from its narrow entry to Woodbridge and Melton on the west bank and Sutton Hoo and Rendlesham on the east. To get into the Deben from the sea, it is necessary to negotiate some shifting sandbanks, and the working channel is indicated by aligning two triangular seamarks. The river runs roughly north-west, with numerous creeks and mudflats busy with waders on either side. One can imagine the instructions that a local resident of eighth-century Suffolk might have given to a relative visiting from Jutland:

> There are six main reaches from the sea, until the river narrows enough to be fordable; just before the ford, look up to the east; on the terrace above the river there you will see a number of burial mounds. They say that the pagan kings of East Anglia are buried there. Beach your boat beneath them, but pull it well up because the tides still run high at this point. Then walk along the path you will find climbing the scarp; our farm lies in the hollow. It has a hall and seven outbuildings …

The modern yachtsman would probably dock in the marina by Woodbridge Tide Mill, which is flanked by the quays and slipway of an area long worked by shipwrights. It is also still possible to moor on a small jetty on the opposite bank. Just here was Ferry Point, where the ferry arrived after crossing from Woodbridge hard. This was the most common way of crossing the Deben for many hundreds of years, if not thousands. On the Sutton Hoo side there remains a derelict wooden hut, where the ferryman awaited the hour. Our path to the

mounds leads northwards along the edge of the water under a slight cliff. It is bared here and there by cutting back or collapse, to expose the strange strata of the crag, a sedimentary mix resembling crushed biscuits and consisting of thousands of tiny shells and pre-pleistocene fossils. The public footpath enters a beech hanger (full of bluebells in the spring), and then out on to the water meadows. Discreet signs now point to 'Sutton Hoo' as we turn to climb up the scarp. There, on the skyline beyond a little copse, lies one of the most famous archaeological sites in the world.

At this point, rather than race straight up to the mounds, we could pause and take stock, because here the journey over the land and the journey in the imagination should converge. The trip to the Sutton Hoo burial ground is a pleasant one by any standards, but it is less clear why the visitor should make it. There is no stone circle, no Roman walls, no crumbling castle; indeed a cemetery can rarely offer the grandeur of ruins. And yet in a certain manner Sutton Hoo represents the trials and pretensions of a universal ancestry; it is a typical slice of England in which some extraordinary things happened. And although these things are amongst the strangest yet encountered by archaeologists, they prove to be closer to our modern problems and preoccupations than we might imagine.

The landscape over which we walked was exploited from at least 3000 BC. It was an oak forest, gradually cleared so as to become a parkland with oak trees; and then divided into large fields, which seem to indicate the demarcation of the land, and perhaps the assumption of rights of ownership. This happened in the so-called Beaker period of about 2000 BC; the people who used the tall brown beakers also cultivated the fields, and built small round huts to serve their farmers. Their successors in the Bronze Age reverted to pasture, corralling their animals in enclosures marked by fences. But the people of the Iron Age, from 600 BC, redivided the land into a network of small paddocks, some of which bore crops. This remained the basis for production in the Roman period too, so that by the time the Anglo-Saxons began to create their kingdom of East Anglia in the sixth century AD, the Sutton Hoo terrace above the River Deben was a patchwork of grass-covered banks.

This is the place where the people of a new English kingdom decided to create a special burial ground, especially wealthy and especially elaborate in its ritual. Some of those being honoured were cremated, others placed in the soil in coffins; one was buried with his horse, another in a deep underground chamber, another in the centre of a buried ship. The objects placed with the dead were of gold, silver, bronze and iron, textiles, leather and wood; they were both functional and symbolic, home-made masterpieces and exotic imports from Scandinavia, North Britain, France and the Mediterranean – objects selected by the early English aristocracy to play a role in their 'theatre of death'. The burials were covered by earth mounds which, in their original form, towered along the ridge above the Deben, offering a landmark conspicuous from every direction. The great levels of investment revealed by the burials and their contents show that, in the period around AD 600, Sutton Hoo was a shop window for the leaders of the age.

This cemetery also witnessed the beginnings of a darker side of English social control: beside the memorials to the great and good of the seventh century was soon cast the shadow of the gallows, the victims of which, garrotted, beheaded and occasionally dismembered, lay in clusters of graves around one mound and adjacent to a track leading inland away from them. Execution continued intermittently at Sutton Hoo until about the eleventh century, when the gallows was transferred to the tump above Wilford Bridge. There its grim rituals were pursued until the nineteenth century. The Sutton Hoo mounds survived throughout the Middle Ages, unmolested apart from their use as rabbit warrens, visited by sheep and shepherds, a familiar landmark for those taking the track from Ferry Point to north-eastern Suffolk.

But in the late sixteenth century, another revolution in ideology and economy left its impression on the land. No longer protected by superstition or respect, every mound was in this period mined with a deep central pit, and then each ploughed to half its original height. There was another peaceful interval, and then, in the mid-nineteenth century, a fresh generation of pillagers and ploughmen arrived; the mounds were trenched deep and ploughed again. But the fertility imparted by the spreading of the mounds was short-lived. By the early twentieth century, Sutton Hoo had become a barren heath overgrown by bracken, and it was the time of the archaeologists.

The three excavation campaigns of the 1930s, the 1960s and the 1980s provide a history in miniature of the science of archaeology itself. The first of the twentieth-century explorers rediscovered a forgotten site. Employing the techniques of the nineteenth-century barrow digger, they revealed the ship-burial in Mound 1 and the treasure that made the site famous, and hastily completed their work as war overtook Europe in 1939. The second campaign in the 1960s mobilised the resources of the British Museum, completed the excavation of the Mound 1 ship-burial and began the broader exploration of the site. The third, mounted from a university in the 1980s, took as its target the context of the cemetery and the origins of the kingdom that created it.

There are, therefore, a number of Sutton Hoo stories to tell, but they can be marshalled into two: what happened there, and how we know. And it seems logical, if not quite chronological, to tell them in reverse order. This book is thus divided into three main parts. Chapters 1–3 tell the story of how Sutton Hoo was discovered and explored, taking the three great campaigns in turn. Chapters 4–6 attempt a summary evocation of the life and times of this little piece of England over some 5,000 years. The full and detailed results of all the discoveries and studies made so far are contained in two hefty publications: Rupert Bruce-Mitford's *The Sutton Hoo Ship Burial*, which appeared in three volumes in 1975, 1978 and 1983; and the synthesis completed in 1997 by myself and Madeleine Hummler, *Sutton Hoo: An Early Medieval Cemetery and its Context* (British Museum Press), scheduled to appear in print in about 1999. The whole of this book relies on those; the present book is not, as there, a detailed argument designed to convince the specialist, but a narrative sequence intended for the visitor, the student and those who like a good story, and are happy to take a certain amount on trust to get it. Nevertheless, it is hoped that the photographs, figures and footnotes included here will provide the reader with an adequate foundation in fact.

Chapter 7 looks to the future. Thanks to the generosity of the Annie Tranmer Charitable Trust and its Trustees, Valerie Lewis and John Miller, the site was in 1997 given to the National Trust for England and Wales, and the Heritage Lottery Fund has contributed a grant of £3.6 million to its development. The news has delighted Sutton Hoo's many friends all over the world. As the property of the National Trust, the Sutton Hoo site can now be conserved and presented, as befits a 'Burial Ground of Kings', for everyone, for ever. The story of how this all came about is described in Chapter 7.

The Sutton Hoo story does not end with this book; in some ways it is a story that *can* never end. The site has acquired a broad range of followers, from the mystic to the sceptic, and it has been very stimulating to meet them during numerous site tours and in the question times following more than a hundred public lectures that I was invited to give about Sutton Hoo in Britain and abroad. It was particularly interesting to note how some questions and observations returned again and again, as though even when apparently answered, they needed to live on and be heard once more. These questions, which my responses often failed to satisfy, seem to reveal a need beyond knowledge, a need to conserve the pleasure of still not knowing. The sensible books leave these uncertain matters out, giving an impression of authority and completeness; but I include them because I think they give a useful record of what interested us in the late twentieth century, and what we found hard to understand. Accordingly in Chapter 8 I present the fifty questions I was most often asked, and without requiring or expecting any permanent title, the answers I gave to them. Sutton Hoo is a living site and a constant provocation to thought and the imagination.

My own involvement with Sutton Hoo over fifteen years has been that of a digger and writer about early medieval (Dark Age) Europe; I have not dedicated my life, as some have, to this monument, although I have loved it and tried to serve it well. It is an awkward site to dig, and in many ways still keeps its secrets hidden from the most sophisticated technology. It is an awkward site to interpret, too, since it raises strong convictions in amateur and professional alike. But that, in a way, is one of its attractions. The exploration of the site is challenging and the interpretation of its meaning always controversial. Both have needed the support of friends and professional colleagues at home and abroad, of whom only a prominent fraction are listed in the Acknowledgements.

University of York
1 February 1998

PART 1

THE SUTTON HOO STORY

Investigations

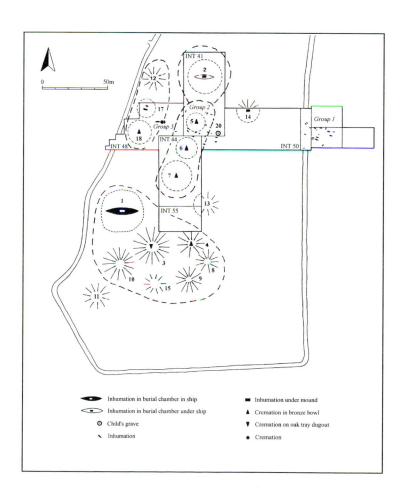

Fig. 1 The numbered burial mounds at Sutton Hoo.

1 MRS PRETTY DIGS UP A SHIP
Excavations at Sutton Hoo, 1938–9

Fig. 2 Frank and Edith Pretty. A photograph taken in the 1920s. By courtesy of Russell Carver.

At Sutton Hoo in south-east Suffolk, a large white Edwardian mansion, with a wood-panelled interior, stands in a garden punctuated with rhododendrons and pine trees on a promontory overlooking the River Deben. In 1926, this house was purchased by Colonel Frank Pretty, retired commanding officer of the 4th Battalion of the Suffolk Regiment; and buying the house with him was his newly married wife, Edith May Pretty, née Dempster, member of a distinguished engineering family whose business achievements included the building of gasometers in the Manchester area (Figs 2, 3). Sutton Hoo, then an estate of 400 acres, was a tangle of sandy heath and woodland, home to a multitude of rabbits. The Prettys could enjoy fine views from the large bay windows of the house to the west over the River Deben to Woodbridge, Melton and the railway line that connects them. From the windows on the south side, across the windy heath, a small group of scarred burial mounds could be seen, lying up against the spinney known as Top Hat Wood (Fig. 3).

Edith Pretty was an adventurous traveller and one of the first women magistrates, as well as the owner of an exceptionally beautiful piece of England. But fate had two shocks to deliver. In 1930, at the age of 47, Edith Pretty found herself pregnant, and in due course was delivered of a son, Robert. Four years later, her husband died, and she and her young son were left alone in the fifteen-bedroom house. In what must have seemed long days over the next few years, Mrs Pretty suffered from ill-health and withdrew from many of her public commitments. She sought consolation in the counsel of a spiritualist medium, making regular trips to London for guidance from her mentor. Whether she hoped to make contact with her husband cannot be said, but like many another before her, she may have found some relief and reason, during the perplexity of bereavement, in the feeling that the world of the dead was an accessible and sympathetic one.[1]

It is not unlikely that these circumstances had some influence on her decision to begin investigation of the burial mounds

Fig. 3 Sutton Hoo (now Tranmer) House, with the burial mounds in the foreground, in 1985. Nigel Macbeth.

visible from the large south-facing bay-window. The impetus, according to some accounts, was provided by friends and relatives, among them a nephew, a dowser, who insisted that gold was to be found; while others speak of shadowy figures around the mounds after dusk, and a vision of a man on a white horse. But, whatever her sensitivity to the attentions of solicitous phantoms, Mrs Pretty was no stranger to scientific archaeology. Even as a child she was well-travelled, and had seen the pyramids in Egypt. When her family were the tenants at Vale Royal in Cheshire, her father was given permission to excavate and expose the plan of the Cistercian monastery which adjoined their house. She would have been aware of the responsibilities of excavating burial mounds, and had already refused to allow enthusiastic amateurs to try their hand. In her case, a keen eye and an educated curiosity would have encouraged investigation as surely as any interest in the other world. Moreover, she required no permission from elsewhere, and in this she was following a 400 year old precedent: the prerogative of post-Reformation landowners to investigate and upturn, with shovel, spade, pit and trench, the mounds that had survived on their land.

In her need for an archaeologist, Mrs Pretty contacted Ipswich Museum whose curator, Guy Maynard, recommended in turn a local man who had acquired the reputation of having something of a nose for an antiquity. So we meet Basil Brown, a self-taught archaeologist and amateur astronomer, whose knowledge of the past was broad, varied and eclectic (Fig. 4).[2] He had visited and

Fig. 4 Basil Brown, at about the time of the 1938/39 excavations. Sutton Hoo Archive.

investigated monuments in East Anglia over many years. Not being himself a landowner, some of his fieldwork called for ingenuity, bicycling around the lanes and using binoculars (when access was not permitted) to study exposed sections of sand and crag. He had taught himself to excavate, too, and had the confidence of one who knew the soil and seemed to know instinctively what had happened to it. He was the first to reveal the character of the Sutton Hoo cemetery, and his sensitive definition of the Mound 1 ship amounted to excavation of genius. But in spite of Brown's undoubted talent, it would not do to romanticise his abilities. A contemporary archaeological colleague, Richard Dumbreck, described him in these terms:

> ... a character; his pointed features gave him the, not inappropriate, appearance of a ferret and were invariably topped with a rather disreputable trilby hat, while a somewhat moist and bubbling pipe protruded dead ahead from his mouth. He had ... gravitated to archaeology without any real training thanks to a quite remarkable flair for smelling out antiquities ... His method was to locate a feature and then pursue wherever it led, in doing so becoming just like a terrier after a rat. He would trowel furiously, scraping the spoil between his legs, and at intervals he would stand back to view progress and tread in what he had just loosened ... The sad thing is that with training he might have been a brilliant archaeologist ...[3]

But there was no doubting his absolute dedication: his assistant John Jacobs remembered later how Brown had gone out in a rainstorm in the middle of the night to tend the Sutton Hoo excavation: 'I think he would have slept there if he'd had his bed.'[4]

Alerted by Maynard, Basil Brown armed himself with 'appropriate literature on the Bronze Age, Iron Age, Roman and Anglo-Saxon periods, and some suitable excavation reports'. Mrs Pretty gave him 30 shillings a week, accommodation in an upper room of the chauffeur's cottage and the help of two labourers from the Sutton Hoo estate, Bert Fuller and Tom Sawyer. She instructed him to put all the excavated soil by the side of any trenches made in the mounds ready for refilling, so that they could be returned eventually to their original appearance.

The work began at Mrs Pretty's instigation on the largest of the burial mounds, that known to us as Mound 1. On 20 June 1938 Mrs Pretty produced a long probing iron of her own design, and invited Basil Brown to drive it into the mound until he hit something solid. This he did. An excavation followed, to a depth of 6 ft (1.8 m), whereupon the 'something solid' was determined to be a stone of no particular significance. At Basil Brown's suggestion, the next day the team left Mound 1 for the time being and pro-

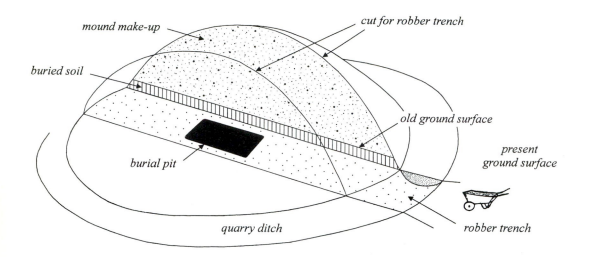

mound make-up

cut for robber trench

buried soil

old ground surface

present
ground surface

burial pit

quarry ditch

robber trench

Fig. 5 How burial mounds were made and dug.

ceeded to try their hands on a smaller mound, the adjacent Mound 3. Here Brown was better able to demonstrate his technique of chamber-finding, a method as effective as it was traditional.[5] Burial mounds are, in general, made of earth and stones heaped over the ground surface. The burial itself is put into a hole (the 'chamber') which is backfilled with the subsoil that came out of it. In places where the ground surface and the subsoil are a different colour, as on sandy sites, the backfilled burial chamber is easily distinguished. An excavator, knowing this, simply has to drive a trench horizontally through the mound at about the level of the old ground surface; the backfilled chamber will soon appear as a square or rectangle of different coloured soil at the bottom of the excavation trench. Even when the trench is mucky with the continual coming and going of the excavators, the pit containing the burial should still show up. If, however, it has already been visited by a previous expedition, the contrast between the old ground surface and the refilled burial pit is often much less clear, and the pit, in consequence, harder to find (Fig. 5). Excavators refer to an unrecorded trench cut by an earlier expedition as a 'robber trench' on the assumption that its primary purpose was to capture the grave-goods.

Spoil from the excavation trench can be piled up beside it, as in Mrs Pretty's injunction; or it can be removed down the trench and tipped in a fan beyond it. If the mound is too tall and the make-up too soft, the sides of the excavator's trench will collapse; a safer procedure, therefore, is to cut back the edges to form terraces along their length, and to barrow the spoil out along the trench. The trench in this case serves as the main thoroughfare for the excavators and the inspecting antiquaries.

Finding the level of the old ground surface can be assisted by digging a pilot trench in the side of the mound, and Brown began in this way, digging a pilot trench on the east side of Mound 3. Then, using the traditional technique, he found the buried soil, and the supposed burial pit, a mere 2 ft (60 cm) down, but its edge was so ragged that he introduced a second trench at right angles to the first to determine the form of the pit more clearly. By 25 June he had done so, 'at least to my own satisfaction', and was ready to empty it. The pit descended to a total depth of 9 ft (2.7 m) from the top of the mound, occasioning trouble with landslides. Brown realised he was not the first to enter the mound, although not, perhaps, that the pit he was engaged in defining was dug by earlier excavators. It was about 40 ft (12 m) across and had been backfilled with turf, black earth and broken clay pieces. At the bottom of the pit was a rectangular piece of decayed wood 5 ft 6 in (1.67 m) long by 1 ft 10 in (56 cm) wide. It could have been a coffin, but more nearly resembled a tray with rounded corners, and carried on it little heaps of cremated bone which proved to derive from a human and a horse. The scraps of finds that remained included some sherds of pottery, a lump of corroded iron, later found to be an axe-head, part of a decorated limestone plaque, fragments of bone inlay from a casket and the lid of a ewer, of Mediterranean origin. Brown thought the 'tray' might have been part of a boat; Maynard thought it was the bottom of a domestic chest or trough. It broke up while an attempt was made to lift it.

The visitors, official and unofficial, arriving on Tuesday 28 June were even less sure of what had been found. The formidable J. Reid Moir, bespoke tailor of Ipswich turned palaeontologist, and at that time Chairman of the Ipswich Museum Committee, demanded a new trench. Mr Spencer, museum assistant, told an indignant Brown he did not understand the soils in that part of the country. Vincent B. Redstone FSA, local historian of Woodbridge, pronounced that the pit was a dew-pond, and required another hole to be dug 6 ft (1.8 m) into the subsoil; upon which Fuller and Sawyer were nearly buried, and Mr Redstone was left to dig a third hole himself. A month later Basil Brown was recollecting in tranquillity this hail of advice with the wry comment, 'with a little diplomacy I got out of bother and the pit survived and finds followed on the Thursday'. On Saturday 2 July the excavation was nominally finished, but as late as 19 July Brown was cutting another trench to the central pit, to suit Mr Reid Moir, which 'proved the eastern limit of the grave to everyone's satisfaction' (Fig. 6).[6]

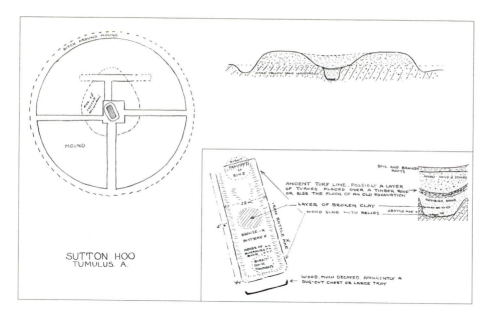

Fig. 6 Plan of 'Tumulus A'
(Mound 3) by Basil Brown.
Sutton Hoo Archive.

This first excavation was hardly auspicious, but 6 July found Brown clearing bracken from Mound 2. He dug a test pit on the south side, throwing back into it a defunct metal bucket.[7] He laid out his trench on a compass bearing approximately east–west, following the orientation of the wooden 'tray' just found under Mound 3. Almost immediately he discovered some pieces of iron and, with an act of recognition that was to be fundamental for the exploration of Sutton Hoo, decided that one of them was the remnant of a 'ship rivet' (Fig. 8). These resembled bolts a few inches long, originally with a domed head on one end and a squarish plate on the other, and were used to secure the strakes of early medieval ships.[8] More rivets were to come, and by 14 July the edge of a burial pit was clear to Brown, although Maynard had noted a previous 'robber' pit. Mound 2 was big and the sides of Brown's excavation collapsed no fewer than three times (20, 22 and 28 July). In between the cutting back and carting away of collapsed mound, Brown looked for and found a boat to go with his rivets: the base of the burial pit was 'boat-shaped without any question' and some of the rivets were still *in situ*. The scraps of finds included a beautiful piece of blue glass, a gilt bronze disc, iron knives and the tip of a sword blade.

Undaunted by his encounter with another robbed burial, on 30 July Brown cleared the bracken from Mound 4, dug a test pit on the east side and drove a trench westwards into the mound. This mound too had been robbed, and the grave pit was very shallow. Nevertheless the cremated bones of humans and animals were found, with fragments of bronze and textile. Brown was able to make the important interpretation that the burial

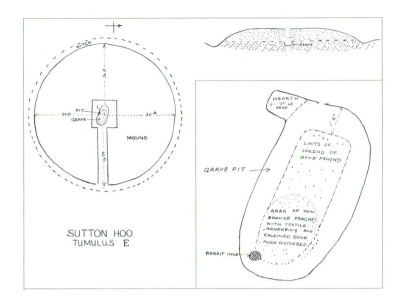

SUTTON HOO
TUMULUS E

rite consisted of cremated bone wrapped in cloth and placed in a bronze bowl (Fig. 7).

So ended the 1938 season; three mounds had been trenched, and each had turned out to have been the subject of previous explorations. The fragments of objects that had been found suggested something of the former riches of the graves, and gave an indication of their date: the imports from Mound 3 were early medieval, while the ornament on the disc from Mound 2 was Anglo-Saxon. Probably all the mounds were Anglo-Saxon, and one at least had contained a boat. In his diary and notebook Brown never seems to express much surprise, but he could be forgiven if he had; he may have expected the Sutton Hoo mounds to be of Bronze Age date like so many others in the vicinity (as on Martlesham Heath), if not Viking as Maynard had expected. Being Anglo-Saxon certainly made them special, but their condition was hardly encouraging. The trenches through the three mounds were backfilled, and incorporated into the backfill of Mound 2 was a pair of steel roller-skates, no doubt belonging to young Master Robert Pretty, then aged eight.[9]

A second season was already under discussion in the autumn of 1938; if Edith Pretty's expectations had not been fulfilled, her appetite was whetted and her instinct persistent. When work restarted on 8 May 1939 there was no hesitation. Basil Brown was accompanied by Mrs Pretty to the mounds and a brief conversation ensued. 'I asked which one she would like opened,' wrote Brown in his diary, 'and she pointed to 1 (Mound 1), the largest barrow of the group, and said "What about this?" and I replied that it would be quite alright for me.' The helpers this year were to be John Jacobs, the gardener at Little Sutton Hoo,

Fig. 8 A ship-rivet, found in the 1939 excavation. Courtesy of Peter Burman. Photograph by John Bateman.

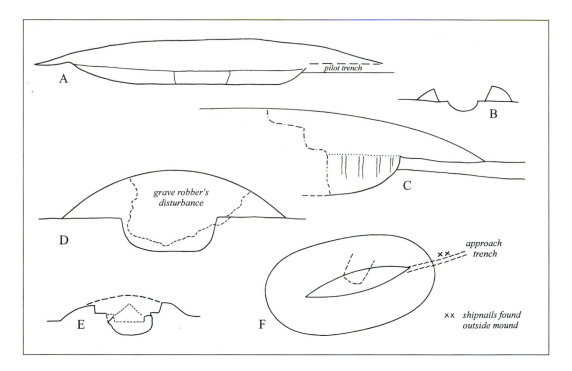

A

pilot trench

B

C

D

grave robber's
disturbance

approach
trench

E

F

x x shipnails found
outside mound

Fig. 9 Maynard's sketches of the robber trench through Mound 1, from a letter to Miss Allen. Sutton Hoo Archive.

and William Spooner, Mrs Pretty's gamekeeper, although Jacobs was busy in the garden until the following day. Brown made a survey, and then his trench, 4 ft (1.2 m) wide and laid out east–west, was driven into the mound from the west.

One can imagine the scene, Brown with his battered trilby and his 'moist and bubbling' pipe, Jacobs and Spooner with spades and shovels ready to cut the turf and load a wooden wheel-barrow, of a kind more normally used to transport weeds and dead-heads from the flowerbeds. Perhaps the job was viewed as little more than a nice rest from the routine of gardening. But a change of mood was not long in coming. About midday on Thursday 11 May, Jacobs called out, 'Here's a bit of iron', and held up a ship-rivet. Brown immediately stopped the clearing operation. Carefully exploring the area with a small trowel, he uncovered five more rivets in position on what turned out to be the wooden prow or stern of a ship. It was then that inspiration took the helm. Brown reasoned that the rivets he had just found should represent the line of a vanished wooden hull. If so, he would have to dig up and over the rivets and descend on them from above, leaving each one in position. He would then be *inside* the ship, and by locating the plate of each rivet, he would be able to define the inside of the hull. Instead of trying to follow the vanished surface of the buried soil, Brown's trench now dipped down into the hollow of a buried ship. By 19 May he had learnt how to define the rivets in position: a pink patch in the yellow sand gave warning of the presence of a rivet, and a light brushing would reveal the red knob of corroded iron, surrounded by crusty sand. Rivet after rivet was revealed in this way at intervals of 6–9 in (15–23 cm), until so confident was Brown of predicting their positions that he could afford to leave a protective coat of sand over the rivets, while tracing the inner surface of the hull.

As the lines of the vessel descended deep into the ground so did Brown's trench, always cutting into the face of the mound, until the inevitable occurred. On 30 May the trench collapsed, but Brown, veteran of so many collapsed trenches, was free within a few minutes. Amongst the tonnage of fallen earth were sherds of sixteenth-century pottery, which had obviously been introduced into the mound at a later date, probably by grave-robbers. Maynard on a visit observed the shadow of a previous trench in the face of Brown's cutting (Fig. 9, D). Brown himself described the intrusion as a pit with a 'Treasure seekers' hearth' at the bottom. He left a standing sample of its fill of black sand and red ash, in the form of a tall column that Jacobs christened 'the lighthouse'.

As Brown phlegmatically cleared up the mess and cut back his giant trench in an effort to make it safer, the archaeological world was beginning to stir. Searching for parallels for his buried ship, Maynard had made discreet inquiries of the museum on the Isle of Man, which held records of the Viking ship-burials which had been excavated there. But archaeological inquiries cannot be kept discreet for long, and the rumour that a Viking ship had been found in Suffolk soon made its way to the coffee room of the Department of Archaeology at Downing Street, Cambridge, then the central node of archaeological gossip.

On 6 June, alerted by the rumour, if sceptical of it, Charles W. Phillips, Fellow of Selwyn College, Cambridge, paid a routine visit to Guy Maynard, ostensibly to collect papers relating to the newly-formed Prehistoric Society. 'I found him somewhat distracted,' said Phillips, 'but judicious questioning soon revealed the cause'. In the company of Maynard, Phillips met Mrs Pretty at her house and together with Maynard the party made its way to the burial mounds.

> I was not prepared for the astonishing sight which met me when I came round to the actual work. There I saw a very wide trench cut right down into the substance of the large oval mound on its longer axis to reveal clearly the gunwale outline of much of a large boat which was interred below the level of the old ground surface. At a quick estimate it could hardly be much less than one hundred feet long. The work had been done with care and as yet there had been little attempt to remove any of the sand which filled the vessel. I could not wonder that Maynard had been daunted by this apparition.[10]

Phillips advised Mrs Pretty to exercise caution with her excavation and made telephone calls on her behalf to the British Museum and the (Government) Office of Works. As a result of these discussions on the telephone, a site meeting was hastily convened, and on 9 June Christopher Hawkes (for the British Museum), R.S. Simms (for the Office of Works) and Guy Maynard (for Ipswich Museum) met Charles Phillips and Mrs Pretty and her team of excavators.[11] It was decided that to excavate further would require a more experienced team and first-rate equipment, but the summer of 1939 was an awkward time to assemble them. War, if not yet certain, was threatening. The British Museum and the Ministry had other things on their minds than a research excavation. The first of these organisations was engaged in packing its treasures into cases for storage in the London Underground in anticipation of the *blitzkrieg*; while the second was preoccupied by matters of greater moment than an archaeological dig, namely the building of air-strips and the sandbagging of the dockyards. But if the times were inauspicious, there was no going back on the Sutton Hoo discovery. News of the find had already leaked out, and at the first relaxation of scientific interest, others, less scientific in motive but no less energetic in execution, would soon be on the scene. There was nothing for it but to try to gather the necessary resources with all speed. Brown was instructed to stop excavating and the meeting dispersed.

Basil Brown, who was never greatly in awe of authority, took little notice of the injunction that had theoretically been put upon him, and he continued to excavate without a pause for nearly four weeks. It is probably as well that he did so, since it meant that someone was always on site and could repel any attempts at trespass and pillage. His work remained careful and intelligent, and he now had an independent source of advice on ship-burials – Mr and Mrs Megaw of the Isle of Man Museum who had visited the site on 8 June. Predicting where the burial would lie, Brown desisted from following the rivet pattern to the lower strakes amidships, leaving a dark rectangle – the collapsed burial chamber – in position. By 3 July he had successfully excavated most of the Sutton Hoo Mound 1 ship and was clearing a clay deposit amidships 'exactly above the place where I expect the chief lies'. He had also had a little poke at a cauldron, part of which lay exposed on the surface, noting the hollow sound given out by the adjacent skin of wood, through which he pushed his finger. He covered up the chamber area with hessian and continued to define the ship, consulting a large volume (in Norwegian) on the Oseberg ship-burial excavated in 1904.

The British Museum and the Office of Works had, in the interim, arrived at their decision: to place the responsibility for the

Fig. 10 Charles Phillips overseeing excavation, in discussion with Basil Brown, watched by Edith Pretty (in basket chair). Those working in the chamber, partially visible, are probably (left to right) T.D. Kendrick, W.F. Grimes and Sir John Fosdyke. Photograph Ann Carver, courtesy of Russell Carver.

completion of the excavation on to the shoulders of Charles Phillips. At the end of June, Office of Works officers contacted Phillips at Little Woodbury in Wiltshire, where he was helping Gerhard Bersu to reveal that classic Iron Age settlement, and requested him to undertake the completion of the Sutton Hoo excavation. Once he had been asked 'to take it on', Phillips accepted stoically the exacting and novel task which lay before him: 'I didn't see how anyone was going to take it on. But since no one knew anything about it anyhow, and as long as you were a reasonable and sensible person, it seemed to me we might as well have a bash; so a bash we had'.[12]

The team was to consist of friends or colleagues summoned from their holidays or awaiting call-up, and the total resources amounted to £250 in expenses, with the additional provision, from the depot at Framlingham Castle, of twelve scaffold poles and a tarpaulin – for which, remarked Phillips dryly, 'little use could be found'. A shepherd's hut on wheels and the interior of

cars would offer the only shelter. Fir cones from Top Hat Wood would provide the fuel for camp-fires for making tea. On 8 July, nursing an injured thumb, Phillips arrived and assumed control. His attitude was a bit bellicose, observed Brown, but the handover between Brown and Phillips seems to have been respectfully done. Phillips was to take responsibility from now on, both for making decisions and for keeping the records, and Brown was to be designated his assistant. On 11 July, Ipswich Museum was invited not to interfere: following a heated discussion, Phillips made it clear to Maynard, in no uncertain terms, who was now in control. Although Phillips was in charge, much diplomacy was still required, as he wrote later, 'to steer the course of this excavation through all these assorted and often intangible obstacles'. For then, as now, many people and institutions felt they had a stake in so mighty a find. On 13 July, the excavation began of what transpired to be the most richly furnished burial chamber ever discovered in British soil (Fig. 10).

Charles Phillips was a large man and he decided that as far as possible the deposit in the burial chamber should be spared his weight. He therefore mainly stayed out, and the work of excavation and recording was done by the friends and colleagues he had recruited (Figs 11, 12). Stuart Piggott (later Professor of Archaeology at Edinburgh) and his wife Peggy (later Curator of Devizes Museum) answered the call on their holiday and arrived on 19 July. The Piggotts were to be the principal excavators of the centre and west of the chamber, and Stuart was the maker of the plans. O.G.S. Crawford, founder of the periodical *Antiquity* and chief archaeologist at the Ordnance Survey, arrived on 24 July. He was to be the creator of an invaluable photographic record. With him came W.F. ('Peter') Grimes, his assistant at the Ordnance Survey, later Director of the Institute of Archaeology at London, who was to be the excavator of the eastern half of the chamber. Another who came to assist at a crucial time was John Brailsford, while John Ward-Perkins (Director of the British School at Rome), Grahame Clark (the future Disney Professor of Archaeology at Cambridge) and his wife were there on important days. 'Under the conditions of the time,' commented Phillips, 'it would have been difficult to have gathered a more valuable group of workers, witnesses and general advisers.'

The excavators worked individually and in a somewhat ad hoc manner, at the east end, at the west end and in the centre, lifting off the layers of compressed decayed wood or blackened sand and revealing, defining and freeing each object. On 21 July the first piece of jewellery was encountered, a little gold and garnet pyramid, a find which greatly raised the temperature and expectations of the team. 'We were working quietly away in our usual morning

Fig. 11 In the chamber: Stuart Piggott draws a plan with the aid of a planning frame, W.F. Grimes relaxes. A photograph taken by O.G.S. Crawford, the editor of *Antiquity*. Sutton Hoo Archive.

routine,' remembered Peggy Guido, 'when quite suddenly as I was trowelling and brushing, one of the lovely garnet and gold ornaments was revealed. Of course from that moment on we were immensely excited'. The responsibility weighed heavily on Charles Phillips. When acquainted with the find, he said 'My godfathers!' and for the rest of the day was heard to murmur 'oh dear, oh dear'.[13] This brilliant object, a pyramidal-shaped strap-mount, was merely a humble precursor. The following day brought a veritable feast of golden objects: gold plaques in the form of patterned birds and animals from a purse-frame, which it could be seen had contained a handful of gold coins; buckles with garnet inlay which had connected the 'Sam Browne' of the buried man's parade-dress; and a great hollow buckle of solid gold, its surface alive with the raised forms of interlaced animals (Col. Pls I, II).

That night in the Bull Hotel at Woodbridge, which served as the excavators' base, Piggott remembered being asked the inevitable question: '"Well, old boy, found any gold today?" "Oh yes," I said, "my pockets are absolutely full," and as I spoke I was holding the box containing the great gold belt buckle in my rather sweaty hand in the pocket of my coat; and "Oh" they said "that's splendid, you must have a drink". "Yes" I said, "I need one"'.[14] Met at Woodbridge railway station, T.D. Kendrick, the Keeper of British and Medieval Antiquities at the British Museum and *eminence grise* of Anglo-Saxon art, had to steady himself when Phillips showed him, in the station waiting room, one of the simpler buckles as a glimpse of what was in store: 'When he saw the buckle, he was both astonished and elated, astonished because of its beauty and perfection, and elated because I was able to tell him that it was part of a much larger collection of pieces in the same style'.[15] All were agreed that the dazzling polychrome jewellery, and thus the burial itself, should belong to the early seventh century AD.

Over the next two days, Piggott excavated at the west end of the chamber, bringing to light a whetstone and a tangle of metal pieces, which were later to resolve themselves into the sceptre, the standard, the shield and the Coptic bowl. Then the excavation of the eastern half began. A great silver dish, which at first was thought to be a shield, was found and on its surface were uncovered splinters of burnt bone. The next day (25 July) the dish was lifted and Grimes began to disentangle the pile of objects beneath. At the west end, meanwhile, work continued with brush and knife: the gold and garnet shoulder-clasps had been found, and then the sword. On 27 July an iron 'lamp-stand' (the standard) was lifted on its plank, and a purple mass of metal at the west end lifted *en bloc*. This purple heap was placed on the grass in the sun beside the excavation trench, and a few minutes later the excavators were surprised to hear a sudden click: the heap had sprung apart to reveal a nest of ten silver bowls, many in pristine condition. A scatter of iron sherds which proved to be the remains of a helmet was recovered on 28 July, and the west end was then declared completed. On 29 July the pile under the great silver dish was finished, with the lifting of a mailcoat and an axe hammer which lay at the bottom. Then the three cauldrons at the east end were lifted. Little now remained, and on 30 July the team took a day off and then dispersed. Grimes and Crawford departed and the Piggotts resumed their painting holiday.

It had been one of those magical excavations that few are given to experience: when every day brings a new discovery, and each find discovered reveals the glimmer of the next. Moments of disciplined restraint and stiff upper lip, while photography and drawing are undertaken, are followed by gasps of excitement and jubilant chatter, taking stock and racking the imagination for every eventuality before the tense commitment of raising the object from the ground. Given the conditions of the day, the operation had been carried out with intuitive efficiency thanks to the considerable native talents of the participants. Luck also blessed the enterprise, and it is unlikely that much was missed. South-east Suffolk has summer weather of a maritime variety: bright sunshine, interspersed with fresh breezes and wet squalls. Phillips reported that the firmness of the sand was remarkable and only the heaviest rain ran in and cut channels in the exposed sand. The strata were more vulnerable to a combination of hot sun and strong winds, causing the ship rivets to drop out. Fortunately, as Phillips recalled, there was very little rain or strong wind in the whole of this menacing summer.

The chamber and its treasures could be seen as anomalies, marking the smooth yellow and buff sand which filled the ship. Organic materials, including most of the timbers, had been generally eaten up over the centuries by decomposition in the fiercely acidic sand. A black line signalled a plank, end- or side-on; but where planks had been densely deposited broad side up, they had devolved into corky mats, sometimes stiff enough to be pressed. Textiles survived as pads, like the unburnt newspaper in a bonfire. Red stains marked the presence of buried iron, and purple signalled silver. Nothing prepared them for the gold; a couple of sweeps with brush or trowel and the yellow metal gleamed back as fresh as if it had just been dropped.

The little team had mainly been equipped by Mrs Pretty, the landowner. The ideal tool for approaching the level of the hull or burial chamber proved to be 'a stout coal-shovel at the end of a long ash handle'. This was used to lower the surface in horizontal slices and throw the spoil well away from the excavation. When objects were encountered, the excavators changed to 'small fine brushes of the pastry type, and penknives' and the loose earth was removed by dustpan and brush. Mrs Pretty's bellows were brought into service to blow dry sand from the objects as they appeared. Jugs and basins from her bedrooms and an empty Chianti bottle provided water for washing. The objects were put into sweet bags obtained from the shops in Woodbridge, or packed in moss from Top Hat Wood and placed in tobacco tins, the ubiquitous receptacle of the pipe-smoking era. Complex objects or groups of objects were rolled on to a plank or strapped up and removed *en bloc* (Fig. 13).

Interviewed in the 1960s, W.F. Grimes recalled the working conditions in the chamber:

> There wasn't time to get any special tools made … The two pieces of equipment that were used were a curved packer's needle which was very sharp when it started out, and an ordinary glue brush. I have no doubt that we did in fact stand on quite a number of the objects a number of times … (but) you could have danced on that jewellery if it was in the sand and you would not hurt it … not that we did! The amount of gold leaf that was blowing about (from the shield) was frightful. We couldn't do anything about it. That's one of the difficulties in excavating in the open air, in the wind.[16]

Such disarming statements increase, rather than diminish, confidence that this was a controlled excavation of measurable success.

In an exhilarating seventeen days Phillips's team had emptied the burial chamber of 263 objects of gold, garnet, silver, bronze, enamel, iron, wood, bone, textiles, feathers and fur (Fig. 14). There was even a ladybird and the crushed remains of a flowering plant. Every Dark Age object that had been imagined, and a few that had not, seemed to be represented in this burial. But there was one obvious absence. The excavators found no trace of a body, which gave rise to an initial theory that there had never been one; in this reading, the monument was a memorial, a cenotaph, to someone who had died at sea or whose corpse was not available for whatever other reason, for burial. But among the more experienced excavators (like Piggott) the absence of the body occasioned no surprise: 'owing to the acid nature of the sand no visible trace of the skeleton remained – a condition which is however familiar to excavators in such soils', an opinion that Piggott gave at the inquest held on the discovery, and one that proved influential with the coroner.[17] The excavation was like a lucky dip; first at one end of the chamber, then at another, then in its centre, objects would emerge out of the mass of black and yellow backcloth of collapsed decayed timber and sand. Now that we know what we know, we can think of a thousand things to look for and a thousand records to make. But in archaeology it was ever thus; the brave pioneers of one generation permit the scientific gravity of the next.

The site was now public knowledge; a premature press release by Ipswich Museum had stimulated a torrent of unwelcome attention. Two journalists crossed the Deben in a rowing boat and came up through the woods; others in aeroplanes flew low over the site and the press pestered Phillips in his lodgings, but intrusion on the ground was discouraged by a force of two policemen, paid for by Mrs Pretty, who were on guard twenty-four hours a day. The official (and accurate) press release attracted little attention; but this was 1939, and the international situation was providing the media with more urgent matters. On 31 July the finds were sent off to the British Museum for safe keeping and Phillips and Brown made their way through the trodden rectangle of the chamber checking for surviving finds. One more coin from the purse turned up, and some more fragments of the helmet and the mailcoat. The chamber was empty; now the study of the ship could begin. On 8 August a team from the Science Museum, which included Lt Commander Hutchinson and A.S. Crossley, arrived to carry out a full survey of the ship which stretched for 90 ft (27 m) along the great east–west cut through the mound. The lines of the hull were marked by the rows of iron rivets spaced 6 in (15 cm) apart, and the lines of the frame by the strips of grey-black powder and crusty sand left by the ribs, which crossed the

Fig. 12 Grimes excavating the iron 'standard'. Crawford, Sutton Hoo Archive.

Fig. 13 Some of the finds, packed up and ready to go. Crawford, Sutton Hoo Archive.

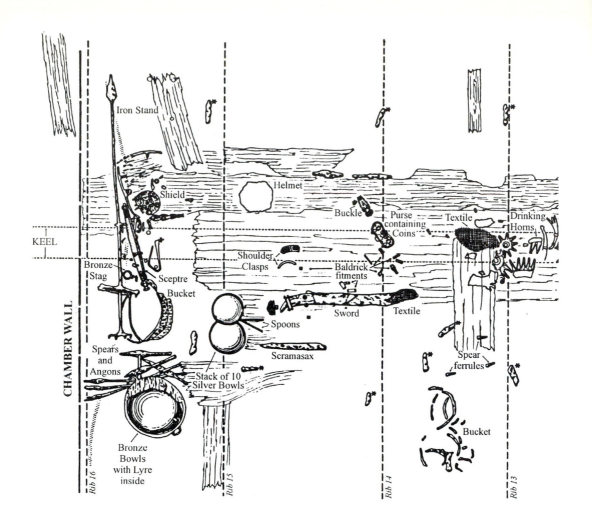

Iron Stand

Shield

Helmet

Buckle

Purse containing Coins

Textile

Drinking Horns

KEEL

Shoulder Clasps

Baldrick fitments

Bronze Stag

Sceptre

Bucket

Sword

Textile

Spoons

CHAMBER WALL

Spears and Angons

Scramasax

Spear ferrules

Stack of 10 Silver Bowls

Bucket

Bronze Bowls with Lyre inside

Rib 16

Rib 15

Rib 14

Rib 13

Fig. 14 Composite plan of the Mound 1 burial deposit, based on SHSB 1, figs 111, 112 and Phillips 1940. Redrawn by Elizabeth Hooper.

ship at 3 ft (90 cm) intervals. This was the dusty ghost of a wooden clinker-built ship, an impression marked upon a great sweep of sand. Commander Hutchinson, who undertook the recording of the ship, must have had a frustrating task, and few of his records have survived; but enough information was recorded to allow a somewhat schematic plan of the ship to be drawn up at the Science Museum in September 1939. Hutchinson was accompanied in his work by Mercie Lack and Barbara Wagstaff, two photographers who were present on site from 8 to 25 August and who between them took 447 photographs, 45 colour transparencies and an 8 mm cine-film (Fig. 15).

On the afternoon of 14 August, the North Suffolk coroner, L.H. Vulliamy (deputising for the East Suffolk coroner) convened

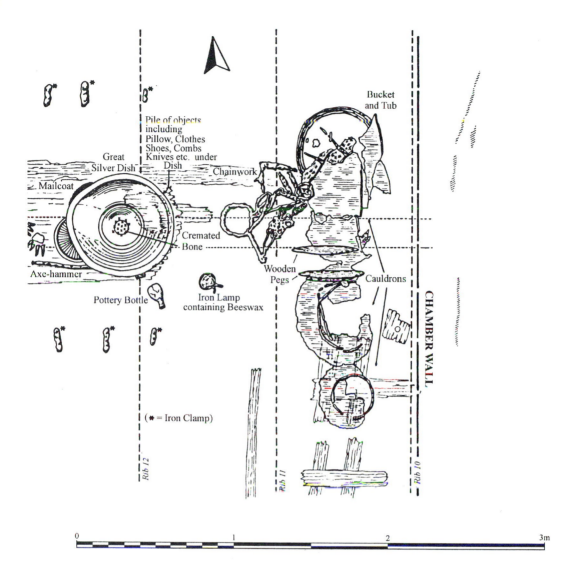

Bucket and Tub

Pile of objects including Pillow, Clothes Shoes, Combs Knives etc. under Dish

Great Silver Dish

Chainwork

Mailcoat

Cremated Bone

Axe-hammer

Wooden Pegs

Cauldrons

Pottery Bottle

Iron Lamp containing Beeswax

(✷ = Iron Clamp)

Rib 12

Rib 11

Rib 10

CHAMBER WALL

0   1   2   3m

a Treasure Trove Inquest at Sutton Parish Hall where the gold and silver objects brought back from the British Museum were put on display. Its purpose was to establish the ownership of the finds under an English law, ancient but still in force, which related to buried treasure. If it could be shown that those who buried a treasure intended to retrieve it, then that treasure belonged to the Crown. But if not, then the treasure belonged to the landowner. The rationale of this law remains obscure, but at its base may lie a belief that anyone burying precious metal in a hoard is probably avoiding tax; whereas anyone burying it in a grave intends it to accompany the dead to the next world. At some time, most probably in the sixteenth century, when many assets of the Roman Catholic church were privatised, landowners became eligible to reap the harvest of such superstitious practices, and thus claim ownership of grave goods found on their land.

With little difficulty, the authority and good sense of Stuart Piggott and Charles Phillips persuaded the coroner that the Sutton Hoo discovery, for all its strangeness, was indeed the burial of a person, an important person, who had died in the seventh century AD, 1,300 years previously, when England had scarcely begun. It was a public burial, performed in the presence, indeed with the necessary assistance, of a large number of people. It was obvious that if anyone had meant to retrieve the treasure, they could easily have done so. Although the attribution of motives to people long dead is hardly a matter for scholarly speculation, let alone the law, there could be few doubts in this case and the jury found that the treasure was buried without intention to defraud the Revenue and now belonged to the landowner, Mrs Edith Pretty. The Crown, as Phillips ironically noted, had thus failed to establish its claim to the regalia of one of King George VI's remote predecessors.

The local discussions which followed this verdict of a Suffolk jury are not well recorded. Charles Phillips mentions family pressure to keep the jewellery, but Mrs Pretty's own position is less certain. Her spiritualist counsellor soon came to stay with her, and Phillips took a stroll with him that evening on the heath, volunteering his opinion that a presentation of all the finds to the nation 'would be a splendid gesture'. Though she was no doubt assailed by advice on all sides, the decision in the end was Mrs Pretty's alone. In a short space of time the accredited owner of the 'million pound grave' announced that she was to give its contents to the British Museum, thus making the most generous donation to the Museum ever made in the lifetime of a donor. Mrs Pretty was offered the honour of Dame of the British Empire, which she declined.

Amongst the visitors who were lucky enough to see the ship at the time of its excavation was the great Anglo-Saxon scholar Hector Munro Chadwick, of Clare College, Cambridge, who had been tracked to his Herefordshire hideaway and told of the discovery. Driven by his wife at his preferred speed of 20 miles per hour he made his way to Sutton Hoo, arriving on 18 August. Chadwick's knowledge was and arguably remains unrivalled, and he is said to have immediately identified the ship-burial as that of Raedwald, who was king of East Anglia from about AD 599 to his death in about 625. This identification, together with his reasons for believing it, was soon published by Chadwick and repeatedly endorsed by other scholars for fifty years. Raedwald was mentioned in the genealogy of a family called the Wuffingas, whose name had survived in a British Library manuscript. According to

Fig. 15 The ship in the later stages of excavation. The 'shepherd's hut on wheels' can be seen in the trees top left. Sutton Hoo Archive.

the Venerable Bede's *History of the English Church and People* written at Jarrow before 731, Raedwald held sway over all the provinces south of the River Humber. He had flirted briefly with Christianity before returning to his pagan loyalties, though he placed in his 'temple' altars to both Christian and pagan deities.[18]

As Piggott remarked at the inquest, the question of who was buried in the ship was 'a matter more for the historian than for the archaeologist to decide'. There was no archaeological indication, in the form of an inscription or even a body, as to whose burial this was intended to be. But Raedwald became and is still the favourite candidate for both the subject of the Sutton Hoo ship-burial and its explanation. The burial was rich – the richest ever seen, in fact – so that it was logical to ascribe it to a king. It was found in East Anglia, so it would be a king of East Anglia. It was dated to the early seventh century by the finds, so it would be a king of East Anglia who died in the early seventh century. As the largest mound at Sutton Hoo, the burial would be appropriate to the one East Anglian king who was credited with lordship over a large part of England. It contained metalwork with Christian insignia, such as the silver spoons and the silver bowls, and metalwork with pagan symbols, such as the gold and garnet jewellery with its interlaced, biting beasts – personal property and regalia that was bright with secular power or religious confusion. It suited Raedwald very well (Col. Pl. III).

The excavators of Sutton Hoo had entered a world that seemed to be the reality on which the poetry of the Dark Ages was founded. The most famous Anglo-Saxon poem of them all, the epic *Beowulf*, ends with a description of the burial of the hero in a 'broad high tumulus, plainly visible to distant seamen', following his fatal encounter with a dragon fifty feet long, itself the guardian of the treasure in a barrow. The poem had begun 3,000 lines earlier with the description of the funeral of Beowulf's father Scyld, buried in a ship which was apparently pushed out to sea:

> Rime-crusted and ready to sail, a royal vessel with curved prow lay in harbour. They set down their dear king amidships, close by the mast. A mass of treasure was brought there from distant parts. No ship, they say, was ever so well equipped with swords, corselets, weapons, and armour. On the king's breast rested a heap of jewels which were to go with him far out into the keeping of the sea ... High overhead they set his golden standard. Then surrendering him to the sea, they sadly allowed it to bear him off. And no one, whether a counsellor in the hall or a soldier in the field, can truly say who received that cargo.[19]

Although *Beowulf* does not describe the burial of a ship in a trench on land, there are numerous echoes of the ritual worlds inhabited by both the *Beowulf* poet and the Sutton Hoo burial party. Beowulf was a Geat (from Sweden) and his adventures took place in Denmark. East Anglia too, and the early English, and their kings, had now joined the dark and beautiful world of early Germanic myth. It was an ironic moment to do so. The England of 1939 was about to enter a bitter struggle against the latest pan-Germanic adventure, and the site of Sutton Hoo was itself being prepared for war.

On the site, the team had thinned to a small group whose task was to complete the recording of the boat: Phillips, Brown, Hutchinson, Lack and Wagstaff. They reached a satisfactory point on 25 August, after removing a few carefully levelled and located ship rivets and gunwale spikes, and the work was then brought to a halt. It was quite impossible for this small team to refill the huge excavation trench, with the mountain of earth that had been extracted from it. On 3 September, Britain declared war on Germany, and Sutton Hoo estate workers covered the scar of the ship-burial with bracken.

2 THE BRITISH MUSEUM'S TREASURE

Research and excavation, 1940–82

The excavators of the ship-burial departed in the autumn of 1939, leaving the great trench open, apart from its blanket of bracken to discourage the inquisitive, and the site could return to its former tranquillity. But it did not stay tranquil for long. The threat of German invasion persisted throughout the rest of that year and the next. East Anglia was an old maritime frontier, featuring the Saxon shore forts, such as Burgh Castle, and the Napoleonic fortresses, such as Languard, witnesses to earlier threats of invasion. But this time the invasion, if it came, would come by air as well as sea, and draglines were soon busy creating a grid of deep ditches all over the flat heath of Sutton Walks, to inhibit the landing of enemy gliders. These ditches came right up to the Sutton Hoo burial mounds, where they can still be seen: long slots, with humps of soil at regular intervals on each side, all now grassed over (Fig. 16, Col. Pl. IV). As well as forming part of the anti-glider barrier, the Sutton Hoo site had another contribution to make to the war effort: in 1942 it was requisitioned as a training ground. Infantry used the mounds as background for target practice with the .303 rifle, the 88 grenade and the 2 inch mortar. They also practised 'platoon in the attack' and 'platoon in the defence', the defenders digging two-man slit-trenches on the flanks of Mounds 1, 2, 6 and 7, and the attackers presumably emerging from Top Hat Wood to be greeted by a hail of blank ammunition. Then the Sherman tanks arrived, and frustrated by the flat lands around them, aimed for the mounds. These provided useful training for drivers, none more than Mound 1 which now took the form of two lobes at either side of a great cleavage at the bottom of which lay the ship-impression concealed by dead bracken: a challenge to the driver of a tracked vehicle and fine terrain on which to practise attacking over trenches or land carved up by high explosives.[1]

Fortunately for Sutton Hoo, these manoeuvres soon came to the attention of Lt Ted Wright, discoverer of the Ferriby Bronze Age boats on Humberside and later a Trustee of the National

Fig. 16 Sutton Hoo at war. The
mechanical excavator is digging an
anti-glider ditch, the remains of
which are still visible today (see Col.
Pl. IV). Artist's impression by
Victor Ambrus.

Maritime Museum, who was able to put a stop to them. The site
slept again under the whine of the valiant Spitfires and the chug
of farm machinery trying to keep the country fed. In 1942 Edith
Pretty died, the family subsequently moved away and Sutton Hoo
House was sold. But, in defence of the site against any less
scrupulous successor, the Pretty family retained, by deed of
covenant in perpetuity, the right to excavate there and to dispose
of any finds which came to light.

In fulfilment of Edith Pretty's bequest, the finds from the ship-
burial now belonged to the British Museum; they spent the war in
a disused arm of the London Underground where they sought protection, like so many London citizens, from the bombs of the Third
Reich. At the end of the war in 1945 the boxes were retrieved and
returned to the British Museum where they were gingerly
reopened. The man charged with bringing the ship-burial to publication was not Brown, Phillips, Piggott or Grimes, but an assistant
keeper in the British Museum's Department of British and
Medieval Antiquities, Rupert Bruce-Mitford. He was confirmed in
his appointment in 1940 while in uniform at army camp. 'You will

also be responsible for Sutton Hoo,' wrote T.D. Kendrick, Keeper of British and Medieval Antiquities, in his letter; 'Brace yourself for this task'.[2] The task in question became Bruce-Mitford's life's work: the form of most of the objects now displayed and published is owed to him and the team he later gathered about him. All the team members had to work out the attributes of a unique assemblage, rapidly retrieved and sparsely recorded; to bring order to material in widely different states of preservation; and to interpret an extraordinary range of artefacts some of which had a shape or structure never seen before.

The finds had been recovered as fragments, into which they had broken when the timber burial chamber had collapsed under the weight of the mound; and the way in which the pieces fitted together was by no means obvious. The story of the stag indicates the nature of the problems facing the British Museum team, and the persistence and ingenuity required to solve them. The little bronze stag had been found at the west end of the chamber, together with an iron ring and bronze pedestal, which fitted together into a single assembly: a bronze stag on an iron ring supported by a bronze pedestal which had clearly become detached from something else. An early suggestion from Charles Phillips was that the stag should have stood on the crest of the helmet, a suitably totemic position, like the boar which stood on the crest of the Anglo-Saxon helmet from Benty Grange in Derbyshire. But the assembly of stag, ring and pedestal would have amounted to an extravagant and unstable helmet crest, and in any case had not been found near to the helmet, but next to the end of the iron 'lamp-stand'. This was a long piece of iron with a cradle or grid on the shaft and a small flat cruciform plate at the top. The grid and the plate had terminals in the form of stylised heads of bulls. At the base was a point with two scrolls, suitable to place in a leather frog for carrying on parade (Fig. 76). The object was interpreted by Bruce-Mitford as a standard, equating to the 'tufa' mentioned by Bede as being carried before Edwin, king of Northumbria, on his progress in 'city, town and countryside'.[3] The stag would set off the summit of the standard nicely, and for twenty-five years it was restored in this position. But during analysis in 1970 one of the team realised that there was no convincing means of attaching the bronze pedestal (bearing its ring and stag) to the top of the standard. So, what had it become detached from, if it did not belong to the standard? The next candidate was the large whetstone which had lain just to the north of the stag. The whetstone had a knob at each end, featuring human faces in relief, and was associated with bronze fittings. This composite object was ingeniously interpreted by Bruce-Mitford as a sceptre, its base an upturned saucer of bronze which provided a seating on the royal

Fig. 17 The 'sceptre', as restored through the researches of the British Museum team. British Museum.

knee; at its head could have stood the stag, a British work of art signifying perhaps a domination of all Britain (Fig. 17).4

In a effort to provide an unambiguous confirmation of the latest hypothesis, the bronze composition of the pedestal was determined in terms of the properties of the metals that made up the alloy: copper, tin, lead, zinc and other metals. The 'fingerprints' of the composition were taken from the stag, the pedestal, the standard and the bronze fittings associated with the whetstone. This exercise confirmed that the alloy of the stag had no association with the standard, but shared with the bronze fittings on the sceptre an unusually high admixture of gold. Furthermore, the upper knob of the whetstone was stained with iron rust, most easily explained as corrosion weeping down the upright stone from an iron object – probably the iron ring that carried the stag and that could have been mounted on its end. Thus this nimble little animal, the chosen logo of Sutton Hoo, posed briefly on the helmet, tried the standard and finally alighted on the sceptre.

The dead man had clearly been buried in parade dress, and piece by piece his accoutrements were reassembled: the splendid 'Sam Browne' (baldric) with its gold and garnet fittings, the purse, the sword, the spears and the shield carrying its dragon and falcon symbols. The helmet, which had corroded into a brittle iron shell, had been shattered into a hundred or more fragments of curved iron, amongst which could be seen elements of a crest inlaid with silver wire and panels with figural scenes. Reconstruction was first achieved by the conservator Herbert Maryon, who recomposed the pieces as a helmet of a rather 'coal-scuttle' style. It was a form that did not satisfy Bruce-Mitford, leaving parts of the face and neck quite unprotected.[5] In 1970 the restored helmet was dismantled and reassembled. The new reconstruction followed rigorous principles, using only joins that could be demonstrated, and omitting altogether the fragments whose position was equivocal. The basic structure was of iron, but decorative panels of bronze were secured to sites on the face-mask and cheek-pieces by riveted bronze strips. The bronze was tinned and would have had a silvery appearance, imitated in the replica that was made by the Tower Armouries.[6] In a startling symbolic composition, a snake body provides the protective rim across the crown. Its beady garnet eyes and gaping mouth meet the beak of a fierce bird, whose wings make the eyebrows, whose body forms the nose and whose tail forms the moustache of the implacable human armoured face. This was protection, physical and psychological, of a high order, a helmet of a kind imagined by the *Beowulf* poet, such that 'no sword, however sharp and tough, might cripple the wearer when he joined battle with his enemies'.[7] This form of the helmet has become the Sutton Hoo icon and is now used the world over to signify things mysterious, menacing or pagan. It would be hard to say if its aspect, with its heavy metal dome and dark sagging eyes, has borrowed or created the image of the modern helmeted biker in dark glasses (Fig. 18).

The Mound 1 hero was accompanied by a number of still more unusual objects evocative of the life of the warrior leader in his hall. A handful of gnarled and twisted fragments of maple wood from one of the hanging bowls was deduced, from the holes seen in one piece, to have been part of a stringed instrument with peg holes. Initially reconstructed as a six-stringed harp, its form was

a

Fig. 18 The helmet, showing stages of restoration: (a) in pieces as recovered from the chamber; (b) being positioned on a model head; (c) the final form. British Museum (with thanks to Angela Evans).

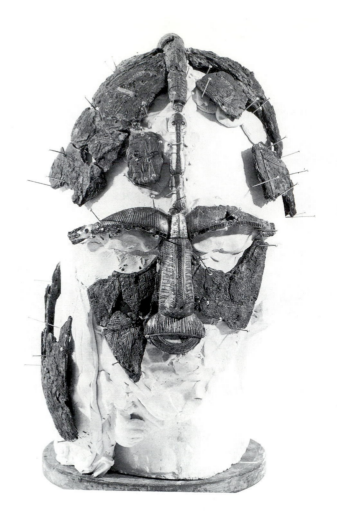

b

subsequently recomposed by analogy with that played by King David in the eighth-century Anglo-Saxon *Vespasian Psalter*; a replica of this instrument (Fig. 19) was played at a concert by one of Bruce-Mitford's daughters. Microscopic examination of the wood pieces had revealed fragments of hair, which indicated that the lyre had been kept in a beaver-skin bag.[8] Drinking horns were remodelled from the metal fragments decorating the mouths, and it was realised that they were based on the horns of the aurochs, a species of wild cattle now extinct. The forms of the crushed cauldrons were reconstructed; the greatest had hung from a chain 11 ft 4 in (3.45 m) long, suggestively cited as indicating the height of the roof-tree in Raedwald's hall. From the pads that had survived, textiles in a dozen different fabrics were discerned: from blankets, cloaks, hangings, tunics and linen; and in the careful

C

examination of every minute fragment, traces of otter fur were found and deduced to be from an otter-fur cap, perhaps worn under the heavy iron helmet.[9]

The Sutton Hoo finds analysis was one of the most thorough ever undertaken. Every scientific technique then available was deployed, and a few new ones developed. By the time publication was completed in 1983, ninety-six individuals had played a part, large or small, in the work. As a result of these researches, the 263 finds were reassigned to the 59 objects, or sets of objects, that had originally been placed in the chamber (see Digest, pp 180–1). Progress had also been made on the question of the missing body of the buried person. At the Pathology Museum at Guy's Hospital, Bruce-Mitford inspected the evidence from a celebrated murder case, the heels of Mrs Durand-Deacon, which were all that

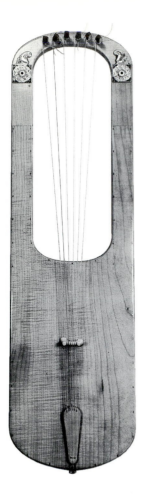

Fig. 19 The lyre, as reconstructed. British Museum.

survived from John George Haigh's tank of acid. Bruce-Mitford went on to infer a similar process, if much more protracted, in the acid bath provided by the hull of the Sutton Hoo ship, and showed that in a central area, where the great gold buckle and the baldric lay, the finds carried corrosion products that were slightly phosphate-enriched. The most likely explanation of this was that there had been a body, which had lain in rainwater collected in the hull and burial chamber, acidified by its passage through the acid sand of the mound; so over the years the body had been rendered invisible by decay. It could now be strongly argued, with scientific corroboration, that a body had lain or sat in the west half of the chamber, and the cenotaph theory was itself laid to rest.

While the objects were being conserved, reconstructed in the round and identified or interpreted, attempts were made to discern the background of the burial and to decide with greater certainty its date and who had been buried there. Bruce-Mitford initiated studies of the context of the jewellery, the ship, the region in which Sutton Hoo lay, and of the ship-burials that were broadly contemporary, especially those in the boat-grave cemeteries at Vendel and Valsgärde in Sweden.[10] The art of the gold and garnet jewellery had perhaps the greatest potential for dating and for making cultural links with the earlier and later art of England. Although resembling Kentish and Frankish work, the polychrome jewellery was assigned to a local East Anglian workshop by virtue of a type of little mushroom-shaped garnet which seemed to be confined to the Sutton Hoo assemblage. Bruce-Mitford related the interlacing or ribbon animals, known to Germanic art historians as 'Style II', to their lively cousins depicted in the early Christian gospel books, showing how the work of the Sutton Hoo jewellers should be seen as the missing link between the pagan and Christian worlds in the conversion period of the seventh century AD. In prime place amongst these gospel books (for which Sutton Hoo could now be seen as the forerunner) was the Lindisfarne Gospels, made about AD 698, and Bruce-Mitford turned aside to help bring out the magnificent facsimile and commentary. Now two great British monuments of native art stood clearly at either end of the seventh century, giving the country two stepping stones across the darkest period of its early history.[11]

The perception of the richness and symbolic character of the Mound 1 assemblage had, if anything, increased rather than lessened during the years in which the objects were conserved, identified and studied. The wealth was unparalleled in a British grave; the sceptre and standard, and indeed the ornamental military accoutrements, were unparalleled in any. It was natural to conclude that the Sutton Hoo ship-burial was unique and at the top of the social order; and in pagan Anglo-Saxon England, that meant it was the burial of a king. These assumptions have been justly challenged, but in general the interpretation has proved fairly robust. Now, the question of 'which king?' had again to be addressed, and in spite of Chadwick's confident assertion that it was Raedwald, this was a difficult task to tackle. The historical context of the burial and the identity of the person commemorated depended principally on the date. Three main methods of dating were available: the evidence of history (the documentary record), the evidence of art history (the style of the art) and the evidence of archaeology (scientific dating and behavioural parallels). In theory, these were independent of each other; in practice, the history was then seen as providing the most senior opinion, to which the other disciplines had to conform in order to win acceptance.

The approximate date, from the widely recognised character of the objects and their ornament, was not in doubt, being somewhere in the middle centuries of the first millennium AD, and most probably between 550 and 650. At this period, Anglo-Saxon and Latin writers describe Britain as having a number of kings and kingdoms, the peoples on the east coast being Angles and Saxons and having kingdoms such as Kent, Essex, Lindsey and East Anglia. Sutton Hoo itself is not mentioned in early documents, but the neighbouring village of Rendlesham to the north of it was described by Bede as lying 'within the Province of the East Angles'; while Felixstowe, on the other side of the Deben, is likely to have been named after the Felix cited by Bede as Bishop of the East Angles. So although we do not know exactly where East Anglia was at that time, it seems highly probable that it existed as a territory and that Sutton Hoo was located within it. If kings were buried there, they would be kings of East Anglia.

The kings of East Anglia are listed in a British Library manuscript;[12] no dates are given there but we know some of them from Bede, who mentions one or two in his *Ecclesiastical History*. If a member of East Anglia's ruling dynasty was buried in the Sutton Hoo ship-burial, it could have been Wehha (the first to rule over the East Angles), Wuffa (d.578), Tyttla (d.599), Raegenhere (in the succession, but who apparently did not rule, d.616/17), Eni (likewise), Raedwald (d.624/5), Earpwald (d.627/8), Sigeberht (d.636/7) or Ecgric (d.636/7). It was less likely to have been Anna, who came to the throne in 636/7, or his brothers Aethelhere and Aethelwald, or their successors, who were known to have been Christian, and who ruled as Christians. Raedwald was singled out by Bede as having won pre-eminence for his people and having 'held sway over all the provinces south of the Humber'.[13] Other aspects of Raedwald's career had attracted Bede's attention. Along with every politician in seventh-century England, the king was absorbed by the major question of the day: whether or not to convert to Christianity. Eventually he took the plunge on a visit to Christian Kent, but on his return to the East Anglian province 'his wife and certain perverse advisors' insisted that he renounce it. When, in an attempt at diplomatic compromise, Raedwald set up altars to Christ and to pagan gods in the same temple, the problem was by no means solved and no doubt attracted the contempt of both sides. The temple itself seems to have survived until the end of the seventh century, since Ealdwulf, a later king of East Anglia whom Bede had met, remembered seeing it when he was a boy.

Raedwald's queen, whose name we do not know, was clearly a forceful woman, and she had a high moral character. If she did not approve of Christianity, she was a champion of loyalty and trust. When Edwin of Northumbria was on the run from his enemy, the ferocious Aethelfrith, Raedwald's court was one of the places in which he sought refuge. Raedwald was offered a large sum to despatch him, and was much tempted to do so. But in contrast to Lady Macbeth, Raedwald's queen dissuaded him, saying that 'it was unworthy of a great king to sell his friend in the hour of need for gold, and worse still to sacrifice his royal honour'.[14] Raedwald agreed and Edwin lived on to become the king and champion of a Christian Northumbria. Raedwald was thus special amongst the East Anglian kings and remained the most popular candidate for the person commemorated in the Mound 1 ship-burial. He died in about 624 or 625, and this is consequently the date generally assigned to the burial. The argument from history has been dominant, and it is probably fair to say that the dates obtained from other disciplines have been influenced in some measure by the advantages of conformity with the story of Raedwald.

The art style made a date in the late sixth to seventh century likely; but exactly when in that period? The great silver dish carried a stamp of Anastasius I, who was emperor of Byzantium from 491 to 518, so the burial was at least later than AD 491. Radiocarbon dates were taken from two carboniferous sources: a piece of timber found lying on the bottom of the ship gave a date of AD 656 ± 45, while wax from the iron lamp dated to AD 523 ± 45.

The prime responsibility for a tighter dating was placed on the coins in the purse (Fig. 20). In other archaeological periods, such as the Roman, coins are the excavators' friend, dateable often to within a few years and sufficiently numerous to provide at least some primary find spots from which to argue a date *after which* a burial was made or a building erected. But in the early medieval period, coins are rare, their images derivative and their inscriptions ambiguous. The coins in the purse were Merovingian

Fig. 20 Gold coin from the purse. It was probably issued by the Frankish king Theodebert II at Clermont-Ferrand between about AD 595 and 612. The obverse shows a diademed figure, echoing the effigy of a Roman emperor. The reverse shows a cross, the emblem of Christianity, and the name Theodebert. British Museum.

tremisses, minted in France, but they carry no dates. The coins do carry mint names, as well as portraits, but the names of the issuers were often blundered, or copied to lend them spurious and anachronistic authority. The date assigned to the Sutton Hoo group by French experts was at first AD 650–60, and this was the dating that was accepted for the first twenty-five years after the ship-burial's discovery. But in 1960, the terminal date of the coin parcel was revised by the French numismatist Lafaurie to around AD 625. Thus Raedwald, who died c.625, could now be endorsed by the coins as candidate number 1. In his own independent confirmation of this date, John Kent of the British Museum carried out an analysis of the specific gravity of the Sutton Hoo coins, proposing that the gold content of the Merovingian coinage was reduced through time, as the metal was progressively recycled. By comparing the specific gravity of gold coins from dated hoards, a sequence was deduced which ended with the Sutton Hoo parcel in the early decades of the seventh century. The character of the assemblage remained curious: were the coins currency or hoarded bullion? Could the burial have been much later than the date of the coins' manufacture? The historian Philip Grierson advanced the imaginative hypothesis that the thirty-seven coins, three blanks and two ingots found in the purse, or associated with it, represented the payment of forty oarsmen, a pilot and a steersman, by analogy with the Roman payment of an obol to Charon who brought souls to their rest in Hades. If this was its context, the date of the coin parcel could be close to the date of their deposition in the burial; no obstacle was offered to the identification of the buried man as Raedwald.

The next task was to place Sutton Hoo in the wider context of its district, its kingdom and that kingdom's neighbours. Near the site were two famous places, Rendlesham and Snape, which engaged Bruce-Mitford's attention. Rendlesham is mentioned in Bede's *Ecclesiastical History* as a the site of a palace where, in the seventh century, the East Anglian king Aethelwald stood as god-father at the baptism of Swidhelm, king of Essex.[15] Bruce-Mitford searched the archives and then searched the site itself, concluding that there was an early Saxon cemetery there, and, somewhere as yet unlocated, a palace and an early church waiting to be found. Also nearby was Snape, the site where a ship-burial had been found in the mid-nineteenth century. It was once a cluster of nine or ten mounds on Snape Common, but most had been dug into in campaigns of 1827 and 1862. Little notice of the first of these campaigns had survived in the archives, apart from rumours of gold aplenty; but from the second campaign, the record of a ship-burial, the first identified in Britain and one of the first to be correctly interpreted in Europe, has survived (Fig. 21). The ship was at least 46 ft (14 m) long and marked in the sand by rows of rivets spaced at 5½ in (14 cm) intervals. It had already been robbed, but the grave goods that had survived to be reported included two iron spear-heads, a glass claw-beaker and a gold finger-ring, together with a 'mass of human hair'. Bruce-Mitford reinterpreted the human hair as belonging rather to the fabric of a shaggy pile cloak, like examples from Sutton Hoo and Broomfield, and tracked down the ring, which is now in the British Museum. Snape, which had also produced cremation burials in pots, was clearly a key site for the understanding of Sutton Hoo: complementary, but different.[16]

Bruce-Mitford's researches also took him to the Malären district of Sweden, cradle of the Svear, whose kingdom gave Sweden (Sverige) its name. In this region there were two well-known cemeteries, Vendel and Valsgärde, which contained ship-burials of similar date to Sutton Hoo. Bruce-Mitford helped the Swedish archaeologist Sune Lindquist to excavate one of the ship-burials at Valsgärde, and the Swedish links with Sutton Hoo became ever more important in his mind. The Swedish allusions in *Beowulf*, the similarity of the Sutton Hoo helmet and shield with examples found in Sweden, and above all the rite of ship-burial persuaded him of a strong seventh-century connection.

The Sutton Hoo ship-burial also became a player in a wider field, since in addition to the cultural artefacts it shared with its immediate neighbours, it could be seen to have drawn objects from all over the world known to the Anglo-Saxons (Fig. 22). The thirty-seven coins came from thirty-seven different mints in the heartland of Merovingian France; the silver-ware came from the eastern Mediterranean, in the hinterland of the residual Roman

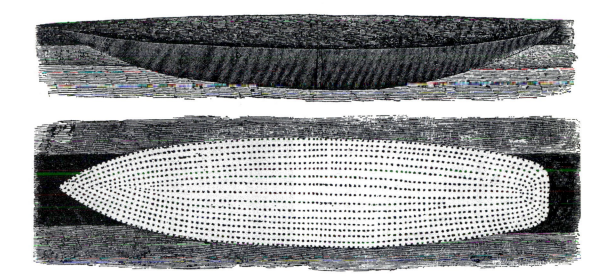

Fig. 21 A plan of the Snape ship found in 1862. After Hele, reproduced in Bruce-Mitford 1974, 120.

empire at Byzantium. There were textiles whose origin could be traced to Italy and the Middle East, possibly Syria, and a 'Coptic' bowl which had probably made its way from Egypt. Here were precious objects which had arrived directly or indirectly across the seas and along the rivers or half-remembered Roman routes, from hall to hall and giver to giver in the diplomatic gestures of a dozen emerging nations of the new post-Roman Europe. The Sutton Hoo burial was becoming established as a closely dated landmark in early medieval history.

There were still some problems, however, that Bruce-Mitford wanted to see solved before committing his studies to print. The ship needed a more accurate plan, since the Science Museum's was rather schematic and Hutchinson's notes had apparently been lost during the war. The chamber had been planned, but was uncertainly related to the ship, the ship trench and the mound, each of which had only vague dimensions. The comparable burials in Sweden had produced horses, sometimes outside the ship, but at Mound 1 there had been no digging beyond the confines of the hull. Could horses have been killed and buried here as part of the funeral ceremony? Certain pieces were missing from the conserved artefacts: could they still be found? In short, the excavation of the Sutton Hoo ship-burial was not complete and should now be finished. A published report would need a plan of the other mounds, still smothered in bracken; and while they were about it, it would be useful to know whether the putative Mound 5, placed tentatively in the gap between Mound 2 and Mound 6, actually existed. This would help with the interpretation of the development of the cemetery as a series of rows of burial mounds. At the same time it would be inter-

Fig. 22 (Opposite) According to Bruce-Mitford's study, the Mound 1 finds are thought to have come from Scandinavia, France, Italy and the Eastern Mediterranean. But the provenance of the sword, shield and helmet are uncertain; all may have been made in East Anglia rather than imported. Also on the map are the locations of scriptoria likely to have made or received insular manuscripts in the next generation. (Hooper/Carver)

esting to investigate the character of a 'Bronze Age hill-top village' beneath Mounds 1, 2 and 3 which had been noted by Basil Brown in his diary.

Accordingly, after much debate and deliberation, in 1965 the British Museum mounted a return visit to Sutton Hoo on a truly impressive scale. The ship-burial site, never backfilled, was to be totally excavated, Rupert Bruce-Mitford taking charge of the completion of the ship trench, and Paul Ashbee, who had considerable expertise in the excavation and interpretation of prehistoric burial mounds, would take the remains of Mound 1 apart and establish its structure. The bioarchaeologist Geoffrey Dimbleby would examine the buried soil and reconstruct the vegetation sequence. Meanwhile, a team from the British Museum's new Department of Prehistoric and Romano-British Antiquities would excavate between the visible mounds to investigate the prehistoric settlement and test for the existence of Mound 5.

All this and more was achieved. For the first time the site was largely cleared of its bracken and a contour survey made. The prehistorians found a Neolithic ditch and Bronze Age palisade, noting also a strong showing of Beaker material (c.2000 BC) beneath Mound 1. Mound 5 was shown to exist, and to have had a robbed burial chamber (which was left unexcavated). Six early medieval burials were found outside and between the mounds. Three of these were inhumations arranged around Mound 5, while further to the west there was a skull buried in a pit, with two unfurnished cremations near by. The skull, which was accompanied by a few scraps of metal, was carbon-dated to the mid-eighth century AD.

The lobes of Mound 1 were distinguished from the spoil heaps of Charles Phillips and Basil Brown and excavated in a grid of square-cut pits – a system pioneered by Sir Mortimer Wheeler. Ashbee deduced that Mound 1 had been constructed from dumps of sand and turf scraped up from the surrounding surface. No quarry ditch or pits were found. Inside the Mound 1 ship trench the mangled remains of the ship were treated with surgical intensity. A great shelter was erected over the trench, beneath which the detritus of the bracken infill and the sand kicked up by rabbits and military manoeuvres was cleaned gently away (Fig. 23). Then appeared the rivets, still *in situ* but subjected to distortions of axis and alignment as though the great ship had twisted in a bed of agony. A detailed plan was made, and in spite of the obvious displacements the ultimate record was made, a 1:1 cast in plaster of paris of the hull skin. This was transformed into a fibreglass positive and the prow section of this sad, sloughed ship-skin was later to appear in a corner of the National Maritime Museum. Diligent sieving of the ship trench spoil brought nineteen scraps of solder, Stockholm tar or unidentified residues,

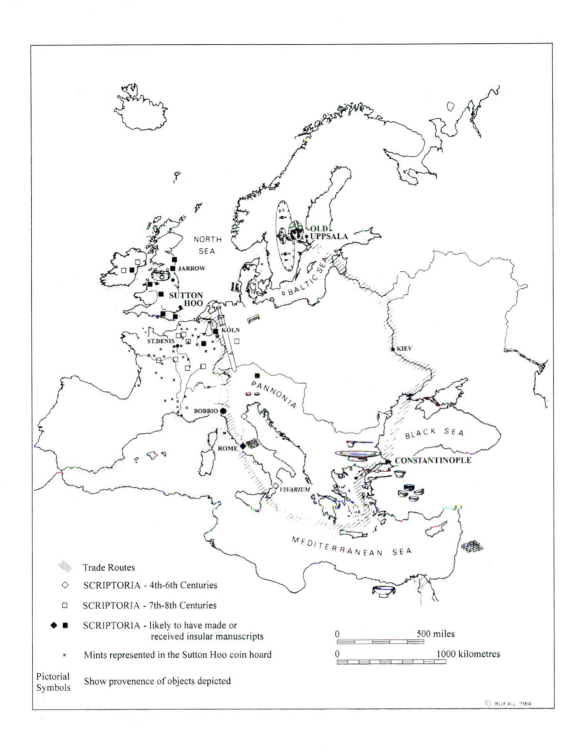

Trade Routes

◇ SCRIPTORIA - 4th-6th Centuries

□ SCRIPTORIA - 7th-8th Centuries

◆ ■ SCRIPTORIA - likely to have made or
received insular manuscripts

✗ Mints represented in the Sutton Hoo coin hoard

Pictorial
Symbols   Show provenance of objects depicted

0   500 miles

0   1000 kilometres

© RUFAU 1984

Fig. 23 The shelter erected over the Mound 1 ship during the completion of excavation 1965–71. G. Keiller.

while reworking of the 1939 spoil heaps produced thirty-four pieces including two small brooches, two buckles and minute fragments of tine from the stag. Under the ship was a long timber stain, probably from an oar. But no horses were found.

The survey of the site itself produced evidence for a total of seventeen mounds of which two (16 and 17) were questionable. Bruce-Mitford proposed that the cemetery had developed along an axis running from Mound 2 to Mound 3, although there was a curious gap between Mounds 3, 1 and 7. The summits of most of the mounds were marked by a little depression aligned east–west. Bruce-Mitford called these 'ship-dents', comparing them to the depressions over the intact ship-graves at Valsgärde (Fig. 24). The Sutton Hoo 'ship-dents' were presumably seen as areas of collapse caused by the subsidence of the deck of a buried ship. The expectation was therefore that other ship-burials remained to be discovered.

In an enormous work of 2,441 pages and hundreds of illustrations, *The Sutton Hoo Ship-burial* was published over the next decade. It appeared in three volumes. Volume 1 (1975) dealt with the ship-burial, its excavation and re-excavation and included all the other information of whatever type and character, relating to the site, the structure of the grave and the mound, that Bruce-Mitford and his team had amassed during thirty years of study. It concluded that the ship-burial was the memorial of Raedwald, king of East Anglia, as Chadwick had long before surmised. Volume 2 (1978) concerned itself with the regalia, objects mainly assigned to Raedwald's kingly and warrior roles. And volume 3, issued in two parts in 1983, described the remaining finds.

There had been some criticism of Bruce-Mitford and his British Museum team for a procedure perceived in some quarters as ponderous and secretive, over the thirty-year gestation of the publication; now they had produced a book that was monumentally generous, in which every aspect and analysis then conceivable of every find was reported and illustrated.[17] By the time it had all appeared there were few people whose mode of existence would allow them the time and the space to absorb the whole of such a work. Its existence provided a quarry of information and ideas, rather than a text-book for the student or a briefing document for the busy researcher. The more casual reader had to rely on Bruce-Mitford's immensely successful *Handbook* to the Sutton Hoo ship-burial, which already contained enough on the finds to engender a lively debate in a student seminar, supplemented by Charles Green's *Sutton Hoo: The Excavation of a Royal Ship Burial*, which was an early attempt to tell the story of the excavation and put its findings into context in East Anglia and Europe. These were later to be joined by an original account of the Sutton Hoo ship-burial by Angela Evans, a member of the British Museum's Sutton Hoo team. The objects themselves were now on display, and were soon to have a gallery of their own in the British Museum's Early Medieval room.

The public would seem to have been served at all levels. The Sutton Hoo ship-burial had sailed majestically into the annals of museum literature, and the material for any reconsideration of the evidence or any reinterpretation of the finds or burial rite was available in the public domain worldwide. The British Museum had done its duty handsomely and only the small-minded could now cavil.[18]

Perhaps surprisingly, it was from Bruce-Mitford himself that the initiative came to question and amend the 'definitive version' and from the late 1970s he was pressing for a return to Sutton Hoo and for more digging there. In a later television programme, he recalled what had been achieved and suggested what should come next. Standing before the cameras on the grass of Sutton Hoo with the mounds behind him, he said he now felt confident about the date of the coins as lying between AD 615 and 635 and confident that there had been a body in Mound 1. Moreover there could be no doubt in his mind that it was the body of Raedwald; the burial with its ambiguous religious symbolism 'suited Raedwald to a T'. Now we needed to know whether Sutton Hoo was *the* burial ground of the dynasty. Were Raedwald's predecessors buried here? Could we find the grave of Raewald's wife? Were there more ships? When did cremation stop and inhumation start? Why did burial continue into the Christian period (as suggested by an eighth-century radiocarbon date on the skull in the skull-pit)? And what was the social and economic basis which lay behind this phenomenal peak of wealth and ostentation? Addressing us engagingly through the camera's lens he announced, 'The answers, my friends, are not blowing in the wind. The answers are lying in the ground. In fact, I'm standing on them'.[19]

Familiarity with Sutton Hoo's world had thus served only to make him all the more curious about it; and his curiosity was shared by those for whom archaeology's task was to supply the gaps to narrative history. This was a clientele that had little interest in the relative dimensions of rivets or indeed in the graves of the common people; the early kings of England were the movers and shakers of their day, and hidden in their spears and cauldrons were signs of their times. Few doubted the general interpretation of Mound 1 as the burial of a king of East Anglia, although there was still room for a side show of scholastic disquisition about which king it was. Most scholars then were unconcerned to question the actual notion of kingship at

Fig. 24 The early medieval mound cemetery at Valsgärde, central Sweden, showing the axial 'ship-dents'. M.O.H. Carver.

all, royalty being accepted as having a permanent and welcome place in the hearts of the British people. But who could resist speculation on who was buried in the other mounds, and whether they were of the pagan or Christian persuasion? For these historians, then, the urge to see more kings was a reasonable one, which deserved gratification.

Mrs Pretty's heir, Robert, owner through deed of covenant of the finds and the right to excavate, had given permission to renew the excavations in 1965. He was ready to do so again, and in partnership with Rupert Bruce-Mitford encouraged support for a new and even larger campaign under the joint direction of Bruce-Mitford and Philip Rahtz, the new Professor of Archaeology at York. In 1978 a small steering committee was formed, backed by the Society of Antiquaries of London and chaired by Rosemary Cramp, the charismatic head of archaeology at Durham University and excavator of Monkwearmouth and Jarrow, Bede's monastery. But not everyone was enthusiastic. Bruce-Mitford had retired from the British Museum and his former colleagues were expressing reservations about another cam-

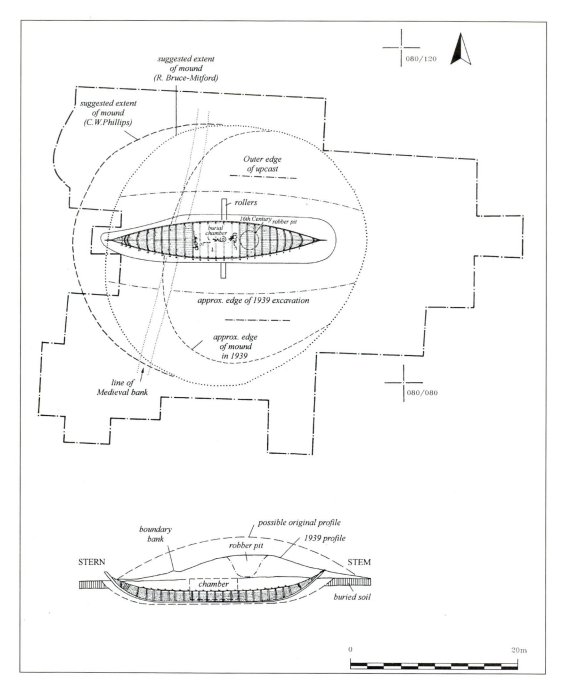

Fig. 25 Plan and section of the Mound 1 ship-burial following the researches of the British Museum team. Composite drawing by Elizabeth Hooper/Annette Roe.

paign. The Sutton Hoo adventure deserved a rest and readers needed time to absorb the tomes with which they were confronted. Archaeology's aims had changed so much during the 1960s and 70s that a 'royal burial' was hardly on the agenda. There was a risk that a return to Sutton Hoo would be construed as a poorly disguised treasure hunt.

These cautious views were countered by those of the steering committee: Bruce-Mitford was the greatest living expert on Sutton Hoo, and would probably occupy the position of ultimate authority to his death and beyond it. It would be foolish to fail to profit by his knowledge and experience, and that of the current team who were just finishing their extraordinary study. However, such reasoning could be flexible: if the British Museum were reticent about a new campaign, maybe another partner could be found for the venture. In an astute political manoeuvre, the steering committee managed to secure the collaboration of the Ashmolean Museum in Oxford, and Robert Pretty put his signature to a letter of agreement endowing them with all the finds that were expected to be recovered.

In this atmosphere of cold war diplomacy, a seminar was held in Oxford on the occasion of a conference entitled 'Anglo-Saxon Cemeteries, 1979'. The conference featured the majority of the country's practising early medieval archaeologists, and a good few from abroad. The seminar was designed to test the will of the delegates for and against a new campaign at Sutton Hoo. But the case for further excavation was weakly presented, rarely exceeding, in its force of argument, an exhortation to the audience to entertain a proper regard for natural curiosity. The relevance of a new campaign to the current world of the conference participants was at best obscure. The excitement of the Sutton Hoo ship-burial belonged in most cases to their adolescence; modern students were wrestling with more exciting theoretical concepts such as the detection of social change, while fieldworkers were taking a few hours off from the manic seven-day week of the rescue excavator. The challenges of the day lay in testing new ideas, or snatching new sites from the destructive machinery of roadbuilders and urban developers, not in reheating yesterday's archaeological discoveries, in which little was promised except more of the same.

It is an astonishing reflection of the tenacity and *sang-froid* of the archaeological establishment of the day that this reception offered no obstacle to their proceeding. This was perhaps not unconnected with the first chill wind which was immediately felt in the nooks and crannies of every state-supported activity following Margaret Thatcher's election as Prime Minister in the same year. The switch to project-funding signalled the end of the state archaeological service which had been created (*de facto*) by underwriting core organisations in county councils and universities. In student seminar rooms, too, the doctrine of self-dedication to the quest of piecing together the past was being questioned. At the conference itself, Ian Hodder pointed out that the analytical approach to Anglo-Saxon or any other cemeteries might be flawed. There would be examples at least where graves did not reflect a real, but a wished-for, society. The evidence of material culture, like that of documents, was no longer the revelation of a simple truth. The intellectual citadel of archaeology had been captured from the natural scientists by those for whom material was not culture, but text.[20]

The loss of confidence experienced by theorists and rescuers in the face of contemporary politics was probably the decisive factor that allowed an apparently anachronistic project like digging more of Sutton Hoo to persevere. Rosemary Cramp withdrew, but the steering committee forged ahead. The provocative flirtation with the Ashmolean proved effective. The British Museum was soon back in negotiation with the Society of Antiquaries, and succumbing to the sensitive diplomacy of the latter's President, Professor Christopher Brooke, had acceded to a treaty to fund a new campaign for five years. Those on the inside who had doubted that this was a good use of the Antiquaries' research money were persuaded that the country needed an archaeological 'flagship' to recover a more glamorous place in the appreciation of the public.[21]

If there was another more intellectual agenda for the new project to address it was not advertised. Indeed, rather than issue a prescription, the Sutton Hoo Committee simply announced its intentions to resume excavations in the *London Gazette*. Interested parties were invited to submit applications for the directorship, accompanied by their suggestions for a programme of exploration. Polemic in favour of the project switched to a 'rescue' theme: the site was in jeopardy from treasure-hunters and rabbits and must be saved by being dug. Right on cue, on 14 February 1982, Mound 11 was found to have had a large hole dug through the top of it, presumably by treasure-hunters. It was a peculiar mound to choose, nearly flat and under a tree; even more strangely, the robbers had got to the level of the buried soil and then stopped, as though making a gesture rather than indulging in a serious pillaging operation.

Few archaeological projects can have been initiated with greater publicity and more hostility than the Sutton Hoo research campaign of 1983. 'We *know* how the Anglo-Saxons buried their kings in the seventh century,' wrote the editor of *Rescue News*, lamenting the waste of resources better applied to sites being lost to the bulldozer. Ostensibly for similar reasons, professional field units were also opposed, most particularly those resident in East Anglia. The Scole Committee, representing the latter, promised that they would formally object to Scheduled Monument Consent being given for excavations at Sutton Hoo. Even the editor of *Treasure Hunting Monthly* condemned the proposed project as selfish and elitist. There were clearly people to mollify before any digging could start. And yet this must have been the most exciting and liberating opportunity that a field archaeologist had ever been presented with: to have the chance to escape, for a moment, from the reactive, fire-brigade mentality of the rescue scene and develop methods and protocols of use to all; above all to address a research question with adequate means and few constraints beyond one's own imagination and skills. How could anyone fail to respond to such a challenge? It was a measure of the paralysis being experienced during archaeology's great metamorphosis (or perhaps of the ethical ambiguity of the Sutton Hoo project) that only seventeen people applied for the job. On 30 October 1982 six were interviewed by the Sutton Hoo Committee, their designs for a new campaign were assessed, and one was chosen. It was in this way that the future of Sutton Hoo came to be placed in the hands of the author of this book.

The successful design suggested that a new research programme at Sutton Hoo could serve the community in three ways: it could bring new understanding to the question of how England began and the character of the society that began it; it could develop new ways of doing field archaeology; and it could give the country a monument which at the time lay in a neglected, bedraggled and vulnerable condition.

In research, the early medieval agenda had already broadened beyond the historical or social equations that had driven the study of Sutton Hoo up to that point. The presence of kings was not sufficient or even necessary to the inquiry. Scholars in Sweden had been reluctant to attribute their mounds at Vendel and Valsgärde to kings, or even to assume that kingship was inevitable. The burial mounds could be the investments of the families of successful merchants. It was clear that at some time kingdoms had formed in the lands around the North Sea. But when and why? The existence of early states was being proposed and tested in other periods, both Classical and prehistoric. If Sutton Hoo was just the burial ground of kings, then there was little point in investigating it further, since the argument would be a circular one: kings are buried like this because these are kings. But if the cemetery could be shown to reflect the politics, social organisation and ideology of its day, then it would be worth interrogating it on these matters. In the new project the questions would be framed in a new way, seeking explanation, rather than discovery from the ground. We would ask, not 'what more can be found there?', but 'why that?', 'why there?' and 'why then?'.

The science of fieldwork was evolving rapidly, too. There was a certain contrast between rescue and research methods, and neither was following satisfactory procedures. Rescue projects had money but not enough time, and were liable to produce too much indigestible data; research projects had too little money and often ideas that were too big to be tested in small areas opened in short summer seasons. Both were infected with the notion that only large-scale excavation made sense. So excavations should be as large and thorough as possible, termed 'total excavation', a strategy justified when applied in the rescue theatre as 'preservation by record'. But these concepts were being challenged by a more scientific procedure dominated by the idea of 'evaluation'. Here the site is thoroughly examined by non-destructive methods, and the underground strata are predicted before any destructive digging is done. The predicted character of the buried site, termed a 'deposit model', is matched to the questions being posed by researchers and the result is a 'strategy', a programme in which the *smallest* possible area is dug that will answer the questions put. The rest of the site is conserved for the future. These ideas had already been tested in some urban rescue work; Sutton Hoo offered an ideal opportunity to see if they could work on a rural site.[22]

The protection of Sutton Hoo for the future was an obvious concomitant of these ideas, and the physical condition of the site in 1983 was catastrophic. Part of it had been scheduled, and the notice announcing that it was 'an offence to damage it' had fallen over and was half buried in the bracken which was growing nearly six feet high. Rabbits burrowed and multiplied in the barrows, and the scars of their old warrens were colonised by brambles. Clearly, the one thing that must not happen at Sutton Hoo was nothing. A 'burial ground of kings' deserved a better fate.

In an attempt to win over the persistent opposition to the project, these new approaches were presented to a public meeting held at University College London on 15 April 1983, chaired by Charles Thomas, the President of the Council for British Archaeology. To obtain a representative professional and avocational sample, all 1,000 members of the Society for Medieval Archaeology were invited – and many came. 'Massive opposition' had been promised by *Guardian* journalist Ann Maitland, who claimed that it was widely believed that archaeologists themselves had vandalised Mound 11 in order to justify the new campaign. But in the event, the opposition was measured and reasonable and largely confined to the archaeological profession itself. The presentation of the programme for the project by its director opened with a slide of the dragon from the Mound 1 shield, and the words: 'There is a dragon which stalks the land, spreading discord ...' It was followed by an outline of the actual research design and its justification, stressing the concept of evaluation as a prerequisite to excavation. Leading East Anglian archaeologist Peter Wade-Martins expressed reservations which were widely held: why now? why this site? Have the results of the previous campaigns, only just published, been properly absorbed? Surely the archaeology being forced on us through imminent destruction should have priority over a new, some would say unnecessary, project? Others objected that the proposed budget (£100,000 per year) was far too small to do the job properly, and others challenged the proposed use of students, which would mean low standards.

These fears were understandable and answers were offered. Many of the objectors were no doubt calling to mind certain old-fashioned, badly resourced university excavations, which now contrasted a little unfavourably with the standards being set by professional field units. But the new Sutton Hoo project was itself to be done by a field unit. The first three years of the programme would be dedicated to an evaluation that would predict what was left of the site and what it could tell us. At that point, and before destructive digging began on any scale, a full *project design* would be prepared, circulated and published in support of our application for Scheduled Monument Consent. Meanwhile the site was being damaged by treasure hunters and rabbits, and furthermore was a complete mess, overgrown by bracken and receiving no care or maintenance. If we continued to ignore it, it would no longer be there to argue about. The money that underwrote the project was not available for 'rescue' purposes; in fact it was only available for research, so if it was not taken up for Sutton Hoo it would be unlikely to be available for rescue projects. But the rescue movement could still benefit by using the project as a laboratory for new techniques. It was hoped that a summer season by the Deben would offer 'rescuers' a stimulating break from their stressful labours elsewhere. It was agreed that the budget was not big enough, and more money would have to be raised. That was the point of choosing a site like Sutton Hoo, which had the power to stimulate new kinds of financial support for archaeology. Using students was not necessarily a prescription for low standards. Students would be trained in formal 'field schools', not used as cheap labour. Units must not operate restrictive practices under the guise of 'professionalism': there had to be a way of getting into archaeology, just as we had all done. Why should students be introduced to field archaeology only on under-resourced, unprofessional field projects? By wel-

Fig. 26 Charles Phillips on his last visit to Sutton Hoo in conversation with the author. Edward Morgan.

coming students, the Sutton Hoo project would help to teach a new generation to dig. But the most important objective of the project was to generate useful research for both the early medieval and the prehistoric periods. The rationale for British archaeology could not remain just 'rescue'; it must be, or become, research-driven, and thus build up the stock of community support and ensure its own survival.

These arguments were largely effective. Winding up the meeting, Martin Biddle, the celebrated excavator of Winchester, announced: 'This has been a turning point in British archaeology. For the first time a project has been presented to the archaeological fraternity before it has happened.' The mood was now more positive and generally supportive, if occasionally sceptical. Later in the year *Treasure Hunting Monthly* revised its position, suggesting that the publicised approach was sensible, and inviting its readers to support it (a service for which the community is greatly indebted). If the cautious approach was to the liking of the archaeological community, this would have to be translated into much patience on the part of the sponsors. The BBC had signed a contract with the Sutton Hoo Committee, paying a facility fee for exclusive coverage. Would they stoically endure three years of scientific fiddling before any new mounds were opened? But their appointed producer, Ray Sutcliffe, liked the scientific approach, and the committee was unwavering in its support. Shortly afterwards the committee reformed as the Sutton Hoo Research Trust with the same membership: Sir David Wilson, Sir David Attenborough and Leslie Webster for the British Museum, and Philip Rahtz, Barry Cunliffe, Michael Robbins and Christopher Brooke for the Society of Antiquaries, with Stanley West representing Suffolk County Council. Together they steered Sutton Hoo away from the heroic age of amazing discoveries and startling finds and embarked on a scientific expedition with a new emphasis and a new vocabulary. 'Evaluation', 'research agenda', 'ethical stance', 'remote mapping', 'project design', 'horizon mapping', 'recovery levels', 'excavation strategy', 'intervention', 'analytical destiny', 'management plan': these were the catchphrases of the new campaign, and broadly represented the programme it was to follow.

The early discoverers, conservators and researchers of Sutton Hoo were giants; and we new researchers saw further because we stood on their shoulders. What we saw, however, led us off in a new direction.

3

THE MESSAGE OF THE MOUNDS
Research and excavation, 1983–98

The new Sutton Hoo expedition was organised in three parts: one devised for the site itself, 'the excavation programme' (including evaluation and strategy); one for the region in which it lay, the 'kingdom of East Anglia survey'; and the third, a programme of 'comparative studies' – formal and informal dialogues with scholars engaged in similar expeditions. The aim was to describe seventh-century society, and determine how it changed, discover what a kingdom was, when and why the people of East Anglia had created one and how they interacted with others across the sea. For East Anglia was only one of a dozen 'kingdoms' which were beginning to make themselves visible around the North Sea coast in the fifth to eighth centuries AD (Fig. 27).

COMPARATIVE STUDIES

The comparative studies, which did much to broaden and deepen the research agenda for the project, were formalised at a series of meetings, beginning with one at Spoleto in Italy in 1983. In this conference, memorable among other things for a small but palpable earthquake, ideas were aired about what a site like Sutton Hoo could mean and how we could know more about it. Current research suggested that burial mounds, or at least big burial mounds, were something new for the Anglo-Saxons in the seventh century, and should have a special meaning for that time. They might have served, as had been suggested for Iron Age barrows in central Europe, as a way of marking the ownership of land. The barrow stood on a hill and 'documented' what the buried ancestor had owned, perhaps by virtue of what could be seen from its summit. Barrows had political meanings, too, and in seventh-century England the erection of a burial mound might have signalled the adoption of a specific political alignment. Barrow building had begun in Kent in the sixth century, in the form of large cemeteries containing numerous small barrows; at the

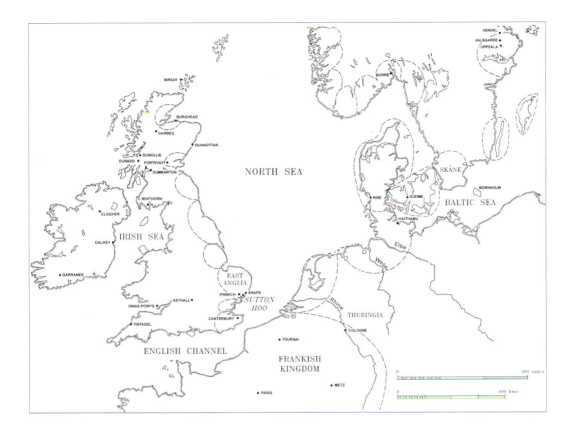

Fig. 27 Early kingdoms of the North Sea: coastal territories suggested by recent research. M.O.H. Carver.

end of the sixth century, the practice appears to have migrated elsewhere, into Anglo-Saxon areas outside Kent. Surely it could be no coincidence that Augustine had arrived in the late sixth century, and that Kent had become a Christian ally of France by then? The barrows of Sutton Hoo and elsewhere could thus be read as demonstrative protests against the creep of Christianity, monuments of anti-Christian defiance. They may even have included the memorials of disaffected Kentish aristocrats, unwilling to bend the knee to Rome. The burying of Christian objects in the Sutton Hoo graves need have no pro-Christian significance. Examples from Nubia showed that the burial mounds erected there at the end of another empire (the Meroitic) had included emblems from half a dozen different religions: a scarab, a love charm in Greek, three lead curses and a gold cross. Whether or not they were the burials of kings, the Sutton Hoo mounds should be political signals, in this case of pagan defiance from a people threatened by Christian encroachment.[1]

The meaning of early medieval burial mounds was pursued in a seminar at Cambridge on 13–15 September the following year, entitled 'Princely Burials'. Such burials, the delegates agreed, must have had some connection with social organisation; the community that made them should have been highly stratified, with an aristocracy on top. What did it mean, then, if a community adopted burial mounds, when it had not previously had them? Wolfgang Böhme showed how the building of burial mounds had begun in the lower Rhine in the fifth century and moved eastwards, reaching the upper Rhine by the eighth. This could mean that communities along the Rhine were becoming socially stratified one after another, building barrows as and when they acquired an aristocracy.[2] But there was at least one other possibility: perhaps the communities always had an aristocracy, but there had come a moment when it became politically imperative to show it. Only then would an investment in such a thing as a burial mound be worth the trouble. What would provoke such an investment? A political threat was one obvious answer, and the coming of Christianity may have been the threat in question. Burial mounds could thus mean either an aristocracy in the process of formation, or one under threat. The Sutton Hoo mounds may have fallen into one or both of these categories.

An opportunity to place the proposed Sutton Hoo research in the wider British context occurred next at Oxford in 1986, at a conference entitled 'The Origins of Anglo-Saxon Kingdoms'. Here the battle lines became clearer between those for whom the Anglo-Saxons had always had kings and those for whom kingship was an innovation of the late sixth century, Sutton Hoo being a dramatic sign of it. A king, according to the latter theory, was someone who could claim jurisdiction over a territory and tax it. The onset of taxation was marked by the arrival of 'manors', settlements that had evidence for storing grain or processing animals on a large scale, like Wicken Bonhunt in Essex. The imposition of tax was also marked on this theory by an absence of grave goods from the majority of graves: the subservient classes among the English no longer needed to indicate their membership of a supernatural tribe by dressing and equipping their dead, but gave the same resources in tax to a new and real authority: the king and the kingdom. The arrival of 'manor' sites and the decline of grave goods in a majority of graves, contrasting the great richness of a few burial mounds, showed, therefore, that kingship was an innovation of the late sixth century.[3] The fuller exploration of Sutton Hoo should test these hypotheses. Had these burials a unique, a royal role in East Anglia, or were they just the memorials of one landowning family among many?

For some, all these forays into interpretation were fanciful; perhaps Sutton Hoo was simply a traditional burial ground, and had a long history of use stretching back deep into prehistory. In the countryside, life moves slowly, and nothing could be understood except by what went before. The significance of Sutton Hoo's prehistory was addressed at a meeting held at Oxford in 1985. No one doubted that a prehistoric settlement existed before the Anglo-Saxon burial mounds, but there were mixed views on how seriously it should be taken. When Brian Hope-Taylor had excavated the first British early medieval palace at Yeavering in Northumbria, a site all the more evocative because it had been known to Bede, he had shown that the great timber halls had stood on a site that was already ancient before the Anglian kings of Northumbria developed it. From this he created a vision of a long-lived folk centre, the scene of ceremonies and gatherings, a special place never forgotten and always significant through the centuries.[4] Could Sutton Hoo have functioned in a similar way? Few thought continuous use to be likely. In a modification of the continuity idea, Richard Bradley showed how the people of the early Middle Ages could recognise the 'vocabulary' of the landscape, choosing for a new development an old site that had either never lost its meaning, or could be readily invested with the properties of a tradition.[5] Others felt that 'continuity' was a 'con'; the Anglo-Saxons saw little and understood less of their prehistoric predecessors. Others again felt that the case was open, and that the prehistoric site at least required its own research programme. The suspected 'Beaker period' settlement was a rarity which should not be ignored; the whole prehistoric sequence should be sampled as economically as possible, and the question of its connection with the Anglo-Saxon cemetery should be left on the table. It would in any case be wrong to give the impression to sponsors that the prehistoric period did not matter; the prehistoric features occurred at the same level, cut into the same natural subsoil, as the early medieval graves. It would not be possible to dig one without digging the other.

These formal meetings – 'focus groups', we should call them now – were extremely helpful for drawing up the research agenda for the Sutton Hoo project. Travels and conversations in Denmark, Norway and Sweden also added immeasurably to the strength of the project design, by showing what problems had been encountered in Scandinavia and the way in which many of them had been overcome. We in Britain were latecomers to the archaeological science of determining social organisation and territorial control in the early middle ages. The Mälaren, around Lake Mälar in the Stockholm region of Sweden, had long been studied in this way, and for south-west Norway, Bjorn Myrhe had produced a fine analysis in 1986 demonstrating the existence of a chain of coastal kingdoms in the fifth to sixth century.

Much of this educational travel was undertaken through the

Fig. 28 The sixth century burial mounds at Gamla Uppsala, central Sweden. M.O.H. Carver.

kindness of the BBC, with whom I was putting together a series of films. We went to Gamla Uppsala, the huge mounds in the Uppland area of Sweden, traditional burial place of the Inglinga dynasty, and scene in the ninth century of the mass sacrificial hanging of men, horses and dogs which had been observed and reported by the missionary Adam of Bremen (Fig. 28). Further up the River Fyris was Valsgärde, the cemetery of ship-graves where Bruce-Mitford had earlier lent a hand, now being slowly brought to publication, with its ships, helmets, dog-leashes and horse-harness; further north still was the famous ship-burial site of Vendel, which in Scandinavia gives its name to the period around the seventh-eighth century. Beyond Vendel, the forest stretches away to the Arctic Circle. These Swedish ship-burial cemeteries, which date from the seventh century to the tenth, are the sites which most resemble that at Sutton Hoo. If they were to provide the model, then Sutton Hoo would contain only ships under the remaining mounds.

We later recorded footage at Jelling in Denmark, the central place of the early Danish kingdom. Here King Gorm had first been buried in a giant burial mound, and then dug up and re-interred in a church on the same spot by his son, Harold Blue-tooth, who, as it says in runes on the great Jelling stone, 'had conquered all Denmark and Norway and made the Danes Christians' (Fig. 29). We visited the Viking ship-burial at Ladby conserved *in situ* in an underground shelter by the Carlsberg Foundation. And in Norway we visited Borre where a new project had been launched to study a cemetery of Viking and pre-Viking mounds grouped beside the Oslo fjord. There could be no doubt of the huge importance of the burial mound in Scandinavia, as a symbol of rank, territorial control and political conviction. How far did England adopt the message of the mounds? Were the people of East Anglia influenced or even aware of Scandinavian ideas? It was important to know if the peoples of the North Sea were in contact in the seventh century – forming a community that might debate the political options and express their choice in monuments.[6]

A meeting at Oxford in 1988 explored the possibility that the mariners of the fifth to seventh centuries enjoyed a regular traffic across the North Sea. If 'blue water crossings', direct voyages between Denmark, Norway and England, as opposed to creeping round the coast, were easy and frequent, East Anglia would have been up to date with Scandinavian thinking in the seventh century and could have been routinely influenced by it. This was a counter to the prevailing notion that the North Sea in the 'Dark Ages' was a forbidding barrier, and became a thoroughfare only with the Vikings. But, surely, the Sutton Hoo ship could also sail

Fig. 29 The great mounds at Jelling, apparently built by Harold Bluetooth to commemorate his parents. After his conversion to Christianity, Harold removed the skeleton of his father from the chamber under the mound on the left and had him reburied in a church on the site, right. M.O.H. Carver.

Fig. 30 *Edda*, a replica of the Viking ship found at Oseberg in Norway, under sail in Heroy fjord in 1988. Soon after this picture was taken, *Edda* capsized and sank. B. Marden-Jones.

and even cross the sea? Some of these bold convictions were tested by practical experience. In the ship-museum at Oslo are preserved the Viking ships that were excavated at Gokstad, Tune and Oseberg. A replica of Gokstad (*Viking*) had been sailed in 1892 through the ice fields and up the St Lawrence to Chicago, to make a telling appearance at the celebrations to mark the 400th anniversary of the 'discovery' of America by Christopher Columbus. In readiness for 1992, a perfect replica had been constructed of the Oseberg burial ship, last resting place of the formidable Queen Åse. Up on the icy coast near Alesund, our film crew was to row, sail and witness the disastrous maiden voyage of this beautiful ship, which was named the *Edda*. Here we learnt that sailing in a narrow keel-less boat before the wind is as thrilling a sensation as life has to offer, but abeam to the wind, the sensation can be perilously short. In the course of learning how to tack with a single square sail, our ship capsized and sank, we crew barely escaping with our lives. If the Anglo-Saxons already knew how to sail and regularly crossed the sea, they would have needed skills of a high order to defeat a head wind; skills we have now nearly lost. Perhaps the Viking gift to history was not the long-ship, but the knowledge of how to tack (Fig. 30).[7]

These adventures, encounters and consultations, and the deliberate policy of sharing the decisions and results with the interested community at every stage (it was small enough), were immensely helpful to the project throughout its life, in particular during the evaluation, when they inspired and guided the project, influencing what was done on the ground and its eventual interpretation. The programme of scholarly exchanges continued until the project's end. In 1989 the seminar series climaxed in Sutton Hoo's 50th anniversary year, with three conferences held at the Universities of Minnesota, Kalamazoo and York. By this time the digging was well advanced and an interim account of what had been found was available to inspire imagination, interpretation and controversy. At the York conference, the last in the series, a mighty feast was held in the Merchant Adventurers Hall. 'Mirth was renewed, laughter rang out and cup-bearers poured wine', and then by way of entertainment, our own poet spoke in the hall. On his feet among the tables, gesticulating and prowling in an imaginary Dark Age heathland, the actor Julian Glover held two hundred diners spellbound in the candlelight, reciting and performing the story of Beowulf, Grendel and Grendel's mother.[8]

THE KINGDOM OF EAST ANGLIA SURVEY

The second theatre of research was to be the geographical region in which Sutton Hoo was situated. In 1986, interested parties from the academic and fieldwork sectors of the archaeology profession gathered at Ipswich to decide how they were going to find the Anglo-Saxon kingdom of East Anglia. It was plain that the most important task was to map its settlements and observe their patterns in the landscape. The shape of a settlement and the size of buildings it contained might be a more reliable indication of social organisation than the form of a cemetery and its graves. A grave might be an investment in the next world, but a settlement would be an investment in this one, and thus reflect more accurately the distribution of resources. The East Anglian region, almost alone in Britain, had used pottery continuously from the Neolithic period to the twentieth century; and, as had been shown by the stunning results of fieldwork at the little village of Witton, Norfolk and Suffolk archaeologists had developed ways of using pottery picked up off the fields to show where earlier settlements were, how big they were and how much land they had under the plough – without doing any digging.[9]

The regional survey designed by the Ipswich seminar divided East Anglia into six sample zones, of which the first to be tackled was the local one, the Deben Valley. The method was straightforward: in each zone, accessible fields were walked in systematic

Fig. 31 (Above) The zones chosen by the East Anglia kingdom survey. Sutton Hoo lies in the one marked 'SE Suffolk'. (Below) The four maps show the prehistoric, Roman and Anglo Saxon settlements located by the fieldwork of John Newman of the Suffolk Archaeological Unit. J. Newman.

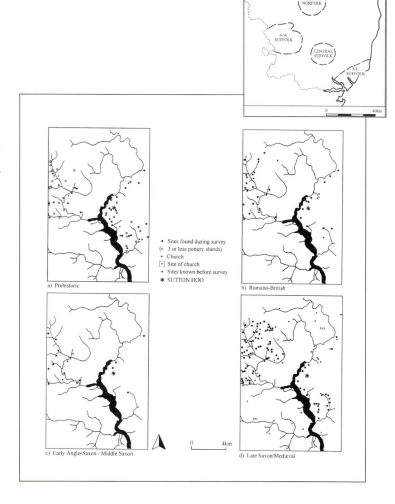

· Sites found during survey
(∘ 3 or less pottery sherds)
✝ Church
[✝] Site of church
▲ Sites known before survey
✳ SUTTON HOO

a) Prehistoric

b) Romano-British

c) Early Anglo-Saxon - Middle Saxon

0   4km

d) Late Saxon/Medieval

strips, and pottery, flint and other materials were picked up off the surface, identified, dated and plotted on a map to the nearest 10 m (33 ft). After covering a number of fields, a pattern began to emerge, which showed the settlement areas of different periods. The fields were then walked again, this time with a metal detector; metal finds would help to distinguish the rank of the settlements, since high-quality metalwork should be confined to the more important sites. John Newman, the Suffolk Archaeological Unit's field officer who led the survey, already knew the area very well, his negotiations with farmers giving him access to a representative sample of land. After five years of examining the fields in optimum conditions he was able to reveal the pattern of shifting settlements from the Neolithic period to the Middle Ages (Fig. 31). The prehistoric and Anglo-Saxon settlements in general were located less than 1 km (0.6 miles) from running water, while the Roman and medieval settlements were more widely deployed. Within the Anglo-Saxon period, special settlements could be distinguished that were long-lived or had a particularly large spread of pottery on the surface of the fields. Using this evidence, Rendlesham emerged as a chief place of the Anglo-Saxon region.

The Deben Valley survey suffered from one disadvantage: little new reconnaissance was possible from the air. Although it was, on the whole, good flat arable land, with excellent cropmark potential, there were problems of access to the sky due to three sensitive military air bases within a few kilometres. The US Air Force offered a little compensation in the form of a flight in a Super Jolly Green Giant, a helicopter with an open back, which provided hair-raising views of the burial mounds in their riverine setting. Other helpful vistas were offered from a hot air balloon, courtesy of Brian Ribbans, a well-known racer. From it one could see the fields stretching east to Rendlesham Forest and Sutton Heath, south to the estuary and the North Sea, north to Wilford Bridge, the first dry crossing point of the Deben, and west to the tree-fringed river with Melton, Woodbridge and Martlesham beyond.

The Deben Valley area also formed the subject of a special documentary study by Peter Warner, in which he examined the early geography of the Wilford Hundred, using documents, place-names and maps. The left bank of the Deben opposite Wood-bridge was notable for its lack of churches: there were none apart from that at Sutton itself, suggesting a 'pagan enclave' which may have endured around Sutton Hoo beyond the period in which parishes were generally created in the tenth to eleventh centuries. Warner also discovered that the seventeenth green of the Woodbridge Golf Course, situated on an eminence above Wilford Bridge, was once called Harrow Pightle, an Anglo-Saxon name indicating a temple site. For another, perhaps not unconnected, reason this place was to have an important role in the later interpretation of the site; it was shown on a map of 1601 as 'Gallows Hill' and carried a little drawing of the gallows itself. This identification received some endorsement later during a round of golf with the secretary of the club, when the information was divulged that some years ago when the land was landscaped (in the service of the world's most exasperating game), several human skeletons had been found. These were presumably the remains of victims who had died on the scaffold.

Exploration of the Deben Valley and the settlement pattern in Anglo-Saxon East Anglia provided the essential geographic context for Sutton Hoo. Now to describe the third theatre of the campaign, the investigation of the site itself.

WHAT TO DIG? THE EVALUATION PROGRAMME, 1983–86

Work on site began in 1983 with a programme of *evaluation*, which aimed at answering the following questions: How extensive was the archaeological site? Which periods were represented? How well had evidence for each period survived? What could that evidence tell us?

Many techniques for mapping buried and invisible strata were applied, in order to look at the surface of the ground, and through the ground and under the ground, to assess what was left of Sutton Hoo, and what it could still tell us, without exposing or disturbing it. The mapping techniques were chosen and deployed in 'zones' which reflected the current land-use: plough soil, pasture and woodland. On the barrow site, the priority was to remove the bracken and gorse, expel the rabbits and clear away the debris (Col. Pl. IV).

Soon the mounds emerged clean and tidy, if still marked here and there by the tracked vehicles of the army. The following spring, released from the tyranny of the bracken rhizomes, a hundred different species pushed up through the leathery turf, their selective growth producing a colourful pattern. Dozens of square and circular patches could be discerned, strongly marked by sheep's fescue and moss: these patches were the ghosts of back-filled and overgrown holes dug by farmers, archaeologists – and treasure hunters. Taking a leaf out of the treasure hunters' book, a metal detector was used to map the fragments of metal on the surface of the site; most of them consisted of bullets and .303 cartridge cases, some stamped '1942', the year in which Sutton Hoo served as a military training area. In the centre of the site was a mass of bottle tops discarded near the old site-hut used by the British Museum excavation team of 1965–71. The surface of the cemetery itself was mapped with an electronic theodolite, and the results enhanced by computer-generated contours. More vividly still, strong lighting thrown across the site at night illuminated all the little dips and hollows captured in the newly cleaned surface (Fig. 32).

Seeing through the turf was accomplished by the current range of geophysical instruments. The different machines were first tested over a trial area which was subsequently excavated: resistivity and fluxgate gradiometry were found to work well and were used in mapping the wide area around the site. The Sutton Hoo evaluation also introduced archaeology to soil penetrating radar, in the form of a pioneering machine built by Mike Gorman for the Scott Polar Institute, Cambridge, to map mountains under the polar ice. This personable and photogenic yellow

Fig. 32 The contours of the burial ground brought out by oblique lighting at night. In the foreground is a hollow way which was in use before 1601. In the background, trial excavations are under way in the centre of Mound 2. Beyond can be seen the lights of Melton. Nigel Macbeth.

Fig. 33 An early archaeological use of soil sounding radar: Messrs Oceanfix using a Japanese instrument on Mound 2. Nigel Macbeth.

Fig. 34 'Ground-truthing'; a test transect through the fields surveyed by surface collection to the south of the burial ground. Nigel Macbeth.

tractor was later to be deposed by a more commercial Japanese apparatus. The timed emissions produced by the radar were reflected from soil/sand interfaces and so affected to look deep into the mounds, detecting a burial chamber under Mound 12 and the robber trench through Mound 2 (Fig. 33).

A fair bit was already known about the underground world of the barrow cemetery, from the excavations that had taken place in 1938–9 and 1965–71. Further previews were achieved by re-excavating a wartime anti-glider ditch and a silage pit dug in the 1950s, both of which showed the strata of the prehistoric site in varied states of preservation. The bracken had clearly been the biggest single agent of destruction, reaching down into the prehistoric pits and into the burial mounds, with rhizomes up to 3 m (10 ft) long. Ideally, a preview was also needed within a mound, in order to assess the degree to which the mounds, the burial chambers and the old ground surface had survived, and to know whether any special means would be required to understand them. For this, a part of Basil Brown's old 1938 trench through Mound 2 was re-opened and re-excavated to the bottom.

The descent was made by following the line cut by Brown's spade and trowel, while protecting the other sides of the shaft (which were composed of his backfill) with shoring. On arrival at the bottom of Brown's trench, the line of his 'boat' could be seen, dark and gently curving on the sandy floor. And there were his marker canes, still where he had placed them in 1938 to show the location of rivets. The boat looked just as unconvincing as it had on Brown's plan, but cutting back at the east end, a dark convex shadow like the profile of a keel was seen by Angela Evans suspended in the section. It was too high to be connected with Basil's flat-bottomed straight-sided boat, and it was this that suggested that the original ship might have been placed, not underground like that in Mound 1, but up on the old ground surface, keel down. Such a boat could have been full-sized and of conventional early medieval type, pointed at both ends. And it was not impossible that some of it, at least, was still there.

The adjoining land meanwhile, under the plough and bearing a crop of potatoes, was examined by 'fieldwalking', from which thousands of prehistoric flints and pottery sherds were collected and plotted. The coarse predictions of the geophysical surveys, the air photographs and the fieldwalking were then subjected to 'ground-truthing' by digging transects across the fields (Fig. 34). The ditches of the prehistoric field system duly appeared, together with the pits containing pottery and flint, datable from the Neolithic to the Iron Age. But in one transect, stretching 100 m (328 ft) away from the eastern edge of the grassy mounds, a lozenge-shaped pit was located that was not of the common

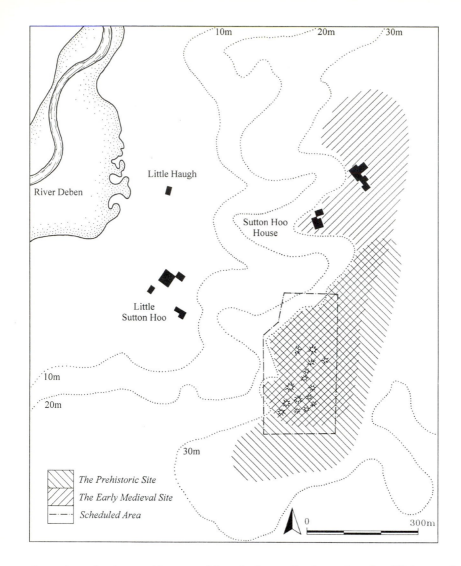

10m 20m 30m

Little Haugh

River Deben

Sutton Hoo
House

Little
Sutton Hoo

10m

20m

30m

The Prehistoric Site
The Early Medieval Site
Scheduled Area

0   300m

Fig. 35 The predicted extent of the prehistoric settlement and early medieval burial ground before the start of excavations in 1986.

prehistoric form. On lowering the fill it was found to contain a long dark smear, at first thought to be a root; but it soon took the familiar shape of a femur and tibia: it was a grave, containing the stain left by a human body. The remainder of the grave was soon excavated and its inmate revealed (Fig. 40).

There was no skeleton, and no bone; the body had decayed to a hard dark brown crusty sand. With gentle trowel and brush, the line of the corpse could be seen or felt for – and so defined in three dimensions: on its back, with its hands together and head tilted forward, in a grave that seemed too small. The grave lay 70 m (230 ft) from the nearest known burial mound. A broader area was opened, and at once more graves appeared. A larger extension still was opened to the east, where there were no more graves; and for another 50 m (164 ft) still beyond that, an absence of graves was gratifyingly, if laboriously, confirmed. In this way an eastern edge to the Sutton Hoo cemetery was located.

Over, on and through the ground, the techniques of evaluation had endeavoured to present us with an inventory of what lay in store. In the autumn of 1985 we were ready to pronounce on the value of the site. It consisted of a large prehistoric settlement complex stretching for some 10 hectares (25 acres) on top of which had developed an early medieval cemetery of some 4.5 hectares (11 acres) (Fig. 35). The deposits in the central area generally lay up to 50 cm (20 in) deep, the prehistoric strata being protected by the early medieval burial mounds; even beneath the mounds, however, it had been badly scrambled by plants, animals and man. Outside the scheduled area, where the land was under the plough, all earthworks had been rubbed out, but the archaeological features were less disturbed because, in recent times at least, they had been protected by cultivation from bracken roots and rabbits. The Anglo-Saxon site seemed to consist largely of graves. There were about eighteen suspected burial mounds and most should yield some information, even if they had already been excavated. From the contacts made around Mound 5 (in 1970) and now on the eastern periphery, we imagined then that flat graves could be present in large numbers. If the density were to continue between the two burial sites, maybe several hundred graves were there to be found. The condition of bodies was severely degraded; sex determination and pathology would be difficult, but there was enough osseous matter for radiocarbon determination. The radiocarbon date received for a body in the eastern periphery was centred on AD 625, contemporary with the Mound 1 ship-burial.

THE STRATEGY

This was the picture predicted by the evaluation; the *strategy* now came into play. What could the Sutton Hoo site be persuaded to tell us, out of all we wanted to know? In the long period of prehistory and the Roman period, the best on offer was the history of land-use – how the land had been divided, cultivated and settled. Location of the settlements would come most readily from the Deben Valley survey and of land boundaries from aerial photography. The best use of excavation, therefore, was to get dates on the field boundaries and establish their character. It would be particularly useful to know when the landscape was first partitioned, since this could signal the arrival of landownership in this part of Britain. Pollen taken from under and outside the burial mounds could confirm or modify Geoffrey Dimbleby's sequence of the environment: oak forest (Mesolithic), cleared in the Neolithic, grazing lands occasionally cultivated for arable (wheat) until the Roman period, grazing throughout the Middle Ages and final reversion to heath in the sixteenth or seventeenth century. Lastly it would be interesting to learn what prehistoric earthworks had been standing when the Anglo-Saxons adopted the place for their cemetery.

Now we had to decide how to interrogate the Anglo-Saxon cemetery itself. The targets were ambitious: the changes in society and the coming of kings, the contacts, alliances and policies of the people of early East Anglia. Would big questions need a big dig? To 'dig the whole thing', which was the mantra of the age, was a prescription that I personally would never accept. We should dig only to answer questions, and they must be questions important enough to merit the destruction of part of a unique monument. If the questions demanded that we should dig the whole thing, they were the wrong questions, and we should think again. A way would have to be found to give a reliable answer to the questions by only digging a part of the site. Is it possible to make such a choice, to say what should be dug, how much and where? This question was on the lips of every visitor, expert, casual or curious: 'how did you know where to dig?'

Our answer was as follows: the story of the politics of early England was embedded in the burial rites practised at Sutton Hoo. So the aim would be to obtain a sample of the burial rites practised from the beginning to the end of the use of the cemetery. Although there was no way of knowing for sure where the beginning and end of the cemetery were, there was a certain logic to be drawn from the terrain. The Anglo-Saxons were likely to have begun their cemetery at the edge of the scarp overlooking the River Deben, and the latest burials should be those furthest inland. If this were the case then a transect should be excavated from west to east, west at the edge of the scarp and east where the furthest burials from the mounds had already been located. The transect was to be 32 m (105 ft) wide, wide enough to catch a burial mound should such a thing have been built there. Within this transect, examples of the burial rites from earliest to latest should appear and signs of any major structural phase should be captured.

Needless to say, there was at least one flaw in this argument: supposing the cemetery did not grow inland in that logical way? Do cemeteries develop in a logical manner? The Anglo-Saxons may have begun their burial at the south end and dug a trail of graves wandering northwards along the scarp. Or they may have clustered them in groups belonging to different families. Accordingly, the proposed east–west transect was paired with a

Fig. 36 The excavation strategy. The cruciform transect indicates the area to be excavated, about one hectare in extent; inset is the hatched area to be surveyed by remote mapping.

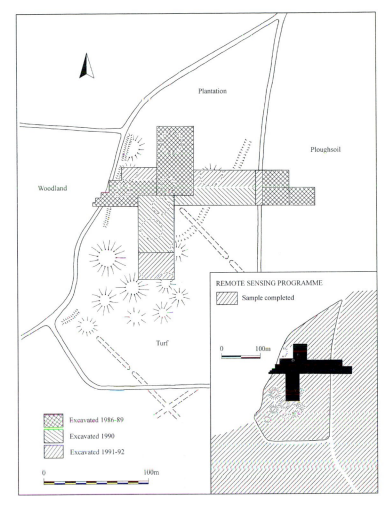

north–south one, so that the design would consist of two transects at right angles; these should catch the axis of growth of the cemetery, whatever it was. The area to be excavated was cruciform: the east–west arms stretched 200 m, encompassing the known limits of the cemetery; the north–south transect, at 100 m, was just long enough, it was felt, to determine the axis of growth of the cemetery (Fig. 36).

The excavation area, so reasoned and devised, was placed at the north end of the cemetery, because most of the previous digging had been done there. Mound 2 had already been excavated, Mound 5 had been started; new mounds had been seen as shallow bumps on the north-west side; the British Museum team had dug eight or more trenches in the area. Our cruciform transect was therefore placed with its centre over Mound 5, its arms stretching north over Mound 2, and south over Mound 7, west to embrace the newly discovered Mounds 17 and 18 and east to

Fig. 37 (left) A hot-air balloon piloted by Brian Ribbans , in use for high level photography of the excavation. Nigel Macbeth.

Fig. 38 (right) The view from the balloon: the far eastern sector under excavation, with the burial mounds beyond. The graves of execution victims can be seen towards the further edge of the open area. Nigel Macbeth.

include those flat graves on the periphery. The excavation area contained eight burial mounds that were to be wholly or partly excavated. The number of flat graves anticipated at that time in the chosen area was two to three hundred on the basis of those found. The area to be excavated was 1 hectare (2.5 acres), or less than a quarter of the known cemetery. Outside and conserved for the future were nine or ten burial mounds in 3.5 hectares (8.5 acres), among them those most likely to be still intact. Conserved for the future would be the best deposits that Sutton Hoo still had to offer. This excavation area was also well suited to the prehistoric strategy: a major ditch system had already been located there by the British Museum archaeologists. There would be buried soils and intact prehistoric strata under the mounds; and there was ample space to map prehistoric features and thus increase the likelihood of producing a good account of land-use over 3,000 years.

Now it remained to cost the excavation, fund it and do it. The Sutton Hoo Research Trust received the proposal for six years' work, like a blueprint from an architect, and scrutinised it; then they accepted it, resolving and minuting at the annual general meeting on 15 January 1986 that 'The Trust has received the Sutton Hoo Project Design ... and approves it in principle. The Trust states its firm intention to complete the excavation and ... its publication.' This was an enlightened and courageous act of faith by

Fig. 39 How horizon mapping worked. The turf was removed by a tracked excavator with a hinged front-bucket (centre right). The exposed surface of the old ploughsoil was then harrowed with the teeth of the mechanical excavator, to simulate ploughing, and the disturbed finds were collected from the surface (centre right). Metal detectors were also used at this stage. The surface was then scraped with shovels, sprayed and trowelled clean (bottom left), and later the defined features were excavated (bottom right). Among the excavated features can be seen (right) a section of the great Beaker period ditch system.

the Trustees, and at the time rather novel. The proposal to undertake a research excavation had been detailed in advance, stating the exact area that was to be opened, why, and with what expected results, how long it would take and how much it was going to cost. This information, integrated into a 'project design', was then published, with the affirmation that it would be supported from beginning to end. It was a significant moment for British archaeology.[10]

THE EXCAVATION, 1986–92

The excavation programme began in August 1986 and continued, in seven seasons, until the spring of 1992 (Figs 37–9; Col. Pl. XI). The cruciform transect was divided into five sectors: north, west, south, east and far east, each of which was stripped and then mapped, and the located features excavated. At first the turf over the barrows was laboriously removed by hand and the prehistoric finds recovered from the topsoil were individually plotted. But it was eventually recognised that their distribution reflected barrow-building, not prehistoric settlement, and a representative sample could be taken by means of surface collection and metal detection. It was thus safe to use a turf-stripper on the mounds and, between them, a mechanical excavator to scrape off the topsoil down to a few centimetres above the yellow sandy subsoil. Then the shovellers went in, followed by the trowellers, and at every stage the ground was sprinkled with water to improve the colour contrast between the subsoil and the pits and graves that had been dug into it. In small areas of 4×8 m (13×26 ft) every part of the 10,000 sq. m (100,000 sq. ft) site was soaked and stroked into its most vivid definition, and then photographed from a tower and surveyed. This procedure, which here acquired the nam of 'horizon mapping', captured thousands of features, some modern, some early medieval, some prehistoric and some natural (Col. Pl. VIII).[11] At first every one of these features was dug, but as our powers of recognition improved it became possible to identify the features of each period and apply selectivity, thus digging less. As a deliberate policy, all the early medieval, a representative sample of the prehistoric and a few of the more puzzling natural features were excavated; so that even in the excavated area many located features await the investigations of a future age.

THE SAND BODIES

The first sector to be opened and mapped was on the far eastern periphery, where we had made contact with a cemetery of 'sand bodies'. When first spotted on the horizon surface, the graves were oblong patches of dark sandy fill against the yellow sand and gravel of the subsoil. The mixed fill was then removed in horizontal slices ('stages') until the first anomaly appeared. If this anomaly took the form of a dark straight line, it generally meant that the grave had a wooden coffin, and that this was one of its sides, a decayed board viewed edge-on from the top. More often, the first thing to appear was a crusty brown lump of sand, the consistency of sugar, which persevered under the trowel and curved away downwards. This was a part of the decayed body itself. Follow the edges of the surface of the brown crust, taking away the softer fill beside it, and the shape would be revealed: a head, an arm, a pelvis, a leg. The whole sand body was eventually revealed, not a skeleton but a brown person. Bone would sometimes survive, but it would be inside the crusty sand jacket, showing that what was being defined was the shape of the flesh itself (Figs 40–42, Col. Pl. IX).

For most of us the shape of a human body is familiar and more or less predictable, and the excavator feeling for the sand bodies in the grave expected to have an easy time of it. Once you have the skull or a leg, you would know which way round the body lay and could say with reasonable confidence where the rest of a person was going to be. But with the Sutton Hoo bodies, it seemed, this was often not the case. A pelvis might be the wrong way up. A head would be found by a knee and a foot would rest on a rib-cage. Some graves contained two people, and one contained three. It became increasingly clear that most of these bodies were buried in positions that were odd: one was kneeling, head to the floor of the grave; one stretched out, hand above the head; another folded forward, another folded back, another sideways; and, strangest of all, one splayed out in a hurdling position, accompanied by a wooden object that seemed to belong to an *ard* or primitive type of plough. Every burial seemed to be different, and the body positions of most, differing from the peaceful norm of a person laid out on their back, indicated some special abuse of the individual that we referred to as 'ritual trauma' or 'deviance'.

A number of excavators tried their hands at the definition of these extraordinary graves; old, young, expert or novice, suspended on planks or cradles and sheltered by windbreaks. All carefully followed the lead of their hands and eyes, with spatula and handspray, and after a week or so of intensive work produced burial positions that were believable ... but grotesque. Burial 24 had his head at right angles to the vertebral column, and teeth, hand and wrist had survived to give a tableau that was both ghastly and sad. Those who saw it all came to a similar conclusion, and it was soon being referred to as 'the hanged man'. Could all these people have perished in a similarly brutal way? Were these the victims of war, execution or sacrifice? Or were all these bodies simply dumped without ceremony, the clients of a shoddy undertaker?

The varied postures, the use of coffins, the large size of some graves, seemingly dug to accommodate the posture, the seventh-century radiocarbon dates that were soon received – these things seemed to argue at first against a medieval execution cemetery. The group appeared to be Anglo-Saxon, with a ritual air. So could they have been sacrificial, and if so, why here? The sacrifices reported by Adam of Bremen at Gamla Uppsala, where men and animals were hanged on a tree, inevitably came to mind. Obligingly, in the centre of the Sutton Hoo eastern group of graves, a large pit was located, of a kind left by a fallen tree; it was surrounded by a set of post-sockets. These, it was realised, were the traces of a gallows.

A convincing interpretation would depend on seeing the large sample of burials that was anticipated. But now there was a big surprise. Throughout the whole excavation sample between the mounds, there proved to be hardly any graves at all. The total number of flat graves *expected* between the mounds was two to three hundred. It was in fact thirty-nine, and they were tightly disposed in two groups; one group was on the eastern periphery, as just

Fig. 40 The excavated sand-body of Burial 17.

Fig. 41 The edge of a coffin, seen in the backfill of a grave.

Fig. 42 (a) The sandman in Burial 30 and (b) the underlying skeleton.

Fig. 43 Applying 'vinamul' to stabilise the sand during excavation of a sand-body.

Fig. 44 The complex of inter-cutting features in the centre of Mound 2. The earliest cut (the vertical lower edge) is that for the Anglo-Saxon burial chamber; the oval pit is the remains of the vertical shaft cut in the sixteenth century; the nineteenth century excavators arrived by trench, cutting a set of steps which can be seen at the edge of the pit, centre; Basil Brown's trench, cut in 1938, came from the east (foreground), his steps descending from the near side. The photograph was taken during the excavations of 1987. Nigel Macbeth.

Fig. 45 Mound 2 being excavated in quadrants, with the robbed burial pit in the centre. The photograph was taken from a kite. Nigel Macbeth.

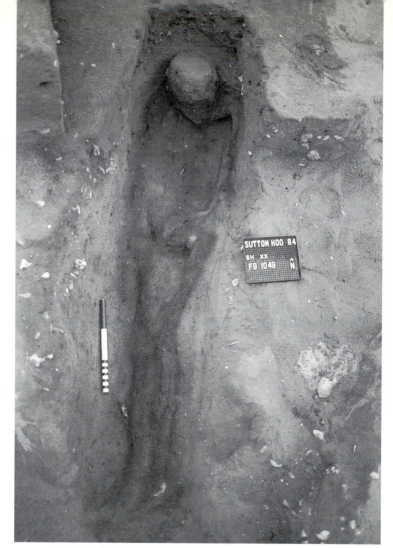

40

41

42a

42b

43

44

45

described, and the other was around Mound 5; and not just near it but radially and tangentially clustered around it in a manner that gave rise to the term 'satellite burials'. The Mound 5 group also included 'deviant' burials, the victims of hanging, to which could be added some compelling examples of beheading and even quartering. Between the mounds, great stretches of sand and gravel were meticulously examined, but apart from the two groups already mentioned, only three graves were revealed, modestly furnished and probably burials of high status children or adolescents. It seemed that to be buried at Sutton Hoo you had either to be an aristocrat ... or a victim. From the radiocarbon dates received, the executions began at both locations at a time which could have been contemporary with the burial mounds. But by virtue of the same dating methods, the practice was found to continue long after mound-burial had ceased. The sand-people were victims of ritual killing buried near gallows that had functioned from about the seventh or eighth century to the eleventh.

DIGGING THE MOUNDS

The excavation of every mound was an adventure in itself, and its potential history was complex. A mound was initially a place of burial, but could theoretically become a memorial where meetings took place. It might then attract grave-robbers, who would cut trenches through it, and farmers who would quarry it for soil. Each mound was not so much an encumbrance to be removed to expose a burial, as a monument with a story of its own to tell. The archaeological problem in digging mounds was an old one: how to see in plan and profile at the same time. To discover the use of the mound surface and the cuts made into it would need inspection in plan over a wide area; but the make-up of the mound would be more visible in section, where the subtle distinctions between turf, sand and soil could be seen by looking sideways at a vertical cut through the heap. To try to gain the benefits of both plan and section, the mounds were 'peeled' against a grid of balks carrying a cumulative section. The sections were drawn when the balks stood about 1 m (3 ft) high – about as high as they could stand without risk of collapse – and then the balks were removed so that the new surface of the mound could again be examined in plan (Fig. 45). Balks were then reinstated on the same lines and the process repeated (Col. Pl. X).

The trowellers on a mound were well aware of the opaque mixture of the material they were trying to clean. The upper levels were hairy with rootlets ('like trying to trowel a heap of dead Airedales' was one assessment). The lower levels were streaked with yellow sand, dark turf stains and clusters of pebbles. Most mounds offered eight horizons, defined in the following way: *Horizon 0* was the surface of the turf. *Horizon 1* was the first surface under the dark soil that supported the turf: the Second World War slit-trenches were seen at this level. *Horizon 2* was the first level at which mound make-up could be seen: but only just. It was riddled with rabbit burrows betrayed by dark curved bands and huge fans of yellow sand. Scarcely a square metre of the mounds was unmarked by rabbit burrows. Our dream of finding ancient activity at this level was frustrated, and was soon abandoned altogether, when we made the discovery that the mounds had been crossed from west to east by parallel grooves of a distinctive kind. The Sutton Hoo burial mounds had in fact been ploughed, and ploughed nearly flat. Once observed, it was hard to see how one could have failed to predict anything so obvious. How could mounds so broad have been at the same time so low? The mounds we were excavating had been very greatly reduced since their construction; perhaps several metres of their height had gone, and the agent of that reduction was (mainly) the plough.

At *Horizon 2* or *3* another common revelation was the second principal agent of any mound's destruction: the so-called 'robber trench'. This was a species of large pit or wide trench cut by earlier excavators whose efforts and discoveries had remained unrecorded or secret. Every mound had been visited at least once by these wanton explorers. In Mounds 6 and 7 the trench took the form of an immense cut 3 m (10 ft) or more wide passing west–east almost through the entire mound. At one end was a set of steps cut in the sand, and at the other the splayed walkway of a wheel-barrow run. The steps were presumably used by the antiquary or landowner, and the wheel-barrow track by his labourers.

The surface of the soil buried beneath the mound (designated as *Horizon 4*) revealed the edges of the burial chamber, but usually little else. This was because the soil *under* the mounds had also been ploughed, most recently between the Iron Age and the Anglo-Saxon period, and presented a dark opaque sandy surface, littered with prehistoric artefacts disturbed by cultivation. At *Horizon 5* the plough marks could be clearly seen. *Horizon 6* was the surface of the unploughed soil, the relic of an ancient forest brown soil in formation after the Ice Age and weathered and exhausted by all that had happened since. At *Horizon 7*, on the surface of the sand and gravel subsoil, the remains of the prehistoric settlement could be seen, brown against yellow, in all their busy detail: ditches, fences, houses, hearths (dishing well below ground level), pits, all accompanied by hundreds and thousands of potsherds and flint implements: a rich assemblage and a vivid sequence unconsciously captured and preserved by the barrow-builders of the early years of the seventh century AD.

Fig. 46 Taking samples from
the floor of the Mound 2 chamber
in order to make a chemical map of
the residues left by the body and
grave-goods. Nigel Macbeth.

Fig. 47 (Below) What was left: plan
of the base of the Mound 2 burial
chamber, showing traces of the
timber lining, the finds left behind
by the robbers and the chemical
imprint of the body and other
vanished contents. Bethell/Royle.

THE EXCAVATION OF MOUND 2

Mound 2 was the first and the largest mound to be excavated, and set the procedure for the rest. The burial rite it revealed was unique. It had clearly included a ship, since at every stage ship rivets were encountered. Not a single one was *in situ*, and the scattered pattern that resulted from plotting them implied that the mound had suffered some immense disturbance (Fig. 48). That disturbance must have been a robbers' trench, even if its edges were by no means easy to see. The quantity, size and shape of the rivets showed equally that somewhere in or under Mound 2 there had been buried originally a full-sized early medieval ship. In the centre of the river of rivets was a large hole, which had been the site of a burial chamber; but since it had been entered twice – by the robbers, and by Basil Brown in 1938 – it was like a nest of Chinese boxes (Fig. 44). Once the sides of the hole had been fully defined, it remained to descend to the bottom and discover the truth about the very curious 'boat' reported by Basil Brown in 1938 (see pp 8, 64). In this soil, the besetting sin of the excavator is failing to get to the real edge; everybody stops too soon. And so it proved here. Basil Brown had not entirely emptied the feature he encountered, and he had defined, not an Anglo-Saxon burial pit, but the tread and backfill of a robbers' entry shaft. Basil Brown's 'boat' was skin deep and its imaginary lines just followed the fans of sand that had washed into the huge hole that the robbers had left open. Behind and under Basil's boat appeared the

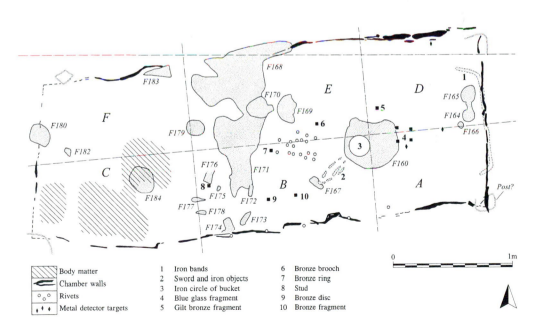

Body matter	1 Iron bands	6 Bronze brooch
Chamber walls	2 Sword and iron objects	7 Bronze ring
Rivets	3 Iron circle of bucket	8 Stud
Metal detector targets	4 Blue glass fragment	9 Bronze disc
	5 Gilt bronze fragment	10 Bronze fragment

Fig. 48 Plan of Mound 2 showing the pattern of ship-rivets and the likely location of the nineteenth-century robber trench.

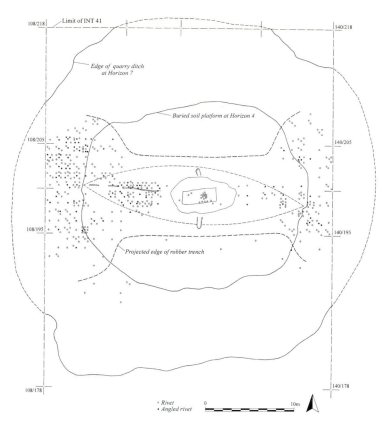

black boards of a rectangular burial chamber 5 m (16 ft) long, 2 m (6 ft 6 in) wide and 3 m (10 ft) deep, in which an Anglo-Saxon had been buried. A ship had indeed featured in the burial rite, but it had been placed not in the hole, but above it, on the old ground surface. Later, the central section of the ship had collapsed, filling the chamber full of rivets and wood pieces for later excavators to find and scatter, or to puzzle over (Fig. 48).

There was little left on the chamber floor, but a dozen or more objects were recovered from the robber trench or from Brown's earlier excavations (Col. Pl. Va). If the body had been missing in Mound 1, here practically everything else was missing too, and it became the site of our most elaborate experiment in the mapping of the invisible. Funded by the Leverhulme Trust, a programme was under way entitled 'The Decay and Detection of Human Bodies on Archaeological Sites'. Phil Bethel, who was responsible for the research, had worked out that sand-bodies were enriched by concentrations of certain cations – aluminium, lanthanum, strontium and barium – which were held as insoluble compounds in places where a body was, or had been. If these compounds could be mapped, it might be possible to determine if and where a body had lain. Accordingly, supervisor Andy Copp took six hundred samples of 30 g (1 oz) each from the subsoil floor of the Mound 2 burial chamber (Fig. 46); the quantity of each element present in each sample was measured by ICP (Inductively Coupled Plasma) emission spectrometry, and the results were spectacular. The tell-tale cations from a body were, gratifyingly, all up the west end; while at the east end were patterns of sand heavily impregnated with copper and iron, which could have derived from bronze cauldrons or iron-bound tubs. A coarse burial tableau had been conjured from an entirely blank patch of natural sand three metres under ground (Fig. 47). Taking it all together, there was enough to identify this as the memorial of a high-ranking male, as lavishly equipped, perhaps, in its original glory, as the burial beneath Mound 1.

CREMATIONS UNDER MOUNDS

A further six mounds were dissected following the procedures developed for Mound 2. It was found that Mounds 5, 6, 7 and 18 had originally covered cremation burials, but each had been thoroughly robbed. In most, the cremated bone and the twisted fragments of grave goods burnt in the fire were scattered along a robber trench and in a vestigial pit at the centre. Here it was even more difficult to penetrate the fog of later disorder; but the burial rite, cremation, was still reasonably clear, and the fragments which remained provided other clues: the cremated person had been accompanied on the pyre by animals, which included horse, red deer, cattle, sheep and pig. The ashes had been gathered up and placed in a bronze bowl, perhaps first wrapped in cloth; or a cloth (found stuck to the bronze) had been used to cover the bowl. The Mound 5 burial, already special due to its 'satellite burials', became more special still when it was found that the skull of the cremated person had been cleft with a sword or comparable blade. Mound 5 had been flattened before the twentieth century, but it could still be seen to have had a different style of construction, the make-up being quarried from pits rather than ditches. Some of these pits were cut by the quarry ditches of Mound 2 to the north and Mound 6 to the south. So Mound 5 could have been among the earliest to be built.

MOUNDS 14 AND 17

The last two mounds to be examined had used burial practices that were individual to them. Mound 14 was the only rich burial that could be readily identified as that of a woman. It had a central burial chamber lined with thin planks set on edge and had been robbed by means of a giant pit. At the base of this trench, near the chamber floor, the fill became very fine and silty, and was full of little fragments of finds, as though a giant blender had been at work.

Fig. 49 First sighting of the two burial pits beneath Mound 17. The mound itself was little more than a platform of buried soil not entirely ploughed away. Nigel Macbeth.

This implied that the robbing team had been interrupted by a rain-storm and, in attempting to complete their ransacking of the chamber during the downpour, had mashed the wet sand of the floor as they groped for the finds that were slipping away from them. Their misfortune was our good luck: the captured assemblage, fragmentary as it was, included parts of a châtelaine (a symbolic key-ring) and allowed us to identify the buried person as a female.

Mound 17 was the last to be dug, in the last month of the last full season in 1991; apart from Mound 1, it is the only mound-burial at Sutton Hoo to have been discovered intact. The mound had hardly shown on the ground surface, and might never have been excavated at all if it had not been for good fortune and the author's persistent hook with a number seven iron. During the evaluation, before the bustle of the full seasons with their crews of fifty to sixty diggers, it was imperative to maintain a presence on site in order to guard the mounds, now mown and as smart as a golf course with their smooth green sward. Indeed they looked as though they should host a game of golf, and several local variants of the sport were invented. One consisted of chipping from the top of one mound to the top of another, and on a good day one could play them in numerical order, beginning at Mound 1 and ending at Mound 14. But the finest practice was to play down

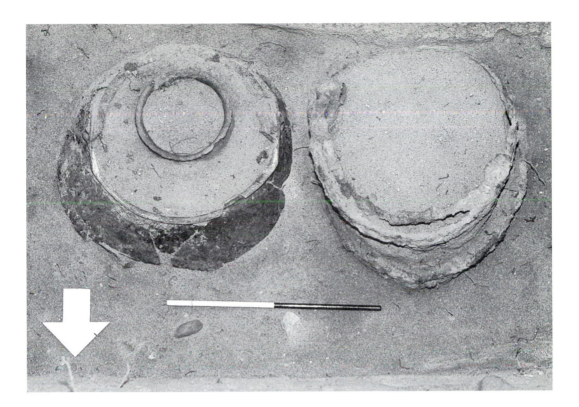

Fig. 50 Grave-goods from the Mound 17 burial: iron-bound bucket (right) and cauldron with a pot inside, pictured as they lay in the ground. Nigel Macbeth.

from the top of Mound 1 on to Mound 12, without hitting the tree which sheltered it, chipping short and hoping the ball would run on under the tree and stay perched up on the slight eminence of Mound 12. It was practically impossible, and I always hooked and left it short, where for some reason it rolled back towards me. In due course, the reason was discovered; when the sun was going down behind Top Hat Wood, a very faint shadow – two, in fact – could be seen in front of the tree; and in this manner two new mounds, Mound 17 and Mound 18, were found and included in the reckoning.

Mound 17 was a patch of soil about 30 cm (1 ft) thick and consisted not of any mound, but of a residual platform of buried soil, not quite ploughed to oblivion, but certainly much disturbed. Off came this soil, with shovel and trowel, and beneath it emerged two oval pits each with a bright yellow band around the edge and a rich dark soil centre like some enormous and luxurious chocolate cut in half (Fig. 49). As veterans of encounters with half-a-dozen robbings we expected the worst: not one, but two, robber pits to empty and sieve for clues to the original burial. With disciplined resignation, the first and largest pit was tackled first: taken down in spits until after 30 cm (1 ft) or so, a surprising neat brown circle appeared in one corner; it should have derived from wood, and looked like the rim of a small wheel. Annette Roe, the excavator, knew that this was unlikely to figure within a robber pit backfill and she took out the next shallow spit with the greatest circumspection. The brown circle persisted, and could now be guessed to be the rotted fabric of a circular wooden tub. A little lower down, at the other end of the grave, there appeared the curved rim of a bronze bowl. It was a satisfying moment when Madeleine Hummler came to get me: 'Come and look,' she said. 'It's the real thing'. There is of course nothing to match the real thing in any of life's moments, and the last few weeks of the campaign were probably the most exciting in all the years of our fieldwork.

Centimetre by centimetre, stage by stage, Annette Roe lowered the surface of the fill, taking out the deposit of the backfilled grave (Fig. 51). No one can say the excavation of a grave is easy, but it is certainly easier to excavate an intact grave than a robbed one: everything is where it should be, one thing warns of another, the excavator is prepared and increasingly alert. The black lines of the coffin boards appeared on each side. Beside the coffin, under the bowl, was a little cluster of bones originating from a handful of lambchops, which, it could be deduced, had once been in a kind of kit bag, with the bowl on top. Beside it was a small lugged cauldron, and next to that an iron-bound bucket (Fig. 50). In the coffin was the skeleton of a young man, with surprisingly well-preserved bones, and a sword as long as his legs. A tiny fragment of millefiori glass and garnet lay near his ear; had we missed a piece of jewellery? No, next to them was a small iron bar showing that a purse or pouch had contained these keepsakes. Under the coffin lay a shield-boss (Col. Pl. VII).

Annette Roe worked on for three weeks with scarcely a break as the light gradually weakened and the weather worsened into winter. She lay on a cot mattress on a board supported by a scaffolding cradle, so that no foot or hand had to put its weight on the funeral deposit. A shelter was built around the grave and a generator provided lighting from 4 or 5 o'clock onwards. The aim was to present the most perfect tableau we could manage, as nearly as possible to reproduce the last view of the mourners before backfilling commenced, with everything showing that was showing then. But some things were too delicate to expose without endangering their survival. The cauldron appeared to be crazed as though ready to break into a thousand fragments; the bucket tottered, its rings of iron only held in position by a jacket of crusty sand.

And at the west end appeared the greatest prize of all: a dark heap of organic traces with the glint of metal peeping out in a half a dozen different places. The pieces, where they could be clearly seen, were small plaques of gilded bronze featuring writhing Anglo-Saxon animal ornament; they had little loops and studs with dark ribbons of decayed leather going away from

Fig. 51 Annette Roe excavating on a cradle in the Mound 17 burial. Nigel Macbeth.

Fig. 52 The British Museum conservation team stabilising objects ready for lifting from the Mound 17 burial. Nigel Macbeth.

Fig. 53 Man-yee Liu working on the 'bridle block' in the British Museum. M.O.H. Carver.

them. It looked like a mass of belts and buckles. Disentangling this was work for a laboratory, not a cold damp dark hole in Suffolk. It was time to call in the British Museum conservation team which had been ready during the six years of the excavation for just such moments as these.

Meanwhile the adjacent pit, smaller than the first, was being excavated, and here too it was apparent that there would be a burial that had not been disturbed. But it contained no finds and no human body; instead there was defined, in precise detail, the large folded carcass of a horse, part skeleton and part sand-body. Now it became clear what had been buried at the west end of the human grave: it was a harness, with probably a saddle and, above that, the wooden tub for the horse's bran, now only a dark brown ring.

After one last photograph in a Force 8 gale, the British Museum conservators swung into action like a team of paramedics at a traffic accident; tub, cauldron and sword were bound up with plaster of paris bandages and lifted when set (Fig. 52). The shield boss was lifted and the spear was extracted from under the heap of harness. Then the soil cube containing the harness, henceforward known as the 'bridle block', was lifted. It was first wrapped in cling-film, and then in baking foil. Then polystyrene foam was generated *in situ* to make a rigid casing. A steel plate was inser-ted under the block, and then the block was turned over, sealed and lifted out of the grave with the back-actor of a mechanical excavator and loaded on to the tailgate of a Ford Granada. Soon it was on its way to the British Museum where it would be dissected into its component parts and reassembled: the first Anglo-Saxon harness to be excavated.

The team returned in the bitterly cold spring of 1992 for a clearing up season. Still to be investigated was the feature in the centre of Mound 17, which proved to be an unsuccessful robber pit; it had arrived at a point situated between the two burials, thus no doubt puzzling and disappointing those who had dug it (Fig. 55). An important group of Beaker period pits adjacent to Mound 1 was also excavated, and a number of other records had to be completed. Then, suddenly, the digging programme was at its end, and it was time to backfill our excavations and reconsti-tute the site. With the use of heavy earth-moving machinery, all the excavated mounds were rebuilt to the height at which they were first encountered in 1983 – that is, except one. Mound 2 was raised to the height to which it would have stood before ploughing had rubbed it down: a magnificent 4 m (13 ft) high, visible now from Melton across the river and imparting to the visitor the monumental presence once offered by a cemetery of such mounds on an open terrace above the river (Fig. 97).

Fig. 54 The sword and buckle from the Mound 17 burial as seen in a xeroradiograph made in the British Museum. British Museum.

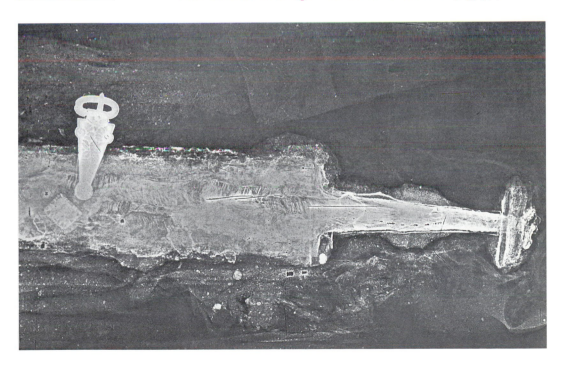

Each generation digs into the past for its own reasons: some for treasure, some for status, some for history. In the 1930s Edith Pretty and her team were led to the mounds by curiosity, and their reward was a jackpot of splendid objects. In the 1960s, Rupert Bruce-Mitford returned to solve specific problems necessary for the definitive publication of the ship-burial. Twelve years later, the campaign of the 1980s had set out to discover a context for the ship-burial, to see if Sutton Hoo could throw light on the origins of an early English kingdom, and to try to understand the message that the mounds had for those that built them and those who were later to see them in the landscape. In this last campaign, the objective was to recount the story of the site as a whole from the beginning to the end – its prehistoric ancestry, its early medieval cemetery and the territory in which it lay. Making sense of the results of the third campaign took place in three main stages. First, there were a great many routine analyses to undertake: of the objects, the human remains, the pollen and the soils. Then the activities implied by these analyses had to be put into sequence and dated; and from this dated sequence of activities, the 'site model' – the story of what had happened on the site – could be compiled. Armed with this story, the archaeologist and the historian could decide on how it fitted into the context of the culture and history of the period; how that context changed the interpretation of what had happened on the site; and how the interpretation of the site might change the current vision of the past that had supplied the context.

All this was attempted in five years of post-excavation work. The examination of the early medieval objects was a simpler task than that faced by the British Museum in 1946. It had challenges of its own, but the interpretation of the new finds could draw on the immense corpus of comparative material assembled in *The Sutton Hoo Ship-burial*, and on the store of knowledge in three of the British Museum's Departments, Medieval and Later Antiquities, Scientific Research and Conservation. The robbed burial mounds had produced many fragments, often tiny, which derived from objects long since smashed and dispersed; these were scrutinised by Angela Evans, a veteran of Bruce-Mitford's own research team. As a result, the terminal of a drinking horn and the stud of a gilded buckle were soon identified in the Mound 2 assemblage, and the dies of the fittings of the drinking horns in the two great mounds proved to be identical. It was apparent that here was a burial of the top rank, originally sharing many attributes with Mound 1, and almost as wealthy. A fragment of châtelaine was picked out from Mound 14, a find decisive in determining that

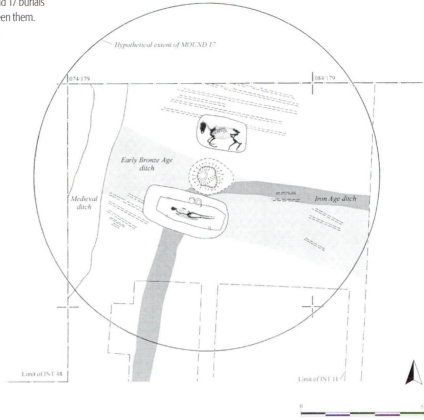

this had been the burial of a woman. Among the cremated bones
dispersed over the scrambled site of Mound 18 was a tiny fragment of a comb, the sole indication that this, like the others, had
been a burial of the early Middle Ages (see Digest, 3).

The most interesting task was the examination of the finds
from Mound 17, this being the only mound burial other than
Mound 1 to have been found intact. Sword, bucket and cauldron
were X-rayed and unwrapped from their protective bandages
(Fig. 54). The little purse proved to have been a cloth-lined
leather pouch containing seven rough-cut garnets, a single garnet
in the form of a bird's beak and a fragment of red and blue millefiori glass. The sword had a pommel of horn and an iron knife in
a leather sheath had lain with it. In the laboratory, a corroded
iron spear-head became two leaf-shaped spear-blades, and these
and the shield-boss, iron-bound bucket, cauldron and a ceramic
pot were all conserved and researched. The toughest assignment
was the examination and restoration of the harness. The block in
which it had reached the museum was first subjected to radiog-
raphy 'in real time' – that is, placed on a turntable in an X-ray
beam, and rotated. The radiographic images obtained at different

viewpoints can be seen immediately and directly on a television screen in an adjacent room. Then the conservators began to dissect the block, lifting the thirteen strap-distributors, seven buckles, five strap-ends and two pendants, all lying within the soil matrix and crossed by the faint tracks of decayed leather. These pieces then had to be assembled in the imagination and on paper, inspired by such analogies as earlier discoveries in Britain and the Continent could provide (Digest, 3).[12]

The horse itself was determined by Terry O'Connor to be a rather thickset male, five to six years old and standing about 14 hands. O'Connor had also identified animal bone in one of the quarry pits of Mound 5 – originally the heads of cattle or horse. Julie Bond found evidence for more animals – horse, red deer, sheep or goat, cattle and pig – among the fragments of cremated bone from the robbed mounds. The precious scraps of human bone, both cremated and inhumed, were searched by Francis Lee for evidence of sex, trauma and age at death – with some measure of success. Most of the execution victims identified were males and mature, but young. In Burial 42 it turned out that two women had been buried face down on a decapitated middle-aged man, for reasons beyond the reach of current science.

A new kind of analysis, micromorphology, was applied to the soil sequence beneath the mounds. Here samples were taken from sections of buried soil, impregnated with resin, baked, and thin slices examined for the characteristic patterns of different natural soil horizons. From this work Charly French was able to show that 50 cm (20 in) or more of podzolised soil had been lost before the mounds were built, due to quarrying or ploughing in the Anglo-Saxon period or before. The sequence of vegetation first deduced by Geoffrey Dimbleby was confirmed in a trench dug away to the west of the burial site in the flood plain of the Deben: here the soils which had washed off the scarp had accumulated. They included a bright band of yellow sand which probably signalled the mound-building period.

The prehistoric sequence was worked out by Madeleine Hummler using the assemblage of pottery and flint, and the excellent comparative data from a century or more of investigation in prehistoric East Anglia. It was the Neolithic people who initiated the clearing operation, but the first systematic division of the landscape could be attributed to the 'Beaker' episode, a Europe-wide ideological movement reflected in burial rite, which no doubt had its counterpart in economic and social reform, as the Sutton Hoo evidence implied. Bronze Age and Iron Age farmers continued to exploit the Sutton Hoo terrace in their different ways, eventually leaving the set of modest earthworks, relics of an exhausted landscape, that the Anglo-Saxons were to see.

The dating of the Anglo-Saxon burials continued to depend largely on finds, since there was, regrettably, no material suitable for radiocarbon dating from the disturbed cremations – the bone itself is calcified and the collagen, which contains carbon, has been burnt away as carbon dioxide. In general, the finds showed very little variation from the dating already achieved for the Mound 1 assemblage. There was no strong reason for dating any furnished grave outside the period 550–650, and perhaps all could be placed in a still narrower band either side of AD 600. The execution burials had generated a set of radiocarbon dates that could have begun in both groups in the seventh century, and continued to the tenth or eleventh century. These burials complemented the results of an important study being undertaken at University College London by Andrew Reynolds, who was demonstrating that the Anglo-Saxon kings of the tenth century had instituted capital punishment at 'killing places'. The Sutton Hoo evidence did not contradict this idea, but it posed an additional question: could the practice not have begun earlier as a natural concomitant of the experimental kingship being attempted in early seventh-century East Anglia?

The experience of excavating at Sutton Hoo for nine years, and in particular of digging Mound 17, suggested that a return to the evidence for the Mound 1 burial rite might also be fruitful. Knowing what was now known, the form of Mound 1 and the ritual that had preceded its construction might be easier to understand. Perhaps it would not be impertinent to readdress some of the questions that had remained from the earlier work of Bruce-Mitford and his collaborators. The rich resource provided by the detailed Mound 1 publication, combined with the records of the most recent campaign, allowed some new hypotheses to be advanced and old ones modified. A model for the burial chamber was devised, drawing on the analogy of the better preserved example excavated in the Oseberg ship. The evidence for a body was reviewed again in the light of the Leverhulme project on the decay of human remains, and Bruce-Mitford's conclusion – that there had been a body at the west end – reinforced. The evidence for a coffin (principally the iron clamps, seen in Fig. 14), suggested and rejected over the years, was re-examined from first principles, comparing the Mound 1 observations with those made at first hand in Mound 17. The split sides of the Mound 17 coffin, its collapsed lid, pressing all the finds into a thin layer at the base, and its curved iron clamps: all seemed to echo the Mound 1 account. A special analysis of the Mound 1 stratigraphy was then undertaken, in which the objects in the chamber were related stratigraphically to each other. From this study it seemed more certain that the chamber had had a floor and that a coffin had stood upon it.[13] It was deduced that the objects had been placed in the coffin, on the coffin, on the walls and on the floor. The same analysis offered an account of the order in which the chamber had been furnished, and how it had collapsed to result in the tangle that was found. New material originating from Charles Phillips and Guy Maynard also helped to propose how the mound was subsequently reduced by ploughing and robbing.

This 'Mound 1 story' was joined by similar chronicles worked out for each of the ten mounds investigated. Putting the mounds in their order of construction proved to be much harder. There were few instances of definable stratification, and all the objects clustered in date around AD 600. Such indications as there were suggested that the cremations came first, led by Mound 5; then the inhumations, including the Mound 17 horse burial; then the two ship-burials, Mound 1 and Mound 2. The best fit seemed to be achieved by supposing that the cemetery had grown from two nuclei, the first based on Mound 5, the second on Mound 1.

Finally, the later history of the Sutton Hoo burial ground was determined, by correlating the excavated evidence for ploughing and tracks with that featured in documents and on a suite of maps from 1601 to the present day. Two separate campaigns of excavation and agricultural exploitation were distinguished, one datable to the sixteenth and the other to the mid-nineteenth century.

From this analysis emerged an outline account of 5000 years of activity in one small piece of England. In particular, the excavation, the regional survey and the comparative studies seem to have gone some way towards helping to interpret the message of the mounds, and looking at Sutton Hoo in a new light: not as a folk cemetery with rich burials, nor as the tail end of a pagan tradition. Sutton Hoo seems to indicate a special moment in English history, when a newly-formed kingdom in East Anglia attempted to pursue an autonomous, non-Christian road to statehood, expressing itself in new kinds of monument. Sutton Hoo might well have been the burial ground of kings, although not all its burials can be seen as royal, nor need all the early kings of East Anglia have been buried there. But the funerary investments found at Sutton Hoo are suffused with the aspirations and anxieties of royal politics, at a crucial moment around the year AD 600.

It remained to create a synthesis from this sequence which would put the events into context and try to explain them, and it is this synthesis which is to be offered in summary form in the next three chapters. It must be emphasised that a definitive version of the Sutton Hoo story can never be given. The model offered in Chapters 4–6 is a construction, a work of interpretation drawing on evidence, of imagination supported by science. If parts of the edifice seem at times too brightly coloured, they rest nevertheless on fairly solid foundations.

PART 2   THE SUTTON HOO STORY

Interpretations

4 PUTTING DOWN ROOTS

Settlement and agriculture at Sutton Hoo,
c. 3000 BC to *c.* AD 600

Fig. 56 The remains of prehistoric settlements beneath Mound 2. The circle of post-holes belongs to an early Bronze Age hut, and the post-row belongs to a middle or late Bronze Age enclosure. Nigel Macbeth.

Pollen grains found in the ancient brown soil show that the Deben Valley was once heavily wooded: there was alder in water-meadows by the river and oak woodlands on the terrace 30 m (100 ft) above it. Leaf-shaped flint arrowheads and a flint axe found in the recent excavations suggest that this wild country was visited by hunters and woodsmen, and to them can be attributed the first great artificial change to the landscape in about 3000 BC, the early Neolithic period in Britain. The process of agricultural exploitation, which began somewhere in the fertile crescent of the Near East in the eighth millennium BC, had its faint echo here 5,000 years later, with the thinning of the trees and the creation of grass clearings which could be grazed. So began a series of local agricultural experiments which were to continue throughout prehistory.

Opening up the landscape, the people of Neolithic Suffolk may have been aware of the special asset that they were destroying, even then. Here and there on the terrace, small pits have been found containing whole pots of characteristic thick-walled flint-tempered earthenware. The pits are often sited around or near large untidy hollows with half-dark, half-bright coloured fill. These hollows were recognised for what they are following the great storm of 1987, which created a host of new examples of the genre: they are 'tree-pits', formed when a tree is pushed over and uprooted and the root mantle left to rot. The close association of tree-pits with pot-pits is by no means secure; there is no stratification to show if they might be contemporary. But both kinds of pit were filled with domestic debris, perhaps as part of a land-clearing operation, or of an episode of abandonment, and together they constitute the only survivors of the first thousand years of occupation. No other marks were made upon the landscape, which was about to experience the most revolutionary change in its history.

Beakers with sinuous profile and geometric ornament are found all over western Europe in hemispherical burial mounds

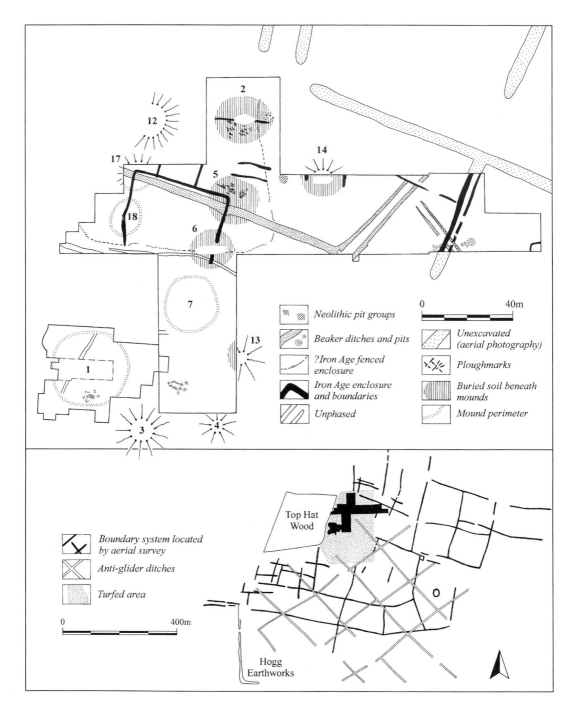

Fig. 57 Plan of the prehistoric sequence at Sutton Hoo.

The legend within the figure reads:

Neolithic pit groups

Beaker ditches and pits

?Iron Age fenced enclosure

Iron Age enclosure and boundaries

Unphased

Unexcavated (aerial photography)

Ploughmarks

Buried soil beneath mounds

Mound perimeter

0   40m

Boundary system located by aerial survey

Anti-glider ditches

Turfed area

0   400m

Top Hat Wood

Hogg Earthworks

with special grave goods, such as barbed and tanged flint arrowheads. In Matthew Arnold's day, these were seen as immigrants from Spain: 'shy traffickers, the dark Iberians' who 'on the beach undid their corded bales'. Now we see this burial rite as rather the harbinger of an ideology that took root widely and exclusively, just as Christianity was to do much later in the same country. And, not without relevance to this parallel, the new ritual was accompanied by a massive increase and reorganisation of economic energy. Restorers of Stonehenge, which was equipped with its trilithons, the people of this period (the early Bronze Age, around 2000 BC) wrought many changes to life and landscape. Much of the evidence comes from burials and ceremonial centres but in East Anglia there are a number of sites which show the ordinary farmers in action. Sutton Hoo is one of them. The dwellings here were round-houses, of which the best example was preserved beneath Mound 2 (Figs 56, 58). A ring of upright posts, up to 300 mm (1 ft) in diameter, supported a superstructure which presumably incorporated wattle and daub walls and a thatched roof; but nothing of this remained. A pair of posts suggested an entrance to the south-east. There was a central hearth, where a coloured faience bead had been dropped. The people used beautifully made and ornamented pots in smooth walnut-brown fabric (Fig. 59), and were cultivators of barley (*hordeum*), oats (*avena*) and wheat (*triticum*). They had access to hazelnuts and oak trees. Next to the house which lay beneath Mound 2 was a massive pit, probably owed to the root-mantle of a tree.

Fig. 58 An early Bronze Age hut, built of upright wooden posts in about 2000 BC. Nigel Macbeth.

Fig. 59 'Beaker' pottery from Sutton Hoo. Nigel Macbeth.

Fig. 60 One of the early Bronze Age boundary ditches, with its many recuts, seen in section. Nigel Macbeth.

But the most significant development lay in the division of the landscape. Great ditches marched across the cleared grassland from river scarp to skyline, undeviating irrespective of quirks in the topography. In this sandy soil, ditches were unnecessary for drainage and, at 3 m (10 ft) across and (probably) carrying a hedge on an adjacent bank, were much larger than was needed to keep out the fiercest cow (Fig. 60). The size of the enclosures so marked is not yet known, but, given a mimimum width of 80 m (262 ft) between ditches, they may have enclosed a hectare (2.5 acres) or more. This can only have been achieved by a commanding or organising hand. These ditches probably signal the imposition of the most fundamental arrogation in human history: the ownership of land. The principal boundary at Sutton Hoo crossed the site from north-west to south-east, where it connected with a double-ditched droveway (Fig. 57). To the north of the main ditch lay the Mound 2 house, with its tree and pit group; another pit group was located beneath Mound 1, with a house probably to the east, accompanied by a rich assemblage of Beaker pottery. The early Bronze Age landscape may be envisioned as an open park-like countryside with mature oak trees and timber roundhouses set in enclosures perhaps a hectare in extent; a landscape that was organised and owned.

One feels that it was the Beaker period that brought to Suffolk those tensions between people and land and person and person that have endured ever since. This fertile region, in easy reach of south Britain, France, Holland and Scandinavia, could never opt out for long from Europe's drama. It was too easy to reach, quick to clear, quick to stock with sheep and quicker to plough. From now on, whatever politics prevailed, the owners were destined to struggle with the acid sand and with each other to maximise their investments, their holdings and their influence.

Without artificial fertiliser, the acid sand of the Sandlings can only tolerate being ploughed for short periods before becoming leached and infertile: the condition known to soil scientists as a podzol. Then it will only support gorse and brambles, unless and until the grass can be allowed to regenerate and the cycle begin again. The oak trees, pride of Suffolk where they remain, and immortalised in Constable's paintings, did not return to Sutton. As the trees were gradually eliminated by fierce winds and by axes of flint, bronze and iron, the sandy soil had little to retain it and it began to drift through wind-blow and rain-wash into the Deben Valley, where it was taken away to the sea.

The early Bronze Age settlement, a peak of affluence for Sutton Hoo, was abandoned; the boundary ditches silted up, and the debris from the houses was swept into open pits and the hollows left by uprooted trees. In the Middle Bronze Age (1500–1000 BC) there followed a pastoral period, in which sheep or cattle were folded in large enclosures built of upright stakes about 200 mm (8 in) in diameter and set the same distance apart. But grain fever returned, probably in the Middle Iron Age (c.500 BC), and with it a new type of small enclosure, known elsewhere as the 'Celtic field', which spread in a ragged network over the terrace. These were the boundary ditches that had been seen from the air. They enclosed fields as large as a hectare (2.5 acres), and as small as 1,600 sq. m (17,220 sq. ft). The soil within some of the fields was ploughed, the marks of the ard preserved in a criss-cross pattern

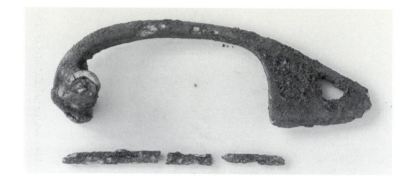

Fig. 61 A Roman fibula from the ploughsoil beneath Mound 5. Nigel Macbeth.

scratched on the surface of the relict brown earth. In others there were narrow trenches reminiscent of the cultivation of vines, and in others small pockets of dark soil suggesting rows of currant bushes or big cabbages.

The use of these fields continued into the Roman period, for a few fragments of Roman pottery and a fibula were dropped and incorporated into cultivated soil (Fig. 61). Insatiable colonisers, the Romans worked every piece of land and water in Europe. Settlement in Suffolk for the previous 3,000 years had been consistently within 1 km (0.6 miles) of running water. Now it crept up on to the clay land and down on to the alluvium. We can expect the soil of Sutton Hoo to have been worked hard, as long as it could bear the load; but the recommencement of the cycle of degradation was inevitable. Soil loss seems not to have been prevented by the embanked enclosures, and by the middle of the first millennium AD, as the fiscal system of the Roman empire collapsed, perhaps over half a metre of soil had disappeared. Turf or scrub grew on an infertile sand 400 mm (16 in) thick. A few trees, among them alder, hazel, oak and beech, stood here and there on the slope. The farmers had gone, but their earthworks were still visible: a network of low banks along the terrace looking out over the ancient tidal breathing of the Deben.[1]

And that is how the Anglo-Saxons found it.

Current terminology designates as 'Anglo-Saxon' the people who were living on the east and south side of Britain in the fifth to the eleventh century AD. We still do not know exactly who they were or where they came from, or indeed whether they were incomers at all. The Venerable Bede believed that there had been a migration of folk from Denmark and North Germany, and that these people had settled on the eastern side of Britain, and had become the English: one race (the English) had dispossessed another (the Britons).[2] In our own time, the ethnicity of people is seen more as a matter of identity-seeking than a matter of biological fact. In both the cultural and documentary record the reality of an actual immigration is hard to tell apart from the wished-for ideal of a single pure ancestry. As individuals, many 'Anglo-Saxons' by Bede's day were probably mongrels of mixed Scandinavian, north German and British parentage, but anxious, for all that, to be seen as a community with a past (even if it meant making it up) and a future (even if it must be fought for). For then, as now, the world was not a park for wanderers to settle where they might, but a hard school in which people competed for recognition and control of territory using force of argument, force of arms, diplomacy, deception, imaginary family connections, imaginary origins or whatever instrument or contrivance proved most effective. Early England, alas, was no garden of Eden: it seems to have been a bustling, stressful, competitive world.

In the fourth century the greater part of the island of Britain was a province of the Roman empire, a contributor to its near-global economy and a subscriber to its ideology which, whether it concerned the rule of Jupiter or Christ, was seen as a component as essential to the welfare of the system as villas, fields, roads and ports and the taxation required to maintain them. It would have been very surprising if the people of Britain, or indeed of Europe, had continued to lend their whole-hearted support to this imperial network for much longer than a century or two. As the British themselves were to find in a later age, after a certain point the adventure palls, whatever measures are attempted to compensate. The abolition of slavery, the extension of citizenship, the denial of the class system, the effective distribution of benefits and the provision of hot baths for all do nothing in the end to suppress the need for freedom or to counter the perverse irritation of predictable security and the *ennui* of efficiency. Anti-imperial thinking was not confined to the Germanic tribes beyond the imperial frontiers. But the naked opposition of these northern tribes offered an alternative politics, and bolstered the hope that the grip of empire would break; the northern European culture would become something to emulate and adopt for those still bound to the imperial production machine. The attraction and fascination of German tribes for Romano-Britons was not that they were German, but that they were tribes. Thus when the political mould began to crumble in about AD 400, the empire no doubt had as many political enemies as friends in the province of Britannia. At the same time, for the German peoples, the empire constituted an artistic and intellectual challenge as well as a honey pot; so while the disaffected within the empire emulated the German tribes beyond its frontiers, the German leaders emulated the empire, incorporating and developing its military equipment and its symbolic language to create something of equal power and unique genius.

East Anglia faces the Germanic lands, as Kent faces France, and this geographical fact has been determinant in much of our history, and continues to be so. In the fourth century, the east coast was the 'Saxon Shore', equipped with signal stations from Yorkshire to Kent to give early warning of the approach of German pirates, and shore forts such as Burgh Castle in Norfolk were used to house the defending forces. It has been suggested that East Anglia was the first part of Britain in which those distinctive Germanic brooches belonging to females were deposited in cemeteries.[3] The females were not, it is assumed, members of an army, so this has been seen as evidence for the first Germanic settlement, either of actual German immigrants from across the North Sea, or of Britons affecting the trappings of the new politics; in either case, in East Anglia, one of the wealthiest areas of Roman Britain, we find the first people signalling (in death) that they wished to be regarded as English.

It is interesting to try to imagine the stress and tension of those hectic days, as generation taunted generation; some yearning for the stability of the years of imperial duty, others restless for the supposed opportunities of anarchy – old stagers, imagining a past that had gone or never was, social rejects, arrivistes and incomers mouthing the new slogans and wearing the new symbols of power, seeing how the land lay and claiming an appropriate ancestry for themselves. That some Britons at least remained in their sequestrated cantonments is indicated by the placename 'Walton', a Germanic term meaning 'foreigner settlement'. One example, by Felixstowe, marked the position of the former fort of the Saxon shore and might have been occupied by loyal descendants of its garrison. In the new world, without tribute or tax, what mattered was land, and to take it, marry it or clear it was the ambition of everyone whose vision stretched further than twelve months. The priority was to see what could be made of the derelict machinery of the imperial agricultural policy, its estate boundaries, arable and stock.

The newly created village at West Stow in Suffolk employed livestock – cattle, sheep, pig, horse – already native to the island; no reason to see immigrant animals here. The little settlement at Witton in Norfolk seems to have had the use of a huge estate – but at first not much of it was under arable cultivation.[4] If the field boundaries remained static, the landscape nevertheless altered in at least two radical ways: the farmer would be found in a new homestead of wooden buildings, rather than an old Roman villa; and transport and travellers would have largely deserted the Roman roads, with their redundant destinations of obselete market towns, to focus their journeys on the arterial network of rivers and seaways. The Saxons were superlative seamen, as the sixth-century Greek historian Procopius complained; they would beach anywhere they pleased, ignoring customs and terrifying the gentry. Now they, and their allies and sympathisers, had the freedom of the seas, and the North Sea between Scandinavia and Britain was probably never busier. At its south end, where the Channel met the Rhine, the Frisians operated. The stage was set for a new Europe of numerous contacts, small lordships and free enterprise.

But the ghost of Rome had by no means been laid to rest. The imperial power safe within the ramparts of Byzantium reached out again and again into the Mediterranean and beyond, in its attempts to reimpose the Christian empire. It reached up through the Atlantic into the Irish Sea, leaving a trail of wine containers and red plates to show where treaties had been directly or indirectly struck with the Celtic peoples of Ireland and western Britain. And across the English Channel the former province of Gaul was being rebuilt as France by Merovingian aristocrats, eager to fill the vacuum left by the Roman empire with something equally overarching, splendid and totalitarian.[5]

The seeds of confrontation between these two world-views germinated and grew throughout the sixth century. On the one hand, the invigoration of the great North Sea adventure, with its conquering heroes, extolling the virtues of enterprise, inventing ancestry, taking land and taking root. On the other, the self-proclaimed heirs of Rome, using Christianity as the propaganda of a new empire led by vigorous Frankish parvenus. Each side, labelled by brooches and fine clothes, worked on the creation of its aristocracy, its ancestry and their legitimacy, with gold and poetry. Each side became surer, more extreme, more provocative as the century closed. The French aristocracy married into Kent; then an eloquent papal emissary, Augustine, arrived at Canterbury, issuing an open invitation to join the recreated empire under Christ. The Roman Christian re-invasion of Britain had begun.[6]

In East Anglia, the spirit of the Germanic settler seems to be indicated by the numerous small villages with their family names, and by the large 'folk cemeteries' in which the deceased men, women and children were dressed in ethnic costume, their *Tracht*, the better to be recognised as forever members of a people. Such a cemetery has been completely excavated at Spong Hill in Norfolk and a large part of another investigated at Snape, situated some 17 km (11 miles) north-east of Sutton Hoo. Most of the deceased were cremated and buried in distinctive urns, with grave goods such as combs, tweezers and brooches. Animals had been cremated too: dogs, horses, cattle, sheep, pigs. Others were buried in coffins, and accompanied by weapons: a spear, shield and occasionally a sword. This was the 'language' of Anglo-Saxon burial, which seems to speak of a network of tribal families which regarded themselves as equal inheritors of the land.[7]

But towards the second half of the sixth century there are signs that this society is being reordered. More graves are rich; and more graves yet have no grave goods. From the mid-sixth century in Kent large grave fields of richly furnished burial mounds salute a new aristocracy. Towards the end of the sixth century, larger and more singular burial mounds spread over the other regions of England outside Kent. New types of settlement appear at about this time: at Wicken Bonhunt in Essex, a planned village with a granary and a large dump of animal bones; at Yeavering in Northumbria, a suite of huge timber halls marks the site said by Bede to have been King Edwin's palace. Just north of the Sutton Hoo cemetery, a scatter of finds including a sixth-century Byzantine bucket suggested a high-status site, perhaps the palace of Sutton Hoo's local potentate (Fig. 63). Documents tell us that at this time there are kings, and they are equipped with genealogies to prove their legitimacy; the ancestors being claimed include both Caesar, the Roman emperor, and Woden, the German god, then metaphorically at war with each other for the soul of Britain. Such genealogies are highly believable in one sense: they do not contain real people much before the mid-sixth century. Kingship in sixth-century England, it seems, is an innovation. With the kings come named kingdoms: Kent, Wessex, Northumbria, Mercia, East Anglia; these too must be inventions of the late sixth century. The primary allegiance of an English person is no longer to a family and a supernatural folk, but to a real territory and its leader.[8]

As part of these dimly observed changes, it is highly likely that some kind of taxation was imposed, since this is the concomitant of territorial control, and thus of kingship, in the sense used here. But there is no need to insist that Christianity be a part of the package. To have a kingdom might be necessary, if only because other kingdoms were gazing hungrily across the Channel. Perhaps kingship was an outcome of the sixth-century *zeitgeist*. But alliances could remain firm, in this case the ancestral alliance with Scandinavia, its aristocracy and its leaders. With varying degrees of urgency all the pagan North Sea polities were adherents of the same *realpolitik*: the promotion of identity and the creation of taxable territories – but without Christianity, centralisation or the French. The temptation to go the whole way and join the Christian alliance was certainly there: alignment with continental Europe would bring immense new trade opportunities in France, Italy and the Mediterranean,

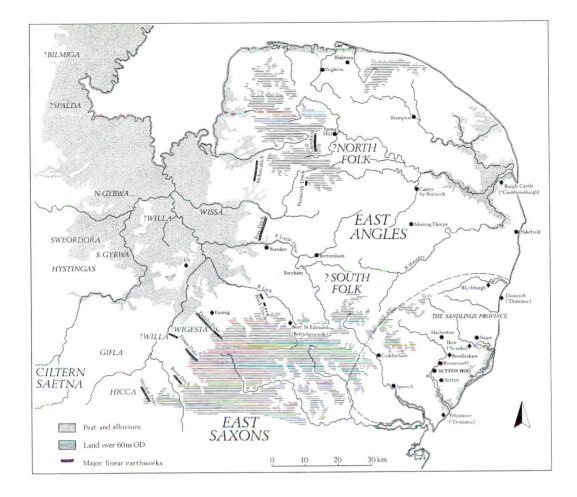

Fig. 62 Early Anglo-Saxon East Anglia. Scull/Pearson.

places that produced gold coins carrying the effigy of the Byzantine emperor, bronze buckets from North Africa, piled cloaks and exquisite silver wares. But the penalties were severe: loss of independence, loss of sovereignty, the inflexible orthodoxies of organised religion. This was a grim choice in which, whatever the temptations of affluence, instinct lay in sticking by one's friends across the sea.

The creation of the early English aristocracy perhaps resulted in a new kind of individual, attracted by things Scandinavian and things Frankish to an equal degree. We must not pretend that we can say very much in detail about these people, whom we usually encounter only in death; but from that we can at least deduce how they liked to be seen by themselves. At Snape one was buried with his horse, one in a small boat of shell construction and one in a large boat, wearing a Roman-style signet ring. These were late sixth- and early seventh-century graves, and represented the new order of the pagan noble.

Fig. 63 The incised pattern from a sixth-century Byzantine bucket found in the ploughsoil in the field to the north of Sutton Hoo House. British Museum, drawing by Jim Farrant.

But there was yet another way to rise above the common herd in death, as in life: burial in a new and separate cemetery on its own site. One family of special means, or one group of self-appointed leaders, did exactly that, finally breaking with loyalty to the folk in the closing years of the sixth century. In the remarkable decade which closed the sixth century AD, in which Columba died at Iona and Augustine arrived on his mission at Canterbury, a new cemetery for this élite family or group was established beside the River Deben at Sutton Hoo: the massive but short-lived investment of a pagan English community. As surely as the churches of Canterbury, Augustine's Gospels, or Bede's *Ecclesiastical History* constitute the political manifestoes of Christian Kent and Northumbria, the burial mounds of Sutton Hoo represent a document recording the defiant bid of the pagan East Angles for independence and international recognition.

5 BURIAL GROUND OF KINGS?

Sutton Hoo, c. AD 600–700

On the terrace on the east bank of the River Deben, in open grassland, in the decade around 600 AD, the people of the Sandlings began the development of a new and special cemetery. Was it then a remote spot? Unencumbered probably, but not remote. The River Deben would have been busy with boats, of both local and sea-going traffic. Opposite Sutton Hoo, the river swelled into a stretch of open water up to 250 m (720 ft) across, where boats could gather and turn when the tide was full. There were well-established settlements – small farmsteads – up and down the river, and at certain places a kind of 'manorial' centre was being created, where the new aristocracy could draw tribute and hold court: possible sites include those located at Rendlesham, Melton, Bromeswell and at a point on the Sutton Hoo promontory itself, where Sutton Hoo House was later to stand. The occupants of some of the new, wealthier, centres may also have created small cemeteries of burial mounds, which in due course would be replaced by churches. Sutton Hoo was thus probably not the only new foundation to be seen on the banks of the Deben in the early seventh century.[1]

The Sutton Hoo site bore the traces of earlier agricultural organisation – the eroded banks and filled-in ditches of a 'Celtic' field system – and it was on the corners of one of these relic fields that the first mounds were raised. At least eighteen mounds were to be erected during the short life of this cemetery, and although the order of their construction is by no means certain, it is likely that the cremations were among the earliest; and of these Mound 5, standing at the north-east corner of the Celtic field in the centre of the site, has primacy. The young person remembered in Mound 5 had died a violent death: the skull had been cut at least nine times by a sword or similar blade. The body was cremated, probably with horses, cattle and other animals, and the ashes wrapped in cloth and gathered into a bronze bowl (Fig. 64). The bowl was then placed in a pit, which was furnished with some delicate bone gaming pieces, a pair of iron

Fig. 64 A cremation is placed in a
pit before the mound is erected.
Artist's impression by Victor Ambrus
of the burial rite used in Mounds 5,
6 and 7.

Fig. 65 Elements of the harness from the Mound 17 burial: two strap-ends with human faces. British Museum.

shears, a silver-mounted cup, an ivory box with a sliding lid, like a little pencil case – perhaps intended to carry a stylus – and probably much else besides, but since lost to tomb-robbers. The burial pit was then sealed or backfilled and a mound heaped upon it. Three groups of mound-builders extracted sand and soil from pits. The most energetic were on the west side, while those to the north dug small pits which were scarcely more than gestures. To the east, horses and cattle were killed, and – whether or not there was feasting – the heads of the animals found their way into the open quarry pits. It seems that at this time, when the quarry pits lay open, a person was also killed, and was laid in the centre of the largest pit on the west side. This person may have been the victim of a sacrifice, of vengeance, of a punishment or a vindictive attack by a stressed foreman. We cannot know; but we do know that this burial marked the first of a series which provide one of the most puzzling and gruesome aspects of Sutton Hoo's usage. The burial of individuals without grave goods was to continue around the mound for the next five hundred years.[2]

When Mound 5 had reached a height of about 2 m (6 ft 6 in), probably as high as it could go, the surplus soil was returned to the pits, where it was soon to grass over, like the mound itself.

The rite of cremation continued to be practised in the line of mounds which had begun with Mound 5. The adult (of unknown sex) buried in Mound 6 had been cremated with a number of animals including a large ungulate (horse or cattle), sheep and pig. These remains were buried in a cloth in a bronze bowl, and the surviving finds were a bronze inlaid pyramid from a sword suspension system, a comb and gaming pieces. In Mound 7, horse, cattle, red deer, sheep and pig accompanied the adult onto the pyre, and the finds included a large multicoloured bead with a hole through it (Col, Pl. V), also perhaps from a sword suspension system, together with bone gaming pieces, and fragments from a cauldron, an iron-bound bucket and a silver-mounted drinking horn or cup. In Mound 4, the burial contained cremated bone from both a man and a woman, together with horse and (possibly) dog. They were accompanied by gaming pieces. In Mound 3 the cremated remains of an adult man and a horse had been probably placed in a bronze container and the container laid on a wooden trough, bier or dug-out boat, and lowered into a pit. Here were placed also an iron axe, a bone box which had carried a Christian chi-rho inscription, a bronze ewer from Nubia and a limestone plaque with a winged victory or angel from Alexandria. An outlier to the west was Mound 18, a memorial to a young adult who had been cremated, and the remains wrapped in cloth and placed in a bronze bowl. Only a fragment of a comb survived from the grave goods.[3]

These cremations, while in every case disfigured by later plundering, seem to share a leitmotif. We could see this group of individuals as young, male, vain and fond of board games; we could also guess that they rode, feasted, fought and, in at least one case, had died in an armed struggle. They had access to domestic animals and game, and to classy imports. They were the new aristocracy of the seventh century.

Not out of place in their company was a young man buried, in a very different way, under Mound 17 (Fig. 66). The place chosen was the north-west corner of the old earthwork which carried Mound 5, 6 and 18, near the edge of the scarp which overlooked the river. Two pits were dug side by side, the sand being thrown up in great heaps to north and south. Some of the sand was washed back in, perhaps overnight, before the funeral cortège arrived. Then, the larger of the two pits was furnished, perhaps with the aid of a pole sloping into the pit like a ladder.[4] Two spears were laid on the base of the pit, and upon them a shield, with an iron boss, its stud uppermost. Then an iron-bound bucket and a bronze cauldron were placed along the north edge. The cauldron must have contained some perishable material, like grain, since an earthenware pot was found sitting within it, the

Fig. 66 The Mound 17 burial: the body is laid in a wooden coffin with a bucket and cauldron (right). The soil block beyond the head of the coffin contains the remains of the harness. Nigel Macbeth.

Fig. 67 The Mound 17 horse. The body of the animal survives partly as bone, partly as body stain. Nigel Macbeth.

grain replaced by sand. Next to the cauldron, on the east side, was a haversack, with the shape of a small kit-bag, containing lamb chops and probably some other foodstuffs of an eternal picnic (bread? or apples?) all trace of which had unfortunately vanished; but these items had propped up a bronze bowl, which appeared at the mouth of the bag.

A splendid harness was deposited at the west end; a snaffle bit with ornamented gilt-bronze cheek-pieces was joined to reins, and by leather (calf-skin) straps to a brow band and nose band; all were connected with strap-distributors covered with gilded bronze disks ornamented with writhing animals (Col. Pl. Vb). There was possibly a 'martingale', too, the sign of a mettlesome steed (Fig. 68). The strap connectors of the bridle were enlivened with axe-shaped gilded pendants; while a set of axe-shaped bronze pendants, covered with silver sheet, probably came from a body harness. And just as the strap ends of human garments so often carry animal ornament, in a neat reversal of the norm the gilded strap-ends of this harness carried little human icons, a set of anxious faces with moustaches (Fig. 65). Leather, wood fragments and bronze pins probably originated as part of a saddle. On the heap of the saddle and bridle was a tapering tub made of solid wood, the sort of receptacle in which to give a horse his bran. And in an adjacent pit to the north lay the body of the horse, killed, we must suppose, to accompany his master. It was a stallion or gelding, five or six years old, which stood to 14 hands.

The moment came for the coffin to be placed in the grave. It was a rectangular box, the lid joined to the sides with four large iron clamps with two nails at each side, hammered into the wood. Inside lay a young man, about twenty-five years old, his sword at his side and a purse by his shoulder. The sword had a pommel of horn and the sword belt a buckle of bronze inlaid with leaf-shaped garnets (Col. Pl VI). The purse contained mementoes or lucky bits: a piece of millefiori, some garnets, a pebble. Whether by accident or perforce, the coffin was lowered on to the stud of the shield and canted over. Inside the coffin, the body of the young man rolled against his sword. Now the grave would be filled in; the spades dug into the heaps of earth on the east and west sides and the sand and pebbles rattled on to the coffin lid. But there was one more object to come, a personal one. A comb was dropped into the grave, hit the coffin-lid and ended up standing almost vertically against the coffin side. One of the mourners had no doubt remembered, probably not for the first time, an unkempt youth, liable to forget his comb ...

Whether dressed like this for life, or just for his journey into the other world, the Mound 17 person conjures up a heroic image worthy of a young Siegfried: mounted on his stallion, with gold and

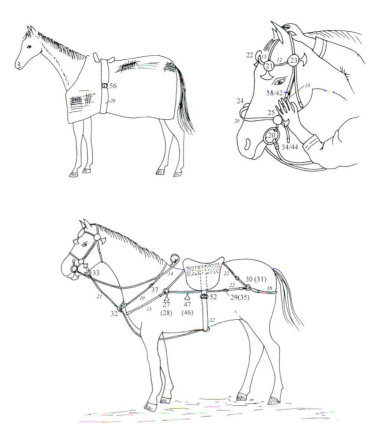

Fig. 68 Provisional reconstruction of the horse harness found in the human burial beneath Mound 17. The numbers in italics refer to strap widths and the upright numbers to the connectors and buckles listed in the Digest of Evidence. Numbers in brackets refer to equivalent items positioned on the other side of the horse. M.O.H. Carver.

silver roundels, strap-ends and pendants dangling and turning; the horn-pommelled sword in its sheath, right arm holding the spears, left arm through the shield strap and left hand holding the reins; and behind, attached to the saddle or body harness, the camping kit: bucket, cauldron and pot, and the haversack with iron rations and a bronze bowl to fill at forest stream or spring. His early death was mourned through the evocation of every young man's dream: to ride out well-equipped on a favourite mount, on a sunny morning, free of relatives, free of love, free of responsibility, self-sufficient and ready for any adventure.

The inhumation rite was used for other burials that lay east and west of the main axis of cremations. One (Burial 12) was the grave of a child, in a coffin less than 1.2 m (4 ft) long. The child could not have been more than seven years old, but he had already been given arms: he wore a small belt buckle and dress pin, and a miniature spear lay inside the coffin. The grave was originally covered by a mini-mound less than 2 m (6 ft 6 in) across. Here was evidence that Anglo-Saxon society at Sutton Hoo, as elsewhere, had reached the stage in which status could

Fig. 69 The day of burial at Mound 17: the cortège arrives. Artist's impression by Victor Ambrus.

be inherited as opposed to achieved. Two other inhumations (Burials 15 and 16) made a row with Burial 12. The first of these was interred in a coffin, wore a leather belt with a decorated plate and carried a knife in a sheath. The second, also in a coffin, wore a belt carrying a châtelaine, the emblem of the well-bred woman, and a leather pouch with draw-strings. The châtelaine included three latch-lifters and a small knife. By the left ear was a hair tie, a leather loop, a pin and a tiny white bead. Although the remains were past recognition, Burials 15 and 16 probably represent, respectively, the bodies of a teenage boy and girl. They may have been marked originally by small mounds, but there was no evidence of this.

Still further to the east, Mound 14 covered a chamber grave, made of thin nailed slats probably from a section of a fence or roof which had been reused to revet the grave. The person had been buried in a coffin and in the chamber was a silver bowl, a least one wooden drinking vessel with silver rim-mounts and facings, a silver dress fastener, some silver wire, two crushed beads, a brooch pin, a cauldron and a bucket. Decisive for the identification of the burial as that of a woman was the discovery of a châtelaine, damaged beyond restoration, but probably including latch-lifters and a knife. This is the only rich mound burial so far discovered at Sutton Hoo that is certainly dedicated to a powerful or favoured female. The others, from their grave goods, seem to commemorate males.

One more example of an inhumation lay to the west of Mound 5, one so disturbed by later depredations that it survived only as a skull in a pit. There were, however, some scraps of metal to show that it had once been a furnished inhumation, and the skull gave a radiocarbon date in the eighth century. This burial was most probably covered by a mound, into which two cremations, both without grave goods, one in a pot and the other not, had been inserted or incorporated. Were these very late returns of the cremation rite, or disturbances from earlier burials? Sadly, little can be said of them, and they must remain as oddities in the Sutton Hoo story.

From these memorials of high rank and varied ritual we now approach Sutton Hoo's funerary climax, Mound 1 and Mound 2, which represent not only still higher rank and more idiosyncratic ritual, but two of the most extravagant funerary investments so far known from Britain. These were the ship-burials, probably the largest and among the latest burials to be enacted at Sutton Hoo.

The land where the Mound 2 burial was to be made was under grass, although it had been ploughed in earlier times. A path bordering the ploughland was still visible and perhaps still in use. The Anglo-Saxon party responsible for planning the burial laid

a

I Polychrome jewellery from the Mound 1 burial. (a) The end of one of the two shoulder-clasps, showing a motif of two wild boars set symmetrically one across the other, as in a heraldic device. The clasps are made of gold inset with garnets and millifiore glass. The boars' tusks are blue glass, and the animals are brought out from the background with filligree gold wire. Width: 48 mm; (b) hemispherical bosses from the scabbard, of gold inset with garnets. Width: 23 mm; (c) dummy buckle (clasp) from the baldric. The garnets include those of mushroom shape thought to characterise the Sutton Hoo workshop. Length 73 mm. These precious objects spent the first night of their rediscovery under Mrs Pretty's bed. All British Museum.

b

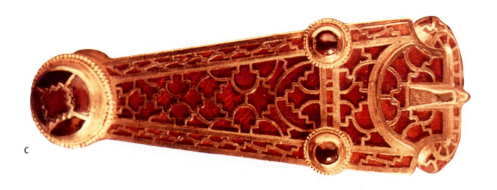

c

II (above) The great gold buckle, which weighs 44.5 grammes. The serpentine creatures entangled on the face are represented by curved beaks and webbed feet. The buckle is hollow and can be opened with two sliding catches at the back. Length: 132 mm. British Museum.

III An evocation of the potentate buried in Mound 1, drawn by Caroline Fleming. The finds in the Mound ship burial include a wide range of textiles, many deriving from items of personal clothing. The dead man may have been Raedwald, a king of East Anglia who died in AD 624 or 625.

IV Aerial photograph of the Sutton Hoo site after cleaning and mowing in 1983. Cliff Hoppitt.

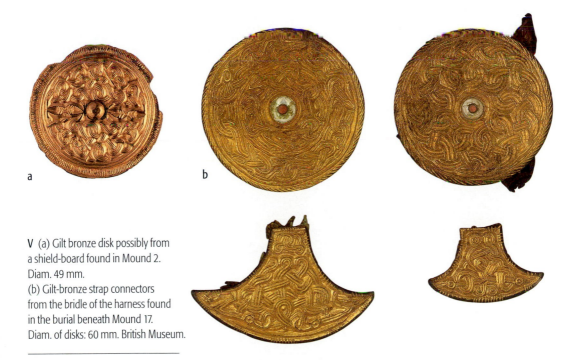

a

b

V (a) Gilt bronze disk possibly from a shield-board found in Mound 2. Diam. 49 mm.
(b) Gilt-bronze strap connectors from the bridle of the harness found in the burial beneath Mound 17. Diam. of disks: 60 mm. British Museum.

VI Sword-harness from the Mound 17 burial. Belt buckle, two sword pyramids, which acted as tag-ends for the straps which secured the sword in its scabbard, a linear mount from the scabbard and a small buckle. The buckle, pyramids and mount are made of copper alloy inset with leaf-shaped garnets. British Museum.

VIII Excavation: preparing the surface with trowel and spray near Mound 5, to reveal Bronze Age ditches, an early medieval burial pit, execution graves, and pits dug by later excavators. The squares are the areas excavated during the British Museum campaign of 1965–71. Rupert Bruce-Mitford looks on (right). Nigel Macbeth.

IX A 'sandman'. The flexed body is marked by thick bars of dark sand which sometimes contain minute fragments of bone. The straight dark edges at the foot and head are residues of wood planks. Nigel Macbeth.

XI The completed excavation in 1991. Aerial photograph by Nigel Macbeth.

X (opposite) Excavation of Mound 6 (foreground) and Mound 7. In the square areas (quadrants) can be seen the coloured sands filling the quarry ditches of the mounds. An army slit trench cut into the near side of Mound 7 (in *c.* 1942) and the parallel lines of a late medieval trackway cut across on its far side. The reconstructed Mound 1 can be seen top right, and the site offices, top. Nigel Macbeth.

XII Edwin Gifford at the helm of his half-sized replica of the Mound 1 ship, *Sae Wulfing*, which is moving at about 7 knots. Photograph by Cliff Hoppitt, courtesy of Edwin Gifford.

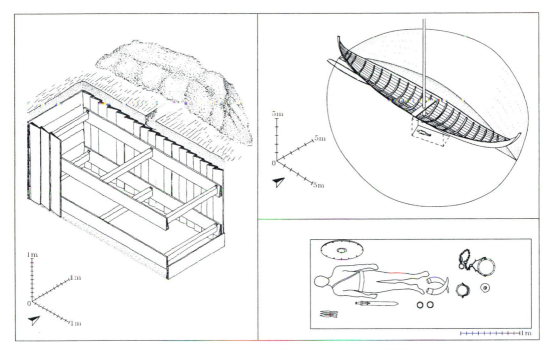

Fig. 70 The Mound 2 burial: reconstruction of the chamber and the positioning of the ship. Carver/Roe/Brennan.

out an exceptionally large memorial. They dug two pits 24 m (78 ft) apart, aligned east–west to the setting sun. A third pit was then placed 13.7 m (45 ft) to the south of one and 27.4 m (90 ft) from the other; this resulted in a right-angled triangle. A fourth pit was dug in an analogous position, so that a rectangle was formed aligned east–west. Over the area of this rectangle the turf was stripped and stacked to be used later in the construction of the mound.

Half way (13.7 m, 45 ft) along the diagonals of the rectangle, the position for the burial chamber was marked. It was to be 1.2 m (4 ft) wide, 3.6 m (12 ft) long and 1.8 m (6 ft) deep from the old ground surface, now stripped of its turf. The brown soil and yellow subsoil excavated from the chamber was heaped up on the north side. The deep pit was now revetted with overlapping vertical planks along its north and south sides, probably held in place with horizontal shoring secured by struts. The short walls to east and west were formed by horizontal planks dropped behind the ends of the long sides. In this way an underground room was fabricated (Fig. 70.)

This chamber was now ready to be furnished, and it was furnished richly. Unfortunately its richness proved irresistible to later visitors, leaving us only scraps and stains to guess at its original splendour. But this much can be said: the burial was equipped with a sword, a spear, a shield with gilt bronze mounts and a baldric which included a gilded bronze buckle. There were drinking horns, a blue glass jar, a bronze bowl and a

Fig. 71 The day of burial at Mound 2. Artist's impression by Victor Ambrus.

silver-mounted box. There were five knives, including two in a double sheath. At the east end was an iron-bound bucket and, perhaps, a cauldron with a chain. The dead man lay at the west end; the rest, and who knows what treasures would have been among them, our imagination must supply.

So far, the burial was splendid, but conventional – a chamber grave. But what came next was, so far as we know, a 'first' for the western world. A stout beam was laid across the mouth of the chamber – or it might have already been in use to prop up the ladder used to load the tomb. The burial party said its last farewells. And then a ship, about 20 m (65 ft) long, was dragged between the marker pits and over the chamber, brushing past the spoil heap, its keel resting on the beam. The hull must have been propped up; if there was a mast it could have remained in place; if there were figurehead and sternpost, they too could remain. Now the chamber had been sealed – by the hull of a large clinker-built vessel (Fig. 71).[5]

How much time elapsed between the placing of the ship and the building of the mound is not known. One imagines that this kind of investment – a richly furnished underground chamber, a ship and a mound – was not a thing to be done in a corner or done in a hurry. It was meant to be seen and remembered, by friends, allies, subjects and enemies, as an extravagant demonstration of continuing power in heaven and on earth. It is even possible that the ship stood for some years, until, perhaps at some anniversary, a new memorial service was convened at which the mound was constructed.

The four corner pits and the position of the ship itself guided the mound-builders; their spoil was taken from a broad if ragged quarry ditch. Two causeways were left, to east and west, to ease loading. Many hundreds of tons of turf, soil and then sand and gravel subsoil were lifted into the ship and around it, and then piled upon it. The mound would have risen against the skyline until only the mast, the prow and sternposts still showed. Last to be added were probably those stacked turves that had been stripped from the mound platform and could be used to prevent large-scale slippage. The stones from the final loads of sand and gravel rolled down into the quarry ditch; and surplus soil, now mixed from transportation, was returned to the quarries. Standing nearly 4 m (13 ft) high and visible from across the River Deben, Mound 2 was a memorial, a monument and a landmark (Fig. 97).[6]

Mound 2 was one of the largest and richest burials known from Sutton Hoo; but not the largest or the richest. This honour belongs to Mound 1, the other and more famous ship-burial; famous to us because it has come to us intact. But it is probable that it was famous then, too, and, notwithstanding the good fortune of its survival, could still have been among the richest burials made in seventh century Britain. Even though it was unrobbed, the uneven survival of materials within the chamber and the circumstances of their discovery mean that several important aspects of the burial rite remain uncertain and controversial: the route taken by the burial ship, the structure of the chamber, whether there was a coffin. Our inferences will always be limited, and some details will never be known, since we cannot now return to the 1939 excavation. But it is worthwhile to try to capture such a pivotal moment of the past. Let's imagine how it might have been.

The site chosen was on flat ground behind a promontory on the river side of the cemetery, south-west of Mound 7. The site was prepared by stripping and stacking the turf, probably from a wide area. There were no corner pits and no chamber to locate. On this occasion the whole ship was to be buried below ground, and the burial chamber placed inside the vessel, amidships. A trench 28 m (92 ft) long and up to 6 m (20 ft) wide was laid out east–west and excavated: descending to 3.5 m (11 ft) below the Anglo-Saxon ground surface, it was the biggest hole yet dug in the burial ground. Nearly 600 cu. m (21,000 cu. ft) of soil and subsoil were excavated and piled up in two large spoil heaps to north and south. These were then cut back, to give a clearance of 4.5 m (15 ft) to the north and 7 m (23 ft) to the south, to allow access to the ship and the burial party.

Fig. 73 Mound 1: fluted silver bowl which had contained the combs and other personal items. Diam. 407 mm. British Museum.

Although little is known about how the ship made its way into the grave, the rivet pattern on the hull indicated that it had been patched and was thus a working vessel, not one especially built for burial. The task of bringing such a huge ship out of the water and up onto the heath seems formidable to us, but must have been a feasible procedure to those accustomed to transport vessels by hand over land, following 'portage' routes from one stretch of water to another. Experiments with some of these land journeys show how they might have been achieved.[7] The Sutton Hoo ships were probably brought up on rollers, having been extracted from the river at high tide at Ferry Point, or even further south, so as to follow the gentlest approach northwards to the burial site. The Mound 1 ship would have to be manoeuvred in position by approaching stern-first from the landward side (east) or by swivelling through 90 degrees on the neck of the promontory; either way the ship would be led between the spoil heaps on rollers until it was over the prepared trench. Then a group of men would put their weight on one end of the ship, so rollers could be eased out at the other; once the weight was removed, the stern or stem could tilt down into the trench. The free rollers removed, those still bearing load would be levered out, or eventually chopped in

half. Canted at a slight angle, the ship now lay in its trench. It was
27 m (90 ft) long, the longest ship so far known from Europe
before the Viking era.[8] It was clinker built, with nine strakes per
side, held together by some 3,000 rivets or clench nails. Such a
massive vessel would surely have been decorated, like those that
came after her, with an ornamented headpiece at the stem and a
tailpiece at the stern, and maybe carvings in wood all the way
down the keel to the waterline or along the washstrake. There is
no reason to doubt that the Anglo-Saxons could execute in wood
what they were able to realise in metal and manuscripts.

The burial chamber was most likely constructed in the ship
once it had been placed in its trench, and analogy with the later,
and better-preserved chamber in the Oseberg ship-burial suggests
how it might have been made (Fig. 74).[9] A series of joists was laid

Fig. 74 Mound 1: a suggested
method of construction for the
chamber. Carver/Brennan.

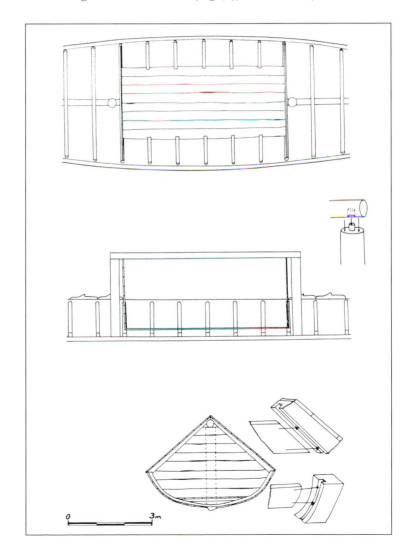

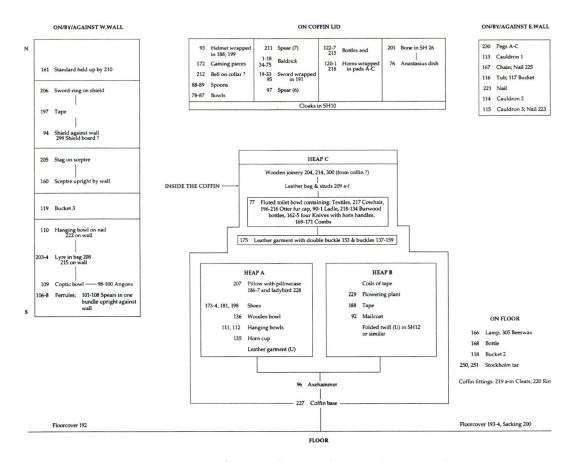

| ON/BY/AGAINST W.WALL | | ON COFFIN LID | | | | | | ON/BY/AGAINST E.WALL |

<table>
<tr><td colspan="3">ON/BY/AGAINST W.WALL</td><td colspan="4">ON COFFIN LID</td><td colspan="2">ON/BY/AGAINST E.WALL</td></tr>
</table>

ON/BY/AGAINST W.WALL

161   Standard held up by 210

206   Sword-ring on shield

197   Tape

94   Shield against wall
299 Shield board ?

205   Stag on sceptre

160   Sceptre upright by wall

119   Bucket 3

110   Hanging bowl on nail
222 on wall

203-4   Lyre in bag 208
215 on wall

109   Coptic bowl —— 98-100 Angons

106-8   Ferrules;   101-108 Spears in one
bundle upright against
wall

ON COFFIN LID

93 Helmet wrapped in 188, 199	211 Spear (7)	122-7 213 Bottles and	201 Bone in SH 26
172 Gaming pieces	1-18 34-75 Baldrick	120-1 218 Horns wrapped in pads A-C	76 Anastasius dish
212 Bell on collar ?	19-33 95 Sword wrapped in 191		
88-89 Spoons	97 Spear (6)		
78-87 Bowls			

Cloaks in SH10

INSIDE THE COFFIN →

HEAP C

Wooden joinery 204, 214, 300 (from coffin ?)

Leather bag & studs 209 a-f

77   Fluted toilet bowl containing: Textiles, 217 Cowhair,
196-216 Otter fur cap, 90-1 Ladle, 218-134 Burwood
bottles, 162-5 four Knives with horn handles,
169-171 Combs

175   Leather garment with double buckle 153 & buckles 137-159

HEAP A

207   Pillow with pillowcase
186-7 and ladybird 228

173-4, 181, 198   Shoes

136   Wooden bowl

111, 112   Hanging bowls

135   Horn cup

Leather garment (U)

HEAP B

Coils of tape

229   Flowering plant

188   Tape

92   Mailcoat

Folded twill (U) in SH12
or similar

96   Axehammer

227 — Coffin base

ON/BY/AGAINST E.WALL

| 230   Pegs A-C |
| 113   Cauldron 1 |
| 167   Chain; Nail 225 |
| 116   Tub; 117 Bucket |
| 221   Nail |
| 114   Cauldron 2 |
| 115   Cauldron 3; Nail 223 |

ON FLOOR

166   Lamp, 305 Beeswax

168   Bottle

118   Bucket 2

250, 251   Stockholm tar

Coffin fittings: 219 a-m Cleats, 220 Rin

Floorcover 192   Floorcover 193-4, Sacking 200

FLOOR

Fig. 75 Mound 1: stratigraphic relationships between the finds, from which was deduced the sequence in which the chamber was furnished. M.O.H. Carver.

across from north to south, coincident with ribs at approximately the level of the junction between strakes 5 and 6. Then a floor of planks was laid on these joists, to run east–west parallel with the keel. The floor stretched from rib 10 to rib 16, a distance of 5.5 m (18 ft), and the clearance over the keel was about 1 ft (30 cm). Now two large upright posts were founded on the keel outside the floor at each end, their upper ends presumably tenoned into a ridge beam. Within the upright posts and on top of the floor, horizontal planks about 2.5 cm (1 in) thick were placed on edge one above the other; they may have been secured in a groove in the rib. As in Oseberg, the rafters may have been cut so that they lay with their lower end 'beaked' on the gunwale and their upper ends resting on the ridge pole. The end walls were continued upwards above the gunwale, each plank being let into a groove cut in the inside face of the end rafters. The end walls would thus be completely secured by ribs and rafters. The lowest plank was secured to the floor by a few nails. The roof was completed with planks laid edge to edge and running east–west over the rafters. But on one side, probably the south, the central rafters and roofing were left off at this stage; only the end rafters were placed in their position so as to lock the end walls in place. The chamber could now be loaded through the open side of the roof (Figs 78, 79).

First to be furnished was probably the east wall, which carried two large oak pegs. On these were hung a cauldron, empty, but with a working capacity of 100 litres, its chain looped up onto a nail, together with two smaller cauldrons and a tub, which completed the food and kitchen provision.[10] Then a large coffin, with dimensions of about 3 × 1 × 1 m (9 × 3 × 3 ft), was either constructed *in situ*, or eased through the open roof, and placed on the floor towards the west end. The lid was off, and the dead man, probably wrapped in a shroud, was laid out at its west end. Into the space at the east end of the coffin, by the dead man's feet, were piled objects of mainly an intimate and personal kind. An axe hammer lay at the base. Then two heaps were begun. That furthest from the dead man's feet ('Heap A') consisted of a leather garment, a horn cup and two little hanging bowls, a wooden bowl and, on top, a goose down pillow in its pillow case. A ladybird had contrived to find its way into the pillow, although not out of it. On either side of the pillow were placed two pairs of indoor shoes, the length of one measurable at size 7 (or size 40 continental): the Mound 1 hero was short and stocky. The heap nearer to the feet ('Heap B') began with a piece of folded twill on which a mailcoat was placed, together with many coils of tape, perhaps for fastening garments. Here a flower was laid.

Both heaps together were now covered by a third ('Heap C') which began with a large leather garment with a double buckle and a number of single buckles. On this lay the toiletries: a fluted silver bowl, containing several combs, four knives with horn handles, seven burrwood bottles presumably containing various ointments, a silver ladle, fragments of textile and an otter-fur cap. On top of the now tottering heap contained by the coffin walls was a leather object with studs, perhaps the equivalent of a travelling bag or suitcase, and on top of that a fine yellow cloak.

Now it was time to say goodbye to the person as an individual and replace the coffin lid, hammering home ten cleats on each side to secure it. But outside and on top of the coffin, the celebration of the person as a statesman was to continue. The remaining two of the three yellow cloaks were thrown over the coffin lid. On them at the east end was placed a great silver dish, imported from Constantinople and bearing the stamp of the emperor Anastasius. On it were food or burnt offerings. In the centre was a group of maplewood drinking bottles and two huge drinking-horns, wrapped in cloth to keep them clean until ready for use. Still further west were placed two spears, one along each edge to guard the parade gear which was deposited in the centre

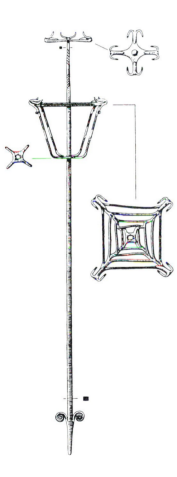

Fig. 76 Mound 1: the iron stand, or standard. Scale ⅟₁₆. British Museum.

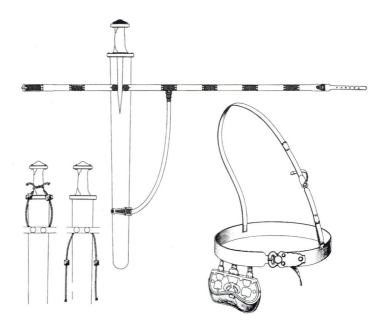

Fig. 77 Mound 1: the form of the baldric, and the methods of suspending the sword and the purse. SHSB II, fig. 423.

of the west end of the coffin. This comprised a baldric ('Sam Browne') with a buckle of solid gold and connectors of gold and garnet; the shoulder clasps resembled those of a Roman officer, but were more splendid and individual than anything worn by a centurion (Col. Pl. I). The baldric supported a purse with a gold frame, its lid guarded by ornamental gold and garnet animals. It contained thirty-seven gold coins, three blanks and two little ingots.[11] On a separate belt was a sword, with pattern-welded blade 854 mm (2 ft 10 in) long, and a wooden scabbard, lined inside with wool. The scabbard carried two little hemispherical bosses, elaborate studs which secured the sword-belt to the scabbard (Col. Pl. I). A connecting strap secured by a triangular buckle led from the end of the scabbard to a swivel on the sword-belt. When the sword was sheathed, the sword pommel was secured with tapes or thongs that had carried little pyramids at the ends. Pommel, connectors, bosses, buckles and pyramids were of gold inlaid with cut garnets: East Anglia's finest jewellery, in a matching set.

Most of the weapons and drinking vessels seem to have been wrapped in cloth to keep them in serviceable condition during the metaphorical voyage.[12] At the very end of the coffin, and still on its lid, was a nest of silver bowls, originally perhaps finger-bowls for the feasting of Christian diners, and two silver spoons. On the coffin lid too was the helmet wrapped up in cloth, and a set of gaming pieces (no one in the Anglo-Saxon world was ever too grand for board games). There was also a little bell on a collar, perhaps from a favourite pet whose mortal remains were to disappear in the dark sand in which all the contents of the chamber were eventually to be immersed (Fig. 86).

The west wall was laden with the symbols of office. An iron standard was wedged between floor and roof. The shield, carrying its dragon and hawk or falcon motifs, stood upright against the west wall. On the south side hung a lyre in a beaver-skin bag, and just below it a large and luxurious hanging-bowl. Further to the south, a bunch of five spears and three angons (a weapon resembling the later pike) were threaded, perhaps symbolically, through the handle of a 'Coptic' bowl and leant up against the wall. The bowl, an exotic item from North Africa, carried images of a camel, a lion and a donkey.

Now the tableau of the dead man was almost ready. There was still space to circulate and admire all these treasures and gifts, which may have been brought together for the first and last time. A few more items were put on the floor: a bucket by the west wall and another by the south gunwale; near the east end of the coffin was an iron lamp with its beeswax cake of fuel. A little bottle containing, perhaps, honey or a condiment, ended up on the floor, but may have started on or near the silver dish. At the west end in the centre, in the midst of the regalia, the whetstone sceptre was secured in an upright position.

The time arrived when enough people had filed along the side of the ship and peered into the chamber; enough speeches had been made and dirges sung; those who were to weep had wept; and those who wished to walk away had gone and the obsequies were finished (Fig. 81). Then the southern half of the roof could be put in place. Once the rafters were in, someone could slip down and light the lamp. But it did not burn for long, since the cake of beeswax fuel was little used. The roof planks were laid in position, and then maybe turfed over for security. It is unlikely that the boat was filled in and the mound constructed immediately. Indeed, it would have been a colossal task, suitable to celebrate an anniversary or a victory in the struggle for survival of the young East Anglian state. But the task was eventually faced, for the ship and its trench were filled in and a mound several metres high was raised. The burial chamber, wedged tightly shut by the pressure of earth, was of enormous strength. It would be many decades, perhaps centuries, before it collapsed and compressed the proudly furnished chamber into a thin fragmented sandwich of woodstain and metal, the form in which it was to be found.

The Mound 1 finds form a wonderful assemblage: many and varied were the objects assembled in this chamber, and the references suggested by them are diverse and complex and operate at many levels in the mind, then and now. The man is a warrior,

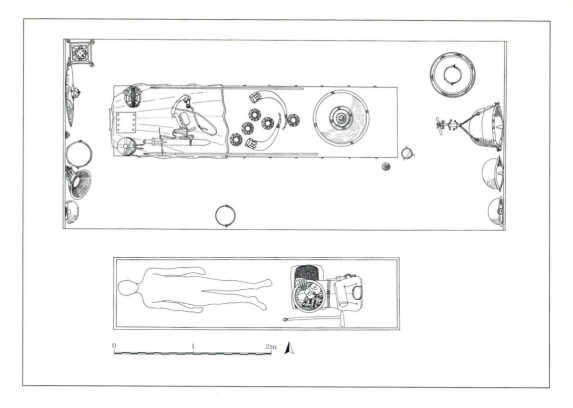

Fig. 78 Mound 1: reconstruction of the furnished chamber, in plan. Carver/Brennan.

equipped for war with helmet, mailcoat, sword, shield and spears. He is a host, ready to put on a feast, with cauldrons, tub, bowls of bronze and silver, drinking horns, wooden bottles, a great silver dish – and entertainment from the lyre-player. He is a leader, dressed in glittering parade dress with highly symbolic accoutrements, his office marked by a standard and a sceptre. For all that, he is a man, with washing and shaving kit, a selection of clothing and shoes, and a soft pillow at the end of the day.

He is also a mariner, and has an axe-hammer to mend the boat and some spare pieces of tar in case it leaks. The placing of the burial in a 'cabin' on board a ship evokes the allegory of a voyage, in this case a voyage to another world from which the traveller was never to return. It puts us in mind of the poetry of the Anglo-Saxons, and of the old English poem *Beowulf* in particular, which refers to the deeds of early heroes and their deaths and burial ceremonies involving ships. Dead heroes go well-equipped to eternal encounters across the sea. Is this Mound 1's simple message? Perhaps, but the funeral was also a public spectacle, an event of the real world, and reality must keep breaking in. The burial makes references to practices in Scandinavia, where ship-burial in the seventh century and later is best known. It includes coins from France, silver from the Byzantine eastern Mediterranean and objects from North Africa. And every item of jewellery and

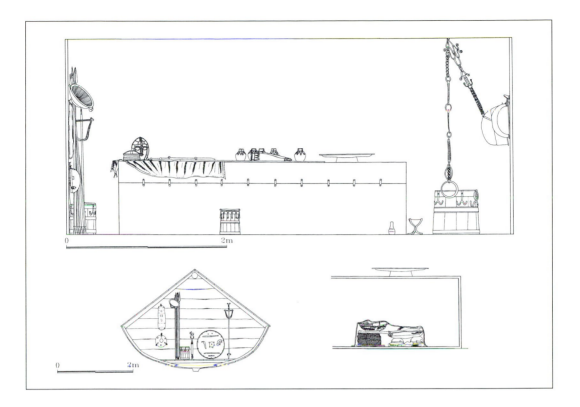

Fig. 79 Mound 1: reconstruction of the furnished chamber, elevation. Carver/Brennan.

Fig. 80 Mound 1: the iron lamp (much reduced). SHSB III, fig. 605.

weaponry included was the result of earlier manufacture, earlier use, earlier choice.

But we would not rely on any one of these factors to explain the Mound 1 ship-burial. For this kind of deliberate deposition is unlikely to have been a direct reflection either of real life or of belief. It was a huge investment, suggesting deep feeling, and bringing forth, from the burial party and its sponsors, a composition that tries to express the fundamentals of loss and hope. In short, the burial is itself a poem, full of references that are interlaced with each other: references to life in the hall, to how a ship is stowed, to the status of the dead person, in reality or aspiration, and at a more personal level to the foibles and achievements of the individual. Looked at in this way, such a burial is a web of allusions, and does not admit of a simple or a single explanation; like poetry it will continue to intrigue us and we shall continue to find within it new meanings to suit our own times. Like poetry its meaning at the time depends heavily on the historical context in which it was enacted. In the interpretation presented here, the Sutton Hoo burial ground as a whole can be presented as a theatre, in which each burial is a composition, offering, with greater or lesser authority, a metaphor for its age. The cemetery is an anthology of statements, connected by certain themes, some of which perhaps can be read clearly enough to allow us to make history from them.

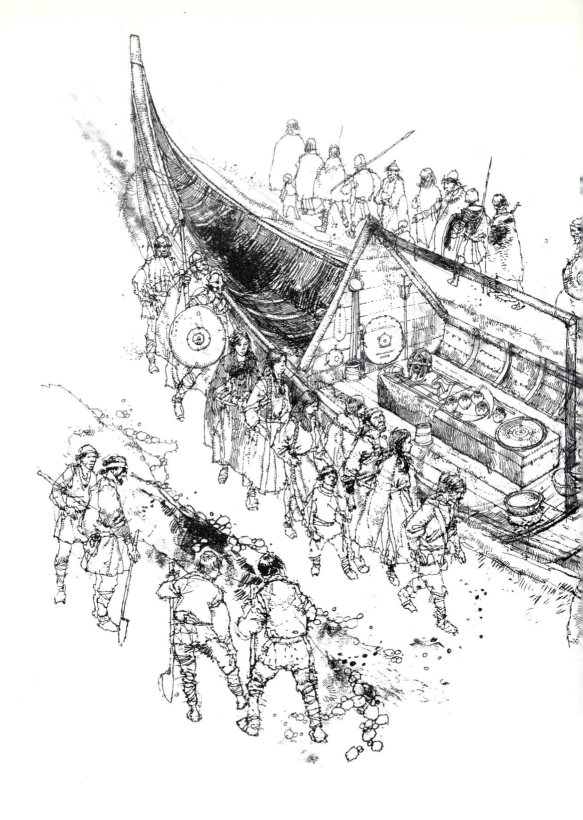

Fig. 81 The day of burial at Mound 1. Artist's impression by Victor Ambrus.

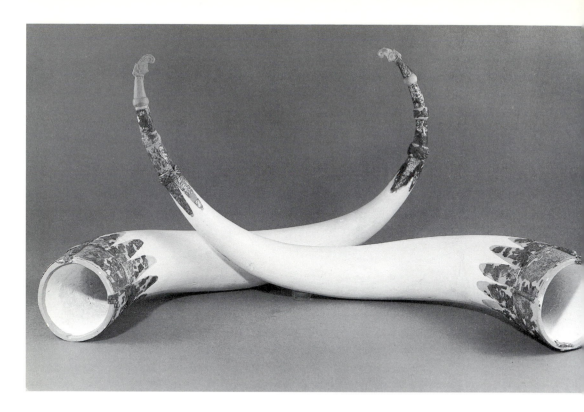

Fig. 82 Grave-goods from Mound 1: the drinking horns. The fittings are modelled onto horns from the now extinct aurochs, a species of cattle. Below: identical curved-beak terminal from a drinking horn found in Mound 2 in 1987. British Museum.

All the mound burials seem to belong to the years around AD 600. The objects in Mound 1 can all be dated on stylistic grounds to the late sixth or early seventh century, and this is also true of the Mound 17 assemblage and of the fragments of finds from the other mounds. The coins, which were Merovingian *tremisses*, provide some more exact indication of date: five out of the thirty-seven coins carry the names of identifiable rulers, and the gold content of this type of coin has been found to vary with time. Both kinds of evidence suggest that at least some of the coins were minted after AD 595 and all may have been minted before AD 613.[13] That is only to say, strictly speaking, that the burial in Mound 1 took place after about AD 613. There is little independent scientific dating because all the burials had poor preservation of bone and organic materials. Radiocarbon dates for Mound 1 were taken from the beeswax in the lamp, which was AD 523 ± 45, and a piece of oak from the bottom of the ship, which was AD 694 ± 45.[14] None of the other furnished graves produced suitable materials; the cremated bone was calcified and had lost its carbon, and the bone had disappeared from the inhumations, leaving only a stain. The unfurnished execution burials in which some bone had survived gave radiocarbon dates from the seventh to the eleventh century.[15]

The evidence for the chronological order in which the mounds were constructed remains frustratingly elusive. The mounds

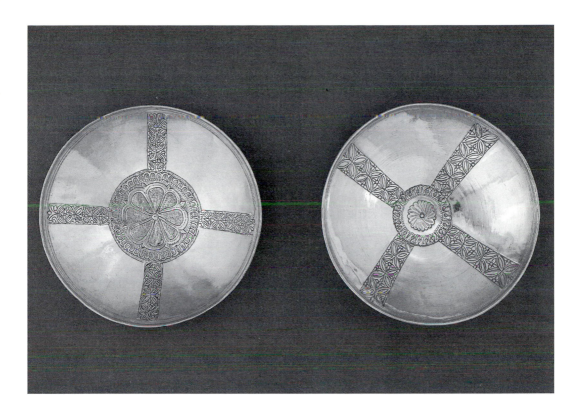

Fig. 83 Grave-goods from Mound 1: two silver bowls from the set of ten. Diam. of the bowls varies from 226–231 mm. British Museum.

were raised in their own space and do not touch each other; and the strata between them was in general quarried or ploughed away. So which came first, Mound 12, 17 and 18 because they are nearest to the river? Or Mound 2 because it is on the highest point? Or Mound 1 because it is the biggest *and* near the river edge? There are a few weak clues from the meagre stratification. The Mound 2 quarry ditch cut a Mound 5 quarry pit, and another Mound 5 quarry pit was cut by one of Mound 6's quarry ditches. Mound 6 and 7 seem to have shared a quarry ditch system and could have been laid out at the same time. At the south end of Mound 7 the quarry ditch curves round: so no more mounds were immediately planned here. Mound 1 seems to interrupt this southward development and alter the geography; a respectful blank space, in which no burials were made, lies at its eastern end. Mounds 7, 13, 4 and 3 surround the space, and mound building then continues southwards in a higgledy-piggledy way: Mounds 8, 9, 10, 11 and 15 seem to have been added looking west of north, as though with their eyes on Mound 1.

From these observations, more intuitive than measured, it can be suggested that Mounds 5, 6 and 7 (all cremations) may have been planned together and may have been the first burials at Sutton Hoo. Another cremation (Mound 18), the horse burial (Mound 17), another inhumation (Burial 56), the children (Burials 12, 15

Fig. 84 Grave-goods from Mound 1: the large hanging-bowl. This bowl contains the model of a fish of the trout family, supported on a pedestal, endorsing the idea that such bowls held water. Diam. 310 mm as restored. British Museum.

and 16), and a rich female (Mound 14) were interred around this founder group. Two great ship-burials followed: Mound 2 in the north (ship over chamber) and Mound 1 in the south (chamber in ship). A secondary development may then have begun, focused on Mound 1. Mound 13 and the group to the south, Mounds 3, 4, 8, 9, 10, 11 and 15, could thus be later than the great ship-burial, but of most of these little is yet known (Fig. 85).

The Anglo-Saxon cemetery at Sutton Hoo can be seen as a short-lived and extravagant ceremonial centre of the late sixth and early seventh century AD, the purpose of which was to provide a focus for a policy of pagan independence. A range of burial rites was celebrated, of which ship-burial and cremation under a mound are the most prominent. These burial rites, new to Britain, show a distinct leaning towards the funerary practice of contemporary Scandinavia.

Sutton Hoo was a very high-ranking and specialised cemetery. It could be termed 'royal' in so far as that word can be given precision in seventh-century England: it is the cemetery of an aristocracy (implied by its wealth), which was dynastic (implied by the suite of cremations in bronze bowls), which claimed a

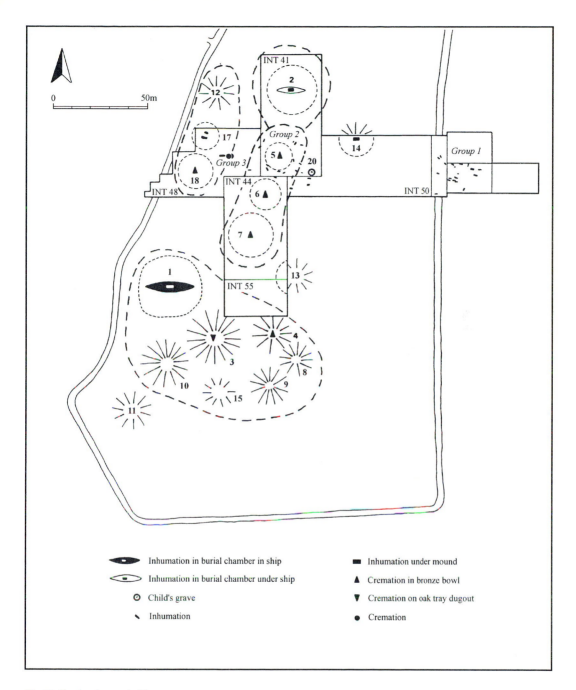

Fig. 85 The development of the Sutton Hoo cemetery. A model. 'Mound 16' has been omitted since its location and existence are uncertain. M.O.H. Carver.

Fig. 86 Reconstruction of the bell from the Mound 1 chamber. It was made of bronze and had a length of chain attached to the top. It is possible that such a bell was worn by a pet animal. SHSB III, fig. 640.

regional supremacy (implied by the symbolic apparatus in Mound 1), and international recognition (implied by the exotic objects). The cemetery lay in the territory of the East Angles, since Rendlesham (to the north) and Ipswich and Felixstowe (to the south) all relate to that province. Since the earliest kings of East Anglia are recorded to have died in the late sixth century, the Sutton Hoo cemetery was initiated at, or just before, the local adoption of kingship itself.[16]

From the choice of burial rite: cremation under mound, and ship-burial, it can be deduced that this was a kingdom which was being created in a pagan mode, in alignment with Scandinavia. This is in contrast to contemporary France, Kent or Northumbria, where kingship was being developed with a Christian ideology and within an alliance of Christian peoples. For the East Angles, the question of conversion to Christianity must have constituted the most agonising dilemma of the day – not so much a question of faith, as a question of allegiance and political judgement. On the one hand were the advantages of a large continental market; on the other, the potential loss of autonomy, loss of contact with kin and allies in Scandinavia and the threat to deeply-held convictions about how life should be lived. Such anxieties are not without analogies for our own times.

The investment in an overtly pagan style of burial at Sutton Hoo may have been directly provoked by the perceived menace of a predatory Christian mission. It was an investment that reached a climax as Merovingian pressure on Kent was gaining ground for the Christian alliance. But in spite of the defiance signalled by the great mounds, in scarcely a generation the Christian argument had been won, and the message of the Sutton Hoo burial ground had become history.

6 THE GALLOWS AND THE GENTRY

An English landscape, *c.* AD 600–1938

There is one more burial rite to explain, one that might have begun with the royal cemetery, but continued beyond its time. The burials around Mound 5 and on the eastern edge of the mounds contained bodies that had been hanged, beheaded or mutilated. Could this have been the work of early English kings?

The first of the burials to be placed around Mound 5 was Burial 53. The body was decomposed and had lost much of its natural form, but was still recognisable as a human, probably lying face down. It had been laid on the base of a large quarry pit to the west of the mound, and not so much buried as covered with planks and branches. All was covered up when soil, surplus to mound-building, was returned to the pit. Graves were later added to the east and south sides of Mound 5 (Fig. 87). Four of them (Burials 44, 45, 50

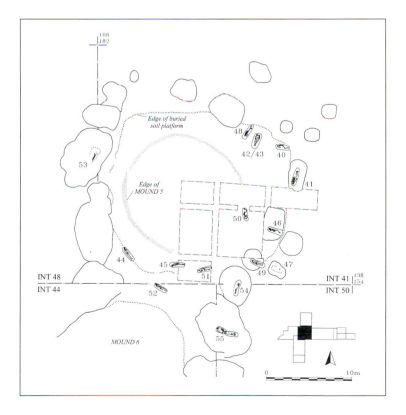

Fig. 87 The 'satellite' burials around Mound 5. These contained examples of execution victims.

Fig. 88 Triple burial (Burial 42/43) of a decapitated man and two women found near Mound 5. The remains of the second woman did not survive well and were inferred from bone fragments by the specialist. .

and 51) were tangential to the mound and against its original edge. The occupant of one of these (45) was buried face down, but the others were relatively normal in the way they lay. The next series of burials was added a little further out, radial to the mound or in its eastern quarry pits (Burials 40, 41, 42/3, 46, 48 and 49). Burial 48 had its head detached and placed below the knee. Burial 40's head had also been removed but replaced askew at the neck end. In the extraordinary Burial 42, a mature male lay on his back, decapitated, and on top of him lay two women face down (Fig. 88). Burials 41 and 46 had been cut into quarry pits which had been partially refilled and turfed over. Burial 49, also in a quarry pit, lay with a 'collar' of dark soil around his neck – seemingly the remains of a rope from the gallows. A third series, furthest away, were Burials 52, 54 and 55, all badly mutilated: Burial 52 had been decapitated and the head replaced at the neck end, although rotated through 180 degrees. The lower left leg was broken. Burial 54 had been decapitated too, but the head was not present. Burial 55 was folded over backwards, and had possibly been quartered.

The earliest of these burials (53) was stratigraphically contemporary with the mound, but no absolute date could be determined for its exiguous remains. The three radiocarbon dates that have proved possible for the group as a whole were 640–780 for the triple burial (42), 860–1040 for Burial 45 and 890–1050 for Burial 40. Burial 55 was cut from a turf line in a quarry pit for Mound 6, on which also lay some medieval pottery, eleventh to thirteenth century in date. These execution burials may possibly have begun in the seventh century with the construction of Mound 5; they certainly continued into the tenth or eleventh centuries.

On the eastern periphery of the cemetery was another group of burials; these were similar, but they were not placed around any mound or even near one (Fig. 90). They lay in two arcs around a cluster of post-holes which seemed designed to support a narrow robust upright structure. And in view of the character of the burials, the upright structure in question is likely to have been a gallows of the simple two-post construction that the Anglo-Saxons knew. The variety of burial posture here was still greater than that observed around Mound 5. The bodies in Burials 19, 25, 32 and 33 were buried face down, with the wrists or ankles laid over each other as though tied. In Burial 19 the arms were behind the back. In Burial 29 the arms had been stretched above the head. Burials 24, 28 and 39 were buried kneeling or crouching. In Burial 21 the head had been removed and replaced in the grave of Burial 22 which followed. In Burial 35 the head had been removed and laid on the shoulder (Fig. 89). In Burial 23 the neck had been broken and head and vertebrae were at 90 degrees to each other. The body in Burial

Fig. 89 An execution victim from the eastern group of burials (Burial 35). The detached head lies on the shoulder.

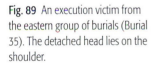

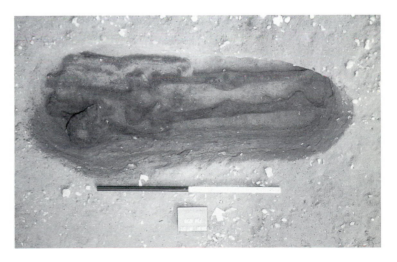

38 was buried on the back with the knees drawn right up to the shoulder. Burial 27 was spread-eagled on the floor of a large grave and accompanied by timber pieces which resembled a primitive plough, but which may have derived from some instrument connected with execution or burial, such as a hurdle, spades or even the gallows itself. Some burials seemed to provide echoes of a less desolate end: the bodies in Burials 17, 18 and 20 were laid on their backs, two of them (18 and 20) placed in coffins. In Burial 34 the body had been placed in a chest or square container of some kind.

Radiocarbon dating was also used to place these burials in time: Burial 17 was dated to 530–710, Burial 22 to 690–830, Burial 30 to 970–1220, Burial 35 to 650–960 and Burial 39 to 880–1030. Wood from a gallows post gave a date of 690–980.[1] The burials in the eastern periphery are therefore probably contemporary with those around Mound 5, and, like them, could have begun at or soon after the time of the royal cemetery and continued until the end of the millennium. In both groups the people buried had been hanged or beheaded. There were some cases of severe mutilation which could have formed part of a ritual killing, or may have resulted from the suspension of the corpse and its subsequent decomposition before burial.

Was this human sacrifice or capital punishment?

This is not perhaps a distinction which we should sensibly make: in this matter the concept of 'punishment' is fatuous, since a person who is dead cannot mend their ways or offer recompense. The Anglo-Saxon laws allowed compensation to be paid for the killing of another person; execution is not therefore associated inevitably, as later, with official retribution for a murder. Public killing, whether sanctioned by judicial or religious belief, must always have been seen as sacrificial, in the sense that the act mitigated a threat. But what threat? The most likely answer is that execution was a necessary instrument for the removal of ideological or political deviants, in which case we are looking for a time when there was a new law and authority to challenge. We are led to the conclusion that the ritual killing at Sutton Hoo represents a concomitant of kingship. Just as the rich burials and the great ships proclaimed that a new era had begun, in which people would give their loyalty to a territory and to a new kind of dynastic leader, so the position of that leader and the permanence of his dynasty and his kingdom needed protection by means of the ultimate deterrent, one that was to disfigure the next thousand years of English history: that is, the public murder of people who do not agree with the king.

Even if such an interpretation is accepted, there is still much to puzzle us about these burials. The radiocarbon dating does not give a precise point in time, and the only confident statement that

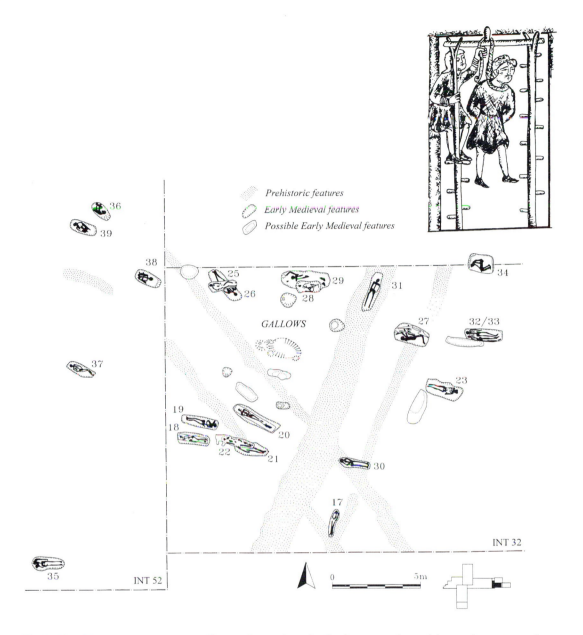

Prehistoric features
Early Medieval features
Possible Early Medieval features

GALLOWS

INT 32

INT 52

0   5m

Fig. 90 Plan of the eastern execution cemetery, showing the post holes attributed to a gallows and, inset, a representation of an execution from the eleventh century Anglo-Saxon manuscript BL Cott. Claudius B IV.

can be made is that the bodies were buried later than Mound 5, and on occasions between the seventh century and the eleventh. In theory they could nearly all belong to the later part of this period, say the ninth and tenth century; and there is some incentive for placing them there. Recent research has demonstrated that public execution at a *cwealmstow*, or killing place, was a feature of later Anglo-Saxon Christian kingship, in the ninth and tenth century, when a politically united England was being constructed from its many regional kingdoms.[2] While accepting this idea, it can however be argued from the Sutton Hoo evidence that execution had begun earlier, and it was the creation of king-ship in the seventh century that may have been responsible for its first appearance and provided its context. If Burial 53 was placed in an empty quarry pit, as seems to have been the case, it must have followed very closely upon the construction of Mound 5, or even, as is argued above, have taken place during the construction of Mound 5, before the surplus soil was returned to the quarry pits. Such a killing might have had a specific context of vengeance: it will be remembered that the person buried in Mound 5 had died violently from multiple blade injuries to the head.

If intermittent executions were carried out at Mound 5, they could have been in progress when Mound 2, and indeed Mound 1, were constructed. The funerals that involved such riches and large ships would thus have taken place beneath the stench and horror of the gallows. If so, these executions – those in the sev-enth century at least – could have carried kudos rather than opprobrium. Or perhaps a demonstration of authority was entire-ly in keeping with the ritual of high-status burial as a whole. Per-haps the gallows were tidied up, or indeed brought into use, to mark the occasion.

But perhaps it is more logical to suppose that the gallows were only introduced as a concomitant of Christian kingship after Sut-ton Hoo had had its day as a royal burial ground. The mounds were, after all, sizeable items in the landscape, deserted, recognis-ably pagan and a suitable place in which to dispose of sinners. But in this case we must ask the question 'Why Mound 5?', since there were then at least eighteen to choose from. The choice of this relatively small mound is more comprehensible if it marked the beginnings of the cemetery or at least the beginnings of the claims of kingship. If prominence was required, there were bigger mounds; if proximity to the passers-by, then Mound 14 would be best, or Mound 2, assuming that the later track patterns echo the former. A compromise would allow the executions to start after the last pagan funeral, but still within living memory. Just as Ealdwulf remembered Raedwald's temple, and could report it to Bede, so King Anna's contemporaries may have remembered the royal burial ground at Sutton Hoo and knew, too, who was buried in each mound.

All these factors may have a bearing on what actually hap-pened; even if what actually happened may remain forever elusive, given the strong feelings generated by this grim topic. For some, the creators and users of the Sutton Hoo Mound 1 shoulder-clasps cannot be associated with such ignoble practices. For others, pub-lic cruelty is an attribute only too probable in seventh-century leadership. On the whole, the story as we have it is not overly far-fetched. If Mound 5 represents the burial of the leader who first needed the claims of absolute rule, and who had died at the hand of another, a revenge killing at the funeral would not be inconceivable. The maintenance of authority in the same family or dynasty, a feature of kingship, would invite further public correction in the event of challenges. Such executions could be events which were compatible with the extravagant funerals of the great.

After the Christian conversion of the ruling dynasty had finally taken root, there would be reasons for leaving the place of execution where it was. Victims of the gallows in this case had not only sinned against the authority of the ruler but against the Christian god, and a pagan cemetery was a proper place to dispose of them. Some, perhaps declared and unrepentant pagans, would be executed and buried next to the mound that had contained, or was thought to have contained, the founder of pagan kingship. Others, Christians who had strayed or rebelled, would be dispatched at the cemetery's edge and near the track. Although they were not permitted to enter consecrated ground at Sutton church, they could be placed in coffins and perhaps even be aligned with the rising sun in the Christian manner.

From the later seventh century, the Christian leaders of East Anglia invested in other ceremonial centres and sites: churches at Rendlesham, and probably at Sutton; monasteries at Burgh Castle, founded by the Irishman Fursa, and probably at Felixstowe, the holy place of Felix, a churchman from Burgundy who became Bishop of the East Angles. He was established in an episcopal headquarters at Dunwich, a site now alas vanished beneath the North Sea. The riverside settlement at Ipswich expanded into a great port, bringing in wine from the new market opened by Christian alliance with the sunny heartland of Europe.

But Sutton Hoo lived on, a dark life but a long one. This grim place with its tall mounds and gibbets remained a landmark, visited intermittently throughout the later Anglo-Saxon period by execution parties. A track reinstated the droveway, which had begun perhaps as early as the Bronze Age, from the Ferry Point inland to the villages of the Sandlings between the Deben and the Alde. Sutton Hoo was the landmark for which the track aimed; it then turned east to Eyke and Orford and north to Wilford. The carts using this track probably trundled back and forth providing a ferry service of their own, run by carters shifting the produce of the Sandlings to the ports on the Deben and the Orwell. On certain mornings some of these carts carried the victims of the current morality, on their way to the now traditional killing-place of the old pagan burial ground.

Probably some time between the tenth and the twelfth century the Sutton Hoo gallows moved. The most likely new execution place was Gallows Hill at Wilford, where it was found to be by the seventeenth century. A map of the Stanhope estates made in 1601 by John Norden shows the place, and provides a little pen and ink sketch of the instrument itself: two posts carrying a cross-beam, exactly as drawn by an Anglo-Saxon artist of the eleventh century (Figs 90, 91). The shift of execution site probably coincided with a change in the routeways. The old route, marked on the same map, went from the ferry through the Sutton Hoo burial ground. But once the bridge had been built at Wilford, all the traffic could go over the bridge and keep dry. The Wilford turn became the new crossroads of the region, and so the message of the gallows was re-established there. Redundant routes fade slowly in the countryside; the Sutton Hoo track was still in existence in 1783, and presumably the ferry was too. But by 1836, when the Ordnance Surveyors compiled their notes for the area, the ferry track had gone; or if not vanished from the site – it is still visible now as a shallow earthwork – it had become obsolete. A new route passed on the west side of the mounds, following along the crest northwards to Wilford, a track that can still be followed through bush and briar along the edges of fields.

During the Middle Ages the area had grassed over and become sheepwalk, and shepherds had sheltered in the hollows of the grassed-over quarries, cooking on open hearths and leaving sherds of coarse pots, to be found in the quarry ditches beside Mound 6 and Mound 14. At certain times, especially when the land had grown too sour to support grazing or the root crops on which sheep relied to get through the winter, the demand for meat was met by the obligingly prolific rabbit, which was farmed in large warrens. The rabbit colonies would be established in specially constructed earth mounds, or better still, contrived out of the existing burial mounds which littered the countryside. In his map of 1601, John Norden uses a characteristic 'cocked-hat' shape to indicate warrens. There are numerous examples sited along the Deben, and some of these may have been former burial mounds. It is highly likely that the Sutton Hoo mounds were also used in this way, as hosts to rabbits.

The period around 1600 proved to be pivotal for the story of Sutton Hoo, just as the period around 600 had been. Two major forces, one old and one new, were about to wake the mounds from their long-respected sleep: agriculture and archaeology. In every quarry pit and ditch of the old Anglo-Saxon earthworks a thick layer of pale sand was deposited over the turf, as though a heathy soil had been pushed in, filling up every hollow. It could perhaps have been blown there – the area has a famous capacity for dust storms, especially after the turf has been stripped and the sandy soil exposed. But the pit-fills contained no 'lensing'

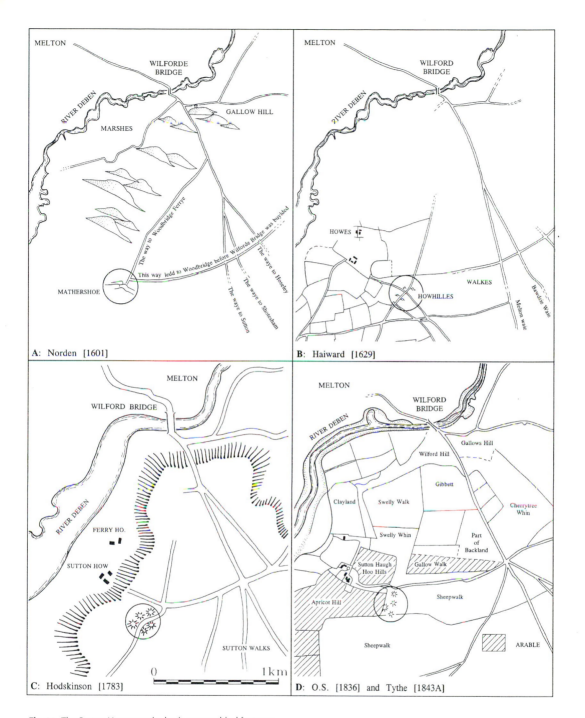

Fig. 91 The Sutton Hoo area; the basic geographical features summarised from early maps, 1601–1843. Annette Roe.

(thin laminar discolourations) which would indicate that layers of sand had been laid down by successive episodes of wind-blow. Neither were there traces of slumping – such as might be seen if the mounds were to erode and fall into the pits and ditches by natural processes. The observed reduction of the height of the mounds and the homogeneous pale filling of the quarries is most readily explained as being due to the mechanical agency of ploughing. If so, this was a major operation, and it can be surmised that a ploughing that filled up the pits and reduced the height of the mounds by several feet (over one metre) would have also erased all traces of a track. But the track was later than this ploughing episode, since it had been seen to run over the back-filled quarries of Mounds 13, 7 and 14. This ploughing must therefore pre-date 1601, when the track in question appears on Norden's map.

There were also later attempts to plough and cultivate land that, as Arthur Young pointed out in his classic late eighteenth-century work *Agriculture of the County of Suffolk*, was really more suitably tended as grassland.[3] When the price of grain went up, as during a war, every piece of land that could bear a crop was ploughed. This happened during the Napoleonic wars of the early nineteenth century and again during the Crimean War when the prices made it a 'golden age' for grain growers. It happened again when Britain joined the Common Market, and the high subsidies for grain led ploughs back on to old acid heaths and humpy slopes which could be persuaded to yield wheat in exchange for a dose of chemicals. The land could not recover easily or quickly from these cereal binges, and the result in the later nineteenth century at least was exodus to Canada and America. On 8 January 1862 Charles Cody of Trimley St Mary wrote to his brother in New Zealand: 'The year 1860 from its extreme wetness was most disastrous to all heavy land farmers and pretty well emptied the pockets of the already needy tenants. At the same time the competition for land is so great that young men generally will be wise to seek their fortunes in one or other of our colonies'.[4] Crag, the fossil shells found under the sand, was ploughed into the soil; and coprolites, supposed fossil reptile excrement, were treated with sulphuric acid to provide super-phosphate, in a process successfully exploited locally by a Mr Fison. But before the days of mass production of chemical fertilisers, the land had to be left fallow and resuscitated with root crops, those turnips and carrots to which Suffolk sheep were fortunately partial, which had been grown on this sandy soil since at least the sixteenth century.

The archaeological evidence and the maps show that the old Sutton Hoo burial ground was ploughed again in the nineteenth century. The plough was used on the slope up to the cemetery from the flood plain (gradient held no terrors for these stalwart cultivators) and a lynchet was built up over the eroded surfaces of Mounds 1, 17 and 12. This happened before 1843, when the area is shown as arable on the tythe map (Fig 91D). There may even have been a third episode before the site returned to bracken heath in the early twentieth century; but that depends on the date at which Sutton Hoo had its earliest experiences of archaeological excavation.

Like agriculture, the use of the gallows and the erection of burial-mounds, archaeological investigation too is a sign of the needs and beliefs of society and it has a history of its own which reflects them. Sutton Hoo, we can be reasonably sure, has been subjected to systematic campaigns of excavation on no fewer than five occasions between the sixteenth century and the late twentieth; it offers us a history of archaeology in a single English field. From the evidence collected, it would appear that the first campaign was the most comprehensive and prodigal of them all. The first hint of the operations was provided by a few sherds of Bellarmine flask (a sixteenth-century gin bottle) found by Basil Brown in a deep pit which had been dug through Mound 1. It was not in fact deep enough to reach the burial, which lay in the centre of the ship nearly 4 m (12 ft) below the old ground surface and as much again below the top of the mound. It was also off centre, a possible, but not a necessary, indication that the ploughing of the mounds had already taken place when this robber pit was tried. The pit would most probably have collapsed, leaving abandoned debris at its base. Another unsuccessful hole was dug through Mound 17; unsuccessful on this occasion because it was placed central to the mound and thus arrived at a point midway between the two graves that lay beneath (Fig. 55).

It is highly probable that every other mound at Sutton Hoo was successfully pillaged at this time with a central pit. An example had been encountered in Mound 3, Redstone's 'dew-pond', and an oval pit appeared to have been used in Mound 14. A great oval opening marks the mouth of the chamber grave in Mound 2. This cannot be attributed to the ship and would be an extravagant access for the later excavators (who came by trench). It would, however, be a credible legacy of tomb-robbers who descended from the top, as seems to have been the sixteenth-century way. Similar pits were found in the very messy Mound 5, which seems to have suffered at least two contemporary attacks by pit. But the most convincing evidence for a campaign of the sixteenth century is the lack of finds recorded from the much-better documented excavation campaign that was to follow in the nineteenth century. We do not know what would have been found during the first campaign, but from the scraps encountered by later excavators one must imagine that it would have included very considerable quantities of gold and silver.

The sixteenth century was a time of known interest in burial mounds, a new kind of interest, neither religious nor scientific. Throughout the Middle Ages, burial mounds seem to have been protected by the kind of superstition that would discourage people from robbing a mound in case they met a dragon or worse. If the thinking of the Reformation reduced such inhibitions, the redistribution of religious land after 1540 must have lessened them still further. The new rich who were receiving the estates of abbeys at the hands of the king were liberated from religious subservience and turned their privatised benefits into capital by the fastest possible route; and if this meant melting down a chalice or pyx, or turning illuminated vellum into gloves, so be it. The new owners of burial mounds were unlikely to have shown less restraint, although there is no need here to suppose any lingering vendetta against the Church of Rome or its equivalent. Burial mounds were recognised and understood, in this case perhaps better than we have done, in that they and their contents were assessed as Crown property, whatever their date. The new owners of Sutton Hoo, the Mathers by 1601, could have easily applied for and won a licence to extract some of the capital value of their holding, for the sake of its development and ultimately for the more widespread creation of wealth.[5]

The second campaign to leave its mark on Sutton Hoo belongs to the mid-nineteenth century, and is dated in this way. On 24 November 1860 the following item appeared in a local newspaper, the *Ipswich Journal*:

> ROMAN MOUNDS or BARROWS. – It is not known by many that not less than five Roman Barrows, lying close to each other, may be seen on a farm occupied by Mr Barritt, at Sutton, about 500 yards from the banks of the Deben, immediately opposite Woodbridge. One of these mounds was recently opened, when a considerable number (nearly two bushels) of iron screw bolts were found, all of which were sent to the blacksmith to be converted into horse shoes! It is hoped, when leave is granted to open the others, some more important antiquities may be discovered. These barrows were laid down in the Admiralty surveys by Captain Stanley during the stay of the Blazer, when taking soundings of the above-named river some years since.[6]

Which mound was excavated in 1860, and what was found? The iron screw bolts must have been ship rivets, and their likely source was Mound 2. Only two ship-burials are known so far from Sutton Hoo, although there may have been others. The early maps suggest that only four or five mounds were easily seen in the nineteenth century, presumably because the others had been so lowered by ploughing as to be scarcely visible in the undergrowth. These should be the five most prominent: Mounds 1, 2, 3, 7 and 10. Mound 2, standing on the highest ground at the end of the row next to the track junction, would have been a natural target. Mound 2, moreover, was discovered on excavation in 1987 to have had a trench cut through it from west to east. Ship rivets were plainly encountered along the length of this trench, and if 'two bushels' (perhaps 2,000 rivets) were recovered for the blacksmith, 800 still remained for collection in 1987. In the centre of the mound the nineteenth-century excavators would have found the great pit – dug, it is suggested, in the sixteenth century – and followed it down. Steps were cut on the west side to gain access to the pit, which was then explored. They seem to have stopped excavating near the base of the chamber, where the earlier robbers had trod. Compacted soil was left against the corners and along the sides. Some scraps of metalwork remained in the chamber, but apart from rivets we must suppose that they found nothing of interest. Disappointed, they left the hole open for a short time, in which it collected copious amounts of silt washed down the steps to create a dished depression, pointed at the west end. It was this that the next excavator (Basil Brown) was to find in 1938, believing he had defined a boat.

The signs were that leave *was* subsequently granted, presumably from Mr Barritt's landlord, to open other mounds. Trenches very similar in design to that traced in Mound 2 were found in Mounds 6 and 7. Entry in Mound 6 was from the west and stopped after the half-way point, where access steps descended to a small ledge, on which presumably the antiquary stood. The west end of the trench splayed out to provide ingress and egress for the labourers removing the soil. The tableau in Mound 7 was more graphic still (Fig. 92). This time the trench was driven in from the east, and the splayed east entrance was scored by the wheels of the labourers' wheel-barrows. The antiquary's stance was at the foot of steps on the west side, just above the pit that had contained the burial. In the pit was a cremation, contained in a bowl. The bowl itself had vanished but had left its shape on the little mound of burnt bone impatiently ejected by the excavator. From his stance, the antiquary could lean over, in top hat and morning coat, eager to see what the earth had added to his estate, hoping for precious objects to put on the mantelpiece or to sell or to exhibit and impress his acquaintances from other parts of the county, even from London itself. The standard of excavation had risen since the trench cut into Mound 2; here

Fig. 92 The nineteenth-century excavation of Mound 7. Artist's impression by Victor Ambrus.

everything was sieved and little remained for those that were to come after. Next in line would have been Mound 1. Did they trench that too? Or was the experience of three robbed cremations in a row too dispiriting? If Maynard's description can be credited, there may well have been a trench cut through Mound 1, but it was too high up to touch either ship or chamber.

The backfilled excavations in Mounds 6 and 7 left a characteristically shaped 'dent' in the top of the mound – not 'ship-dents' as Bruce-Mitford had hoped, but 'trench-dents'. How successful were these diggers of trenches? If they found precious Anglo-Saxon objects, what did they do with them? It is, of course, possible that Mr Barritt or his collaborators had found a heap of treasure and decided to keep quiet about it, because he was a tenant and wished in his turn to escape the rat-race and become a millionaire. But there are several reasons for thinking that he had been unlucky and so had all who were with him. The newspaper article itself makes it likely that the first mound at least had been something of a dud. The burial was not recognised as that of ship, because the 'iron screw bolts' were not then recognised, in their dispersed locations, as ship-rivets. The Snape excavators, digging a less disturbed boat below ground two years later, were more perceptive. If precious objects had been found here, or in the mounds that were later trenched, then it does not seem credible that they could long remain a secret. To put the discoveries of this period into context, 1860 was something of an *annus mirabilis* for the antiquary, who was rapidly being accepted as part of the new scientific vanguard. Sir Austen Henry Layard's *Nineveh and its Remains* had appeared in 1854, swiftly becoming a best-seller, and Charles Darwin's *Origin of Species*, published in 1859, seemed to make a remote past possible everywhere. It was a time for the formation of antiquarian societies, and vicars, lawyers, army officers and gentleman farmers were among the first to join. There was probably more social advantage in flourishing an Anglo-Saxon buckle at such a gathering than in having it melted down for a few guineas of bullion.

Moreover the learned societies of England and Suffolk were no strangers to the Sutton area. In 1860 the autumn meeting of the Suffolk Institute of Archaeology and Natural History convened at Woodbridge, and Roman and Saxon jewellery was exhibited in the lecture hall by Messrs Whincopp, Spalding, Loder, Baker 'and many others'. This was on 24 October, one month before the discoveries were made on Mr Barritt's farm. It does not seem possible for the Suffolk Institute to have remained ignorant of the excavations in 1860, or those that followed, presumably in the spring of the next year, had they discovered anything of value. For in 1864 the British Archaeological Association met at Ipswich, and no mention was made of Sutton Hoo. On that occasion Mr Whincopp was again an exhibitor, as he had been at these gatherings since 1851 when he exhibited to the Archaeological Institute a gold and garnet buckle found at Melton in 1833.[7]

The reporting of these casual finds was unsystematic, and not too much should be made of the failure to mention them. But it is hard to see that a major discovery at Sutton Hoo in the mid-nineteenth century would have escaped the notice of Mr Whincopp or the entire membership and readership of the *Gentleman's Magazine*, the Archaeological Institute, the British Archaeological Association and the Suffolk Institute. We must conclude that there *was* no major discovery. The mounds had either been well turned over by the sixteenth-century campaign, or contained cremations in which little appeared to be glorious. Mr Barritt did not get rich, but his campaign was certainly followed by a last ploughing: the backfilled trench of Mound 7 showed that a plough had been dragged east–west across the mound. But it was a half-hearted effort; the track to the east, disused since before 1836, was not rubbed away by it. The price of grain had presumably fallen again.

The sixteenth century had gobbled up everything it found; the nineteenth century was ready to share objects of beauty and curiosity, but had found little of this character to reward its considerable exertions. At the beginning of the twentieth century, as the Sutton Hoo site turned to heathland and Europe turned once more to war, the burial ground still kept its secret. And it might have done so for many more centuries, had it not been for the construction in 1905 of a new country house on the promontory to the north and the arrival there in 1926 of Mrs Edith Pretty.

A MONUMENT FOR THE MILLENNIUM

7

Fig. 93 Making a silicon rubber mould of a 'sand-body'. The moulds were used to make fibreglass replicas of the sand-bodies to bring the reality home to visitors, who naturally had few opportunities to observe the excavation of these controversial burials.

It has always occasioned surprise, particularly among foreign visitors, that in spite of its prominent role in English history, and its consequent national importance, Sutton Hoo has, until recently, been in private ownership. For students of heritage matters it might not be without interest to consider some aspects of the fourteen-year struggle to convey the site to an institutional owner, now successfully concluded with the gift of the whole estate by the Annie Tranmer Charitable Trust to the National Trust.[1]

As a landowner, Mrs Edith Pretty did not require permission to initiate her excavations of 1938, and under the English law of Treasure Trove was determined as the owner of the finds from the great ship-burial and, by implication, from any other graves. Following her donation of the objects to the British Museum, the site was *scheduled*, that is officially protected under ancient monuments legislation originating in 1882. A notice to this effect, cast-iron in material, although less so in authority, was erected on the site.

This measure does not oblige the landowner to look after the site, only to desist from destroying it. Neither does it provide for public access. But the long-term conservation and presentation of its historical assets to the public might nevertheless be considered as the natural destiny of such a place. This at any rate was the concern of the 1983 campaign, and to devise a secure future for the site was an integral part of the evaluation with which the 1983 campaign started. The process of evaluation was intended to assign a current *value* to Sutton Hoo and to express how that value could best be appreciated by means of a research plan and a management plan. The programme of excavation had involved only a part of the site in the firm conviction that the rest would still be there to answer the questions of another generation. Could that long-term conservation be guaranteed and, if so, how? Public access could also be considered part of the duties of a researcher, either because the research was being done in the name of the public, or because the presentation of a monument

(whose character was about to change irreversibly) should be considered a part of the publication programme. Accordingly, temporary measures for conservation and presentation were immediately put in place.

For *conservation*, the most urgent necessity was to guard the site against treasure hunters, eliminating bracken and rabbits. This custodianship was achieved without a break from November 1983, including over the Christmas holidays when students who would like to get away from it all (particularly with someone else) might spend the festive season in the site-hut with a calor gas fire and bottle of wine or two. In eight years we only suffered three minor attempts at vandalism, none very damaging. The rabbits and bracken were eliminated by the site caretaker, Mr Peter Berry, who became responsible for transforming the tangled, ugly, neglected surface of the Sutton Hoo burial ground into a smooth green monument of which any government would have been proud (Cl. Pl. IV).

Presentation was multi-media in every sense (Fig. 94). The treasures from Mound 1 were already on display at the British Museum in a new gallery in the Early Medieval Room. There was also a small exhibition in Woodbridge Museum, dealing with the history of the exploration of the site. There were books already published. Access to the site itself was agreed with the owners in a limited, controlled way, so that only the dedicated undertook the long walk from the road to the mounds. There they were greeted by volunteer guides from the Sutton Hoo Society, a group which was created locally with the express purpose of making visitors welcome.[2] Over and over again, the guides stood on Mound 1 recounting the discovery of the ship-burial, and then took their parties around to see new discoveries being made. Among these, the execution victims occasioned great interest, and display examples were wrought in fibreglass, made by means of silicon rubber moulds (Fig. 93).

Visitors came from all over the world (Fig. 95), from learned societies, from families needing a day out, from schools, from clubs, from town and country, from overseas and from the next door village; among them were day-trippers, professors and royalty. Eventually, when the excavation campaign was complete, Mound 2 was itself reconstructed, as a reminder to the visitor of the imposing monuments that had once stood here, and how they had been reduced and rubbed away by the using of the land (Figs 96, 97). The most important visitor access was provided by BBC television, which made four programmes about the campaign, each of which was shown a number of times. Through this medium, it could be said that more than 13 million had spent an hour in the company of the Sutton Hoo project.

Fig. 94 BBC camera crew filming for the Sutton Hoo series shown on BBC2, under the direction of Ray Sutcliffe.

Achieving the long-term security of the site was much more difficult, and to some extent the experience offers a parable for the relationship between archaeological monuments, the government and the public which is not without a wider historic interest. The right to excavate was owned by the Pretty family, who had retained it, together with pre-emptive ownership of the finds, under a deed of covenant when they sold Sutton Hoo House. This right was subsequently assigned by Robert Pretty to the Sutton Hoo Research Trust, and under the same agreement the finds from future excavation would continue to be given to the British Museum.

The Trust's actual presence on the site and access to it was, in practice, dependent on the good will of the landowners and tenant farmers, a working relationship that became smoother still when the Trust itself unexpectedly had the opportunity to become a landowner. Metal detection carried out during the evaluation showed up the lines of vanished wire fences, including the southern boundary that separated the land owned by the Tranmer estate from that owned by its southern neighbour, the Sun Alliance Insurance company. This indicated that a few acres of Sun Alliance's farmland actually lay within the Sutton Hoo burial ground. With a little diplomacy and much generosity of time by Sun Alliance (and by John Knight, our honorary solicitor), the Trust was able to take a first piece of the burial ground into its ownership and care.

Fig. 95 Members of the International Society of Anglo-Saxonists advancing from Mound 1 in 1986.

Now the priority became the long-term protection of the site itself; the Sutton Hoo Research Trust did not intend to stay in being for ever; how were we to guarantee its future? The site had always been in private ownership, and therein lay its long-term insecurity. However enlightened might be the owners for the time being, the care of an unproductive piece of land and the maintenance of public access are never going to figure highly on their agenda, particularly if their purpose in buying the estate in the first place had been retirement, seclusion and peace, rather than the edification of visitors. The owner in 1983 was Mrs Annie Tranmer, who together with her principal trustee, John Miller, had given permission to excavate and had lent their sincere support to the archaeological project. Within a few months of the project's beginning, they showed themselves sensitive to the longer term future of the site; and within a short space of time, decided to offer Sutton Hoo to the nation in exchange for relief from estate duty.

It was then that the mood of the new world of English politics became apparent: even if the owner was willing to give the site, the nation did not seem to want it. English Heritage, the government agency designed to manage its publicly owned monuments, was formed in 1983, the year the campaign began. In spite of its own title, English Heritage did not seem to regard the acquisition of the earliest burial ground of English kings as appropriate or opportune and maintained a stoical lack of interest in acquiring it. After several attempts at engaging the attention of the agency had failed, an alternative tack was adopted: an approach was made direct to the Capital Transfer Tax Office. This body agreed in principle to accept Sutton Hoo on behalf of the nation provided that we could find someone sensible to give it to and provided that the duty claimed by the Inland Revenue was nevertheless paid. But who would pay it? The next door to knock on was that of the National Heritage Memorial Fund which had recently paid a handsome sum to prevent the export of the Earl of Warwick's sword. They were most responsive, insisting only that the District Valuer should be consulted as to the real value of Sutton Hoo. The Inland Revue required £350,000 from the Tranmers; it would be interesting to see whether the state was getting a bargain or not.

According to criteria used by the District Valuer, Sutton Hoo was not so much priceless as worthless. As agricultural land, it was obviously most unsatisfactory: it was covered in large hummocks which would impede ploughing, and there was an injunction (that is, the Ancient Monuments Act) that would discourage cultivation in any case. It would fare little better as a recreational place: the hummocks (unless they could be removed, of course) would inhibit a good game of football. It was agreed that it could serve as a picnic area, but the value of such places was not high. The whole site was not expected to reach a value to the community of more than £3,000, that is about £300 an acre.

But what about its value as an archaeological site? It appears that it had none; or if it had a value, it certainly did not have a price. Sutton Hoo, one of the most famous sites in the world and perhaps the second most important one in England after Stonehenge, was not wanted by English Heritage and was apparently worth only £3,000 to a landowner in need of £350,000.

Perhaps someone in another country would appreciate what we were trying to save for our incorrigibly venal nation? J.P. Getty had recently given a large sum of money (and compensation to the developers) to purchase a field, the development of which would have spoiled the vista of Ely Cathedral. It was decided that the Getty Trust would be approached, but to anticipate any questions concerning price, it seemed to wise to be ready with our own estimate, which reflected, in money, the worth that we believed it could claim in terms of archaeological value. This would need ingenuity, since the site was in truth simply undulating sand and turf. The graves might contain finds, but by deed of covenant the finds would belong to the British Museum and could bring no financial value to a landowner. What price, then, a field of historic hummocks?

Fig. 96 Rebuilding Mound 2 (the modern way) in 1993. The original height was calculated from the volume of the quarry-ditch.

The method used was to draw an analogy. If hummocks were history, so were illuminated manuscripts, in which the Anglo-Saxons had also invested much wealth and labour when they ceased to be pagans and became Christian. A burial-mound was the analogue of a *codex*, one like the Lindisfarne Gospels in the British Library; and a flat grave might be considered the equivalent of a folio, or perhaps an illuminated initial. But could these be priced? Fortunately, yes; in the shops of Old Bond Street it used to be possible to find illuminated initials for sale, snipped off their parent manuscripts; they could be picked up for £100. And as for the famous gospel books, some had been lent recently by the British Library to an exhibition at Stockholm, and an insurance figure had had to be quoted for this purpose.

Using these data for the equation, and with Sutton Hoo's expected burials in mind, a price could be computed amounting to £7.25 million. It should be a veritable snip at £350,000 (less the finds). But Getty's staff decided against. Sutton Hoo was worthless to the nation and had failed to get itself exported. It seemed that the Sutton Hoo Research Trust would have to remain its informal unpaid guardians for ever more.[3]

But there was to be another chance, one perhaps more in tune with the times, and more to the liking of Annie Tranmer and her trustee, John Miller, who had been understandably discouraged by previous responses to their initiative. This was the possibili-

Fig. 97 Mound 2 rebuilt. The monument is visible from across the river.

ty that the site might pass into the ownership of the National Trust for England and Wales, a charitable organisation dedicated to the protection of English landscapes and buildings, which celebrated its centenary in 1995. Through the good offices of Elisabeth Walters, a member of the National Trust's Executive Committee, and a most hospitable resident of neighbouring Sutton village, we solicited the interest of Merlin Waterston, the National Trust's regional director, and contact of a gentle and sympathetic kind was shortly made. In 1993 Mrs Annie Tranmer died and the estate passed to her daughter, Valerie Lewis. The trustees of the Annie Tranmer Charitable Trust, National Trust officers and the Sutton Hoo Research Trust were soon in discussion.

The transfer was finally made feasible in August 1997, when the Heritage Lottery Fund awarded £3.6 million for the development of the estate. The Heritage Lottery Fund, under the wing of the National Heritage Memorial Fund, had accepted wholeheartedly that the site was of international importance. Annie Tranmer, her trustee and her daughter had created an opportunity to conserve and present a noble and a precious monument, one fit to stand for the earliest burial ground of English kings. Sutton Hoo was at last safe for the future and for international knowledge, in the words of the National Trust centenary aphorism, *for ever, for everyone*.[4]

8 OPEN FORUM

Fifty questions and a few answers

One of the most enjoyable aspects of working on the problems of Sutton Hoo was the sharing of ideas with audiences. These ranged in number from three million (BBC 2) to three (an adult education class on a snowy night) and in venue from international conferences to village halls. The live audiences are the best, and the best part of the evening is often provided by the questions at the end. These contain insights you did not have, show you common sense where you were trussed up in complexity and send you off in new directions. People in future centuries will also be fascinated by Sutton Hoo and will want to ask of it new questions that we cannot now foresee. As a tribute to my questioners over the years, and with an eye on those to come, I offer some answers to the questions I was most often asked. The future, of course, will bring more of both.

GENERAL

1 What are the principles for interpreting a cemetery like this?

A cemetery is valuable for the archaeologist, not so much for the objects found in it, as for the behaviour ('mortuary behaviour') captured in the burial rites. Interpreting this behaviour is not straightforward. The meaning given to burial varies with the societies that make them, and so does the degree of meaning. Some communities in the past invested heavily in their cemeteries, others did not. Some had free choice of burial rite, others did not. Some communities used burial practice in a way that was traditional, others used burials in an innovative, expressive way. This presents us with a problem, since we have first to discover the context and then decide which level of meaning the cemetery is likely to have.

At one level, we can assess the investment which a burial attracted, by comparing it with contemporary examples. Whatever the intended or unintentional meaning, the wealth is expended by being put in the ground, and therefore is an index of what was available to burial parties for the purpose. Wealth in this case can be assessed by the quantity of gold, silver and bronze, which were known to have value in this period because coins were made from them; also by the complexity of objects, such as (in this case) the purse or the bridle which use different materials and are tricky to make; also by the distance that objects have travelled: the

Coptic bowl, the Byzantine silver. Lastly the size of a mound must be a measure of how much power, if not wealth, lay at the constructors' command.

If these things suggest that Sutton Hoo was an unusually rich cemetery, they do not explain why it developed, when and where it did. To answer these questions, we have to call on the historical context (if we know it) or on analogies with other sites and cultures.[1]

2 What analogous cemeteries are there, and what do they mean?

Mound burial with wealthy grave goods is as old as the Bronze Age in Europe, and elsewhere in the world it is commonly encountered. Everywhere it is deemed to be expressive of wealth. But rich monumental burial in mounds did not happen always and everywhere. The most famous artificial mounds are the pyramids of Egypt, but the ones most often compared with Sutton Hoo are those of early Iron Age central Europe and later Iron Age central Scandinavia. In both cases, the mounds are thought to celebrate the death of successful leaders in a way that would provide a permanent memorial. They probably did this when the community felt itself under threat, so that friends and enemies alike would be assured that the dynasty and its people intended to survive and had the means to do so.[2]

3 What was the 'threat' to the people of East Anglia?

The threat to late sixth-century/early seventh-century East Anglia is likely to have been connected with the Christian mission, which can be read politically, from an insular viewpoint, as the creeping imperialism of the Merovingian kings of France. These had gained control of the central part of the former Roman province of Gaul and were busy recreating a central European union, with Christianity, nominally at any rate, as its driving ideology. Kent had been absorbed into the union and East Anglia was probably next. The East Angles were caught between the trade advantages of joining the union and the perceived betrayal of their Scandinavian allies and ancestors. In other words they feared loss of liberty, autonomy and sovereignty, and had a fundamental difference in outlook: the 'North Sea' vision of independence and enterprise versus the 'united Europe' vision of urban amenity and cultural domination.

And in case any of this sounds familiar, that is hardly surprising; the European problem began here in the seventh century, and its resolution, attempted several times on one side or the other, has never been achieved. Eurosceptics and the Europhiles, then as now, are champions of different world-views, and it is doubtful if they can ever agree.[3]

4 Where did the Anglo-Saxons get the idea of mound burial?

The idea of mound burial was already known to the Anglo-Saxons even if they practised it on a modest scale. There were grave fields of small mounds in sixth-century Kent; and the cemetery of Spong Hill in East Anglia had small burial mounds in the sixth if not the fifth century. The idea of mound burial may have come from the famous burial of Childeric, the Frankish leader buried in a large mound at Tournai in AD 482. Fourteen horses were sacrificed at the burial. The practice continued to develop on the Rhineland along the edges of the Merovingian kingdom. The large mounds of Scandinavia were constructed from the sixth century at Gamla Uppsala.

Mound burial was practised in the Bronze Age in both Scandinavia and central Europe, and the landscape in Britain too was covered in circular mounds, as well as by the earlier long barrows. These too would have been a stimulus to the Anglo-Saxons – who were quite aware of what they were: some of them were reused to bury Anglo-Saxon dead. It is as though the possibility of mound burial was always there in the imagination, but it is only special periods and special circumstances that drove people to act out the dream. It is not impossible that the dream itself had its roots in the Egyptian pyramids. Although archaeologists no longer believe in diffusion as the explanation for the transfer of a particular practice, we are beginning to see that ideas can travel widely and endure long in the imagination without necessarily being turned into material culture.[4]

5 Where did the Anglo-Saxons get the idea of ship-burial?

Similar arguments can be made for the Anglo-Saxon adoption of ship-burial. There are ship-settings in stone in Bronze Age Scandinavia, where upright stones are laid out in the shape of a ship; and burials employ wooden objects, which look like boats, in Bronze Age Norfolk and Humberside. Wooden boats, without rivets, were used to bury certain people at the cemetery of Slusegård on Bornholm from the fourth to the sixth century AD. Proper ship-burial, where a clinker-built ship is placed in the ground, with a mound on top, seems to begin in England at Snape and Sutton Hoo, and in Sweden at Valsgärde and Vendel. It is not clear which country was the earliest, since all the burials are dated around the early seventh century. In England the practice was short-lived; while in Scandinavia it continued for four hundred years, with a major flourishing in the Viking period. This implies that in Scandinavia ship-burial had a powerful and enduring meaning.[5]

6 Is there a connection between Sutton Hoo and Scandinavia?

There are archaeological connections in art and in burial rites, but it would be wrong to exaggerate the link. The shield and helmet from Mound 1 closely resemble examples from Sweden, for example in the cemetery at Valsgärde. On the other hand, in the early seventh century the Swedish and East Anglian cemeteries are our main source of material; in other words the objects may resemble each other because they

are the only examples we have from the period. Cremation under mound and ship burial are common practices in Sweden and in Norway. But from Denmark we have no burials at all from the sixth to the seventh century. The safest deduction is that cremation under mound and ship burial were important to people in Sweden, Norway and East Anglia at a given moment. Many places had contact with each other, but their culture looks similar only when they had a common ideological viewpoint and made similar investments to express it. The likelihood is that the connection between East Anglia and Sweden consisted in allegiance to similar ideological or political agendas.[6]

7 Could the Sutton Hoo burials be immigrants from, say, Sweden?

In theory, yes, they could either have arrived in the distant past or in the era of the Sutton Hoo cemetery. But there is no special evidence to suggest that they did. The problem is that if we are dealing with small mobile populations (as I think we are), they can have much culture in common. They can own land and have relatives in England, Norway, Denmark, Sweden and Saxony at the same time; just as we now have relatives in Canada, Australia or the United States, without feeling we have lost our own nationality. It all depends on the communications, and the communications then were good enough, I believe, to live a life either side of the North Sea.[7]

8 How do you know Sutton Hoo is not Viking?

By its date. The term 'Viking' is used to mean material of generally Scandinavian provenance of the ninth to eleventh century. The date of Anglo-Saxon, Scandinavian and Frankish ornamental metalwork has been sufficiently well studied for there to be no possibility of any of the Sutton Hoo artefacts being as late as the ninth century, when the Vikings were in East Anglia. However, there was a great empathy between Scandinavia and the East Angles, and it is likely that in spite of Christian pressure, contact between them continued from the early Saxon to the Viking period and even beyond.

It is not impossible that Viking burials will one day be found in East Anglia, perhaps even at Sutton Hoo. But none has as yet.[8]

9 Is Sutton Hoo pagan, or could Christians have been buried there?

Modes of burial now, in modern Europe, might be a matter of personal choice, and need not reflect a controlling ideology. But this was less likely to be the case in the seventh century. The burial rites of Sutton Hoo are manifestly and deliberately pagan, and this should mean that a pagan community was responsible for them. It is true that included in some burials were objects that carry Christian insignia, such as the silver spoons and bowls from Mound 1. But these were made in the Christian Byzantine empire. The rite of ship burial and of mound burial has no convincing Christian context. I believe that the burial rite mattered very much; the investment alone was too great for a mound to be raised half-heartedly or on a whim. The execution victims, however, probably belonged to a mainly Christian society (see p. 168).[9]

THE PREHISTORIC SITE

10 Were there any prehistoric mounds at Sutton Hoo?

No prehistoric burials, whether under a mound or not, have been found so far at Sutton Hoo in a hectare of excavation. One must conclude that there was no continuity of burial there and that the Anglo-Saxons did not add to a prehistoric mound burial site. There were prehistoric mounds in the vicinity, however, for example at Martlesham Heath across the Deben.[10]

11 Why was the prehistoric site excavated?

First, to discover its relevance to the siting of the Sutton Hoo cemetery; second, because it would have been technically difficult to exca-

vate the early medieval site without also examining the prehistoric site, which was at the same level in the ground; and lastly, because the prehistoric sequence is of great importance in itself for the understanding of land-use in East Anglia. It has turned out to be an important investigation of farming practice on the acid grasslands over some five thousand years.[11]

12 What was the relevance of the prehistoric site to the siting of the Anglo-Saxon cemetery?

The excavation showed that the prehistoric site was not a 'central place': there was no major settlement, and no monuments. It was agricultural land throughout its life. What it left in the Anglo-Saxon landscape were the shallow earthworks of an Iron Age field system. These were used to site the Sutton Hoo burial mounds, but it would be hard to argue either that the Anglo-Saxons had some feeling for the place inherited through the ages, or that they recognised these earthworks as important monuments. These were prevalent hypotheses in the 1980s that needed to be tested – and were disproved.[12]

THE CEMETERY

13 Why was the cemetery put where it was?

The cemetery may have been sited opposite a supposed Anglo-Saxon palace at Melton or Kingston, although it is mainly the evidence of the placenames that leads us to these places. A rich buckle was found at Melton in 1833 and exhibited by Mr Whincopp at an Archaeological Institute meeting in Ipswich – this might be another pointer to an important site there. It is also worth noting that Wilford represents the first point at which the tidal Deben is easily fordable. There was probably a wide stretch of water for boats to gather opposite Melton. There may have been a palace site where Sutton Hoo House now is. The burial mounds, visible from a distance, would mark the site of the palace and its 'marina'.[13]

14 What does the name 'Sutton Hoo' mean?

Sutton is the southern 'tun', which is a common term for a settlement or homestead in Anglo-Saxon, coming into popular use from the mid-eighth century. Hoo is a spur or promontory or little hill. It does not have to mean burial mound, but often does, since burial mounds are often sited on promontories where they act as landmarks.[14]

15 Why are burial mounds sited on promontories?

So that they can be seen. There is also a theory that they were used as 'documents'; so that, for example, the land owned by a dead person was the land visible from the top of their burial mound. This served in preliterate days to avoid disputes.[15]

16 Do we really know the extent of the cemetery?

The evaluation defined an area of 4.5 hectares (11 acres) for the cemetery, but several uncertainties remain. It is unlikely that burials continued to east or west, since to the west is the scarp which falls away to the River Deben and the land to the east was well tested by an area 16 × 50 m (52 × 164 ft) and found to be empty of burial. It is unlikely that there were many more burial mounds to the immediate north and south, since they would have been marked on the early maps, or found from the air or by geophysical survey. Flat graves, however, could continue along the terrace to north or south.

A kilometre (0.6 miles) north of the cemetery, a field on the far side of Sutton Hoo House has produced, from the plough soil, a fine bronze bucket incised with Nubian warriors and imported from the eastern Mediterranean (Fig. 63) as well as a gold coin of Honorius and some Ipswich ware pottery. These could have derived from more burial mounds, and it seems that there were at least mounds for rabbit-warrens in this area on John Norden's map in 1601. On the other hand, geophysical survey has not produced evidence for ring-ditches, such as

might be expected from burial mounds. The finds might therefore come from a settlement site, appropriately located on the next promontory to the north, which carries Mrs Pretty's house.[16]

17 Do we now have a fair idea what is in the Sutton Hoo cemetery?

Three kinds of graves have been discovered so far within the cemetery: burial mounds, furnished graves without mounds and execution burials. All the larger burial mounds so far excavated have been marked by a surviving mound, even if some were only just visible; so it is unlikely that there are many more to find. The execution burials were tightly clustered in two groups, and it does not seem likely that many more such groups await discovery in this place. The furnished graves without mounds were found close by the mounds, and there may well be more of them. In general, the picture of the cemetery that has emerged from the latest campaign is thought, at this moment, to be representative of what was there.[17]

BURIAL RITES

18 How long did it take to build a burial mound?

The maximum volume of Mound 2, as deduced from the volume of its quarry ditch, was 790 cu. m (27,650 cu. ft) and the volume of a wheelbarrow is 0.1 cu. m (3.5 cu. ft). It takes one man five minutes to dig out soil, fill a barrow and take it up a ramp to add to a mound. This means that it would have taken about 660 man-hours to build Mound 2, assuming they had wheelbarrows or their equivalent. From which one can calculate that it would take around ten man-weeks, that is, ten men working a ten-hour day for seven days, to build a mound this size. This is the equivalent extra workload of an additional harvest; it thus represents a considerable investment.[18]

19 Why were there no ordinary burials at Sutton Hoo?

Let us assume that by 'ordinary' burials we mean the rites of cremation in urns and inhumation with grave goods that were practised in the large Anglo-Saxon cemeteries such as Spong Hill. Sutton Hoo, however, has few certain burials of this kind. At Sutton Hoo we have cremation under a mound, chamber grave, horse burial, ship burial and some simple poorly furnished inhumations. There are three reasons which may help to explain this difference. First, the large Anglo-Saxon folk cemeteries date from the fifth to the seventh century, while Sutton Hoo is dated to around AD 600. Second, Sutton Hoo is a separate cemetery, reserved for the élite; its burials are mostly of high rank. And third, Sutton Hoo belongs to a special moment in history, when burial was used to signify particular kinds of ideology and political allegiance. All these factors make Sutton Hoo look different and look special, at least until other sites as splendid are discovered.[19]

20 Was Sutton Hoo unique, or were there other cemeteries like it?

This is a matter of degree. Rich graves with mounds have been recorded at Taplow in Buckinghamshire, Asthall in Oxfordshire and elsewhere. There is a burial in a ship at Snape, and burial mounds, some with very rich graves, are known or suspected at many sites in East Anglia, in Suffolk and indeed further along the River Deben, for example at Melton, Eyke and perhaps even at Rendlesham. Sutton Hoo has been more extensively excavated in modern times than any other mound cemetery, and has contained one of the very few rich burials to be found intact. These factors are bound to raise its prominence in any discussion.

It is possible that there were many cemeteries of burial mounds like Sutton Hoo, so that by the seventh century every rich farmstead would have one. In this case, Sutton Hoo is the burial ground of just another wealthy family. In the present state of knowledge, however, Sutton Hoo stands out by virtue of being a new foundation of the seventh century, of having cremation under mounds and ship burial which features highly symbolic objects, as well as objects of high value, and of being an execution site. Nowhere in England has quite this combination as yet. It is thus unique at present, and will long remain a candidate for identification as a royal cemetery, that is, one of the highest rank.[20]

21 Why did some burial parties choose cremation and others choose inhumation?

This is a big question for Anglo-Saxon England, and for Germanic Europe as a whole. The question 'what belief lay behind cremation or inhumation?' is not possible to answer as yet. In the context of Sutton Hoo, we can probably say this: by the early seventh century the norm for burial was inhumation. But the circumstances of East Anglia in the seventh century led the élite to choose models that expressed their political aspirations. Some chose cremation under mounds because it was used in Scandinavia and expressed a more anti-Christian stance.

The ship burials used inhumation, but ship burial itself was an even stronger signal of solidarity with the pagan east. Of 263 ship burials known in Europe in the seventh to eighth century, only three are known from England; the majority are in Scandinavia. The other inhumations, in Mound 17 and Mound 14, were high-status inhumations, but probably less politicised in their ritual. Chamber graves are commonly found in Anglo-Saxon folk cemeteries. Horse burials, while not common in Anglo-Saxon England, belong to a well-defined Germanic funerary rite found all over the Baltic zone and the Rhineland.[21]

22 Where were there other ship burials in Britain?

At nearby Snape there was a ship burial and two boat burials. Although rivets have been found at a number of sites, and boat pieces in graves at Caister-on-Sea (Norfolk), it is thought that only Sutton Hoo and Snape represent the use of the boat or ship as a deliberate ritual gesture. They belong to the same period and may have had a similar meaning, an expression of solidarity with Scandinavian ideas.[22]

23 Why was ship burial brought in at Sutton Hoo and Snape and nowhere else?

The élite of Snape and the élite of Sutton Hoo were surely closely related; and both sites may have been situated in the homeland of a family that gained the political leadership of the East Angles in the late sixth/early seventh century. If this family was particularly concerned to build that kingdom in alignment with Scandinavia, this policy might have been expressed in the form of special burial rites. Since Snape is an older folk cemetery, and Sutton Hoo a new élite cemetery, it might be that the family originally buried at Snape, and moved their ceremonial centre to Sutton Hoo when their claims began to extend to a wider territory.[23]

24 Did the Anglo-Saxons practise human sacrifice at Sutton Hoo or anywhere else?

It is possible that the very earliest executions at Sutton Hoo were contemporary with some of the mound-burials, but most seem to belong to the period after the conversion of East Anglia to Christianity. This group does not therefore offer strong evidence for human sacrifice. Elsewhere, there are examples of execution in early (pagan) Anglo-Saxon cemeteries, but most examples belong to the later Saxon period (ninth to eleventh centuries) and can be regarded as killings which were judicial rather than sacrificial in intent.[24]

25 Why were there two execution sites?

This remains unknown. We expected that the earliest gallows would be that on Mound 5 and the later one that in the field, perhaps to correspond with a gradually shifting track. But since the radiocarbon dates apparently make the two execution sites contemporary with each other, I

have guessed, and it is only a guess, that the distinction is that unrepentant pagans were buried around Mound 5 and Christians around the gallows in the eastern field. This suggestion is prompted by the east–west graves and use of coffins in the eastern field, and the fact that Mound 5 is a pagan burial and possibly that of an important ancestor.[25]

26 Did the Anglo-Saxons execute by hanging or beheading, and is it significant?

Both were apparently used here. The significance could be that hanging is Germanic and beheading a Roman method of execution. Perhaps this referred to the identity of the victim; but it is, in any case, entirely appropriate to find both in a community so vacillating over its cultural allegiance.[26]

OBJECTS

27 Who assembled the grave goods and with what model in view?

This is the kind of question to which no one knows the answer, so anyone can give one, based on their own perceptions of past and present. Here is mine.

The Mound 1 assemblage, being one of the few complete wealthy graves we have, shows that the assemblage was highly structured; that it included a wide variety of things, but not everything the Anglo-Saxons could have included. Furthermore, the vast majority of the things included in graves seldom turn up on settlement sites, even in fragments. This means that we must look for an explanation that is special to the burial rather than assuming that the objects represent the dead man's possessions which were in everyday use.

The Germans refer to 'grave gifts', and it is not impossible that many of the objects were gifts made at the graveside by guests in honour of the dead. This would help to explain why there were so many imports. On the other hand, the gift-giving would have to be regulated, like the presents given at a wedding; just as a married couple try to avoid receiving six toasters and one towel, so mourners would have to avoid burying a famous warrior with three shields and no sword.

In Bede's account of Raedwald, there is a clear indication of the degree of influence of his wife in East Anglian politics. It is possible that, here and in general, the burial of an important man was orchestrated by an important woman. The burial is thus 'composed' as a balance between the official and the personal. Official in this case means that the dead man must be armed and equipped to meet the duties of fighting and feasting on behalf of his folk who are still on earth. Thus sword and shield, sceptre and standard, are augmented by cauldron, lyre, drinking horns and finger bowls; for as every politician knows, what cannot be achieved on the battlefield can usually be managed at a party, especially if there is plenty to drink.

The personal thoughts are expressed by the materials in the coffin itself, packed we may assume under the supervision of the dead man's wife: washing bowl, shoes, spare socks, knives for nails and beard as well as some eccentric keepsakes only known to her.

The image in the mind of Raedwald's wife, or the women who buried the young man in Mound 17 and the other male noblemen (one hopes they each had a woman to bury them), must have defined the contemporary world-view, and was designed to do so. Reality and 'everyday life' played a role, to be sure, but was secondary to the great vision of what was suitable to a great leader of a great people. These burials, I think, were meant to signify the future, not the past, and the future of the living as well as the dead.

To know how the women were themselves buried, and their grave tableaux assembled, we should need more complete examples, like the Oseberg ship burial of Viking Norway, the richest female burial known. My perception is that women also arranged the burials of women; so the hand that 'rocked the cradle and ruled the world' also composed the grave and ruled the world-view expressed there. In this sense, pre-Christian women may have been the people's historians.[27]

28 What was the purpose of the coins?

The coins were minted in France where they may have had a use as money, but in England this is most unlikely. It is interesting that each coin appears to come from a different mint. Could it be that they were a form of tribute, not owed, but sent in recognition of the dead man's achievement, each major mint of the then Merovingian empire contributing a coin? Some scholars would say that there is no significance in the mints; this group would result from a handful grabbed at random from a reasonably well-stocked treasure chest. The historian Philip Grierson suggested that the thirty-seven coins, three blanks and two ingots make up the payment of a crew of forty oarsmen and a pilot and a steersman. However, it is not certain that the Mound 1 ship had forty oars. The Suffolk historian Norman Scarfe felt that the coins represented a bribe by Aethelfrith, King of Northumbria, to kill his rival Edwin.

This is speculation, but since the coins were buried in a ceremonial purse, an instrument of office, it is not unlikely that they did represent a symbolic or diplomatic payment of some kind.[28]

29 What was the Mound 1 'standard' and how may it be interpreted?

Bruce-Mitford deduced that the iron standard was an emblem which might have born items of foliage or cloth, and equated it with the 'tufa' carried before King Edwin of Northumbria in procession, as described by Bede:

> So royally was the king's dignity
> maintained throughout his realm that
> whether in battle or on peaceful progress
> on horseback through city, town or
> countryside in the company of his thanes,
> the royal standard was always borne before
> him. Even when he passed through the

streets on foot, the standard known to the Romans as tufa, and to the English as tuf, was carried in front of him.

A Roman standard could have taken the form of a winged orb mounted on a spear. If the Sutton Hoo standard was a *tuf*, its symbolism is more obscure than that. It showed no signs of burning, so had no role as a flambard. It could have carried branches or flowers. Strangely enough, a ritual branch with iron leaves was found in the Lombard burial mound excavated at Zuran near Brno. There are echoes here of a symbol of control, the leader or priest who for centuries called a moot to order by shaking a branch.[29]

30 What was the Mound 1 'sceptre' and how may it be interpreted?

Bruce-Mitford's restoration of the whetstone with the stag on top of it, and the knee pad below, led him to identify it as a sceptre on analogy with the staff of office carried by Byzantine emperors; this may be seen, for example, in the consular diptychs, ivory panels with portrayals of emperors. Other references can be discerned in the composition. The whetstone can be seen as the emblem of the 'sharpener of swords', a leader of warriors. The anatomy and style of the stag suggests it was a British work of art. The heads may be Germanic divinities or ancestors on whom the ruler's authority and his good luck depended.

The object as a whole, therefore, if deconstructed, can be seen to carry a number of messages. One can imagine it as the product of a seventh-century 'regalia working party', which was instructed to come up with something that would impress a Byzantine emperor and a British potentate, but without alarming the champions of pagan independence. It must have received mixed reactions; but whether it was placed in the tomb because it was thought to be a worthy and representative emblem or a ridiculous conceit will never be known.

Bruce-Mitford saw its inclusion in the burial as a sign that the buried person, King Raedwald, had aspired to the rule of Britain. But this particular role may have been more imaginary than real. The recent find of an iron crown and throne at the undocumented fifth- to sixth-century palace at Monte Barro in Lombardy reminds us that there were many potentates at this time able to put on airs which were later reserved to kingship.[30]

SHIPS

31 How did the ships get to the Sutton Hoo cemetery?

They must have been dragged up the slope from the River Deben and along the ground, probably using rollers. Given the great weight of a wet ship, the most likely route would be the gentlest slope, from Ferry Point or further south. Early medieval people were accustomed to the idea that their ships should cross the land to get from one waterway to another.[31]

32 Did the Mound 1 ship go to sea?

We can say at least that it was a ship that had seen some service. There was a patch in its hull, indicated by an additional cluster of nails, so it had been repaired. This suggests a working ship that had been honourably retired rather than a vessel built for a funeral. We do not know whether it went to sea, but it was certainly large enough. There is only just enough room for the Mound 1 ship to turn round in the River Deben at low tide.[32]

33 Could it be sailed?

There was no evidence for a mast or rigging. But then the most likely place for a mast, in the centre of the ship, was covered by the remains of a decayed burial chamber. There was, however, a large piece of timber seen during the excavation, which might have been part of a mast; this has been identified here as the upright post for the chamber.

Edwin Gifford has built an experimental replica of the Mound I ship, at half-size, and demonstrated that she sails beautifully (Col. Pl. XII).[33]

34 How many oarsmen were there?

The evidence for the number of oars comes from tholes and thole pins that were seen along the gunwale; but these only occurred here and there. From these we can say only that there were at least twenty oars, and there may have been as many as forty. A likely number is twenty-eight (fourteen pairs), seven on each side of the mast and/or the chamber.[34]

35 What were the ships used for?

There are very few surviving ships from early medieval Britain. The Sutton Hoo ships are among the largest from early medieval Europe as a whole, so they should be special, perhaps royal conveyances. At Snape and Slusegård (on Bornholm, Denmark) little dugout or skin boats were found in graves, scarcely 2 m (6 ft 6 in) long. We should imagine that between these two extremes all sizes and types of dugout and clinker-built boats would be in use, for ferrying across rivers and lakes, for transport of wheat and cattle, for exchanges and raids across the sea, for pilgrimages and for burial. The answer to this question must be 'everything you can think of, and more'.[35]

KINGS

36 Was there a body in Mound 1, or was it a cenotaph?

No body was found in Mound I, but as Stuart Piggott pointed out at the inquest this was a common circumstance in acid soil. The absence still worried some people and it was proposed that the Mound I ship and its chamber were a cenotaph, that is a memorial without a burial. During the British Museum study of Mound I, an ingenious experiment showed that the grave goods near the west end were enriched with phosphate, so a body could have lain there. In the 1983–93 campaign many 'sand-bodies' were found in graves that had no bone at all; the body was visible thanks to its difference in texture and colour from the surrounding fill of the grave. A special project was also launched, funded by the Leverhulme Trust, which attempted to further the study by developing a kind of 'forensic archaeology' in which chemical analysis was used to determine the decay products left by a human body. Various kinds of meat were also buried in an experiment to see how long it took for the meat to decay and become a 'sand form'. The answer was less than six years.

In the light of these studies we have no reason to doubt that there was originally a body in Mound I. The body would have been subject to very hostile conditions: a few hundred years of rain acidified by passing through the make-up of the mound would have collected in the bottom of the boat. The body would thus have lain in an acid bath until the moment that the hull of the ship had rotted sufficiently for the water to drain into the sand beneath. At this point everything soluble, including the body and its bone, would have been flushed away. If no bone had been present, it would have been impossible for the excavators to see even a sand body, sandwiched as it was between two layers of dark sand representing the decayed wood of the coffin and chamber.

Should another 'Mound I deposit' ever be found, the Leverhulme technique of chemical mapping could now be used to see where it had lain.[36]

37 Who was buried in the mounds?

The evidence from burial and settlement suggests that by the early seventh century East Anglia had acquired a stratified society, probably equivalent to the one that is described in later documents: nobleman (aristocratic landowner), churl (free smallholder) and slave (a chattel, owned and fed by a nobleman or a churl). The distinction between the classes and the grades within them were measured by the *wergild*, the amount of compensation payable by the killer in the event of unlawful killing. For a slave this would have been about 1 pound, the equivalent of eight oxen, for a churl 10 pounds, and a nobleman, 60 pounds.

It is a reasonable assumption that the value of grave goods equated to, or at least reflected, the level of the *wergild*. If someone had been unlawfully killed, it was fair that the killer should at least have paid for the funeral. On this basis, the majority of the mounds at Sutton Hoo would have belonged to the class of the aristocracy. If a pound was equivalent to 240 pence or 8 mancus, this would have bought 560 grains, or about 3.6 g (0.1 oz) of gold. A nobleman of average nobility would therefore have had a *wergild* equivalent to 480 oxen or 200 g (7 oz) of gold: enough to furnish a grave of the kind we find under the majority of the Sutton Hoo burial mounds. Far more than this is implied by the finds in the ship burials, and for this reason we are justified in assuming that they at least are the memorials to people of the highest rank, in this era called kings.[37]

38 Which kings were they?

Archaeology cannot answer this question; it would require, at the least, a material clue like an inscription on a memorial or an engraved ring in the burial or some such sign of the name of a dead person. We have nothing of this kind at Sutton Hoo, so archaeologists can only conclude that they are a group of high-ranking individuals, mainly male.

Historians are at liberty to equate the findings with what is known of named individuals. They can reason which tomb is most likely to have contained which king; and whereas this remains a guess, it is perfectly sensible and interesting to make it. The person buried in Mound 1 has proved to be an irresistible subject of speculation, and on different occasions since 1940 has been claimed as Raedwald, Sigeberht, Earpwald, Raegenhere, Aethelhere and even Saebert, King of Essex.

Now that the whole cemetery can be included in the reckoning, rather than simply Mound 1, the question can be revisited. The Sutton Hoo cemetery is the largest concentration of high-ranking burials in England, a relatively well-explored archaeological landscape. It is situated in East Anglia and dated to the seventh century. The historian will note that there are named kings of East Anglia in Bede's *Ecclesiastical History* and in the *Vespasian* king list. And if the historian believes the sequence of burial suggested here, then it becomes possible to put the kings in individual mounds: so, for example, Wehha (died late sixth century) would be in Mound 5; Wuffa (d.578) in Mound 6; Tyttla (d.599) in Mound 7; Raedwald (d.624/5), who had aspirations to rule a wider realm as Bretwalda, in Mound 1 or 2; his successor Earpwald (d.627/8) in Mound 1 or 2 on the grounds that the East Angles wished to signal a continuation of Raedwald's power. Sigeberht and Ecgric, killed together in 636/7, may have had a Christian burial; or they can be assigned to Mounds 3 and 4. Their successors at least were Christian, and it is likely that the kings from Anna (d.654) onwards were buried in churches or near them. The relative dates of the objects makes it unlikely that any of the mounds so far excavated would have been constructed much after AD 650.

It can be seen that whereas this is pure speculation, and must not be taken as fact, it conforms in certain undeniable particulars. The pagan kings of East Anglia reigned in total for less than a hundred years from the late sixth to the early seventh century. The archaeology of the cemetery also is of that date and duration. It does not matter much who was in which mound; the archaeology has revealed two ship burials and a small group of cremations under mounds, which between them can account for the named members of the dynasty; there are graves here too for the unnamed relatives whose proximity to the ruler earned them the right to be buried at Sutton Hoo.

Thus although the association of Sutton Hoo and the short-lived pagan royal house of East

Anglia has not been proved, there are still sufficient grounds for believing it.[38]

39 How do we know the Sutton Hoo kings were kings of East Anglia?

Sutton Hoo is currently in the county of Suffolk, which is in East Anglia. Its closest archaeological parallels are with Snape, also in Suffolk. It is also within the diocese of East Anglia, which is unlikely to have changed its boundary greatly since the Middle Ages. The best contemporary information we have comes from archaeology, in the form of Ipswich ware, a type of pottery made in the seventh to the eighth century. Its distribution maps out a territory that includes Sutton Hoo, and mainly covers present-day East Anglia. Bede mentions that nearby Rendlesham was in East Anglia. Sutton Hoo also lies north of Ipswich, which is generally considered an East Anglian town.[39]

40 If Sutton Hoo is the royal burial ground for East Anglia, why is it situated at the south-eastern corner of the territory instead of in the middle?

Bearing in mind that the principal means of communication was by sea and the land was the slow way to go, Sutton Hoo was by the front door of the kingdom with fast sea routes to the Waveney, the Wash and the settlements on the rivers that drain into them, as well as to the key points of contact at the Rhine mouth and the west coast of Jutland. If it lay in the centre of East Anglia, it would actually have been one of the most difficult places to get to.[40]

41 What other places were becoming kingdoms at the same time as East Anglia?

The answer to this will come from research currently under way in many countries. There are many problems in defining a 'kingdom' from burial mounds, burial practice or settlements, but insofar as it is valid, there are territories of this type assigned to Medelpad and the Malären in Sweden, a number in south-west Norway, in Jutland, and, in Britain, the north Picts around the Moray Firth, the south Picts around the Tay, Dalriada (Argyll), and the Anglo-Saxon kingdoms of Northumbria, Mercia, Wessex, Essex, Kent and East Anglia. There is still a great deal to know about how, when and why these kingdoms appeared; but they appear to be the foundation for the countries that still exist.[41]

SUTTON HOO AND BEOWULF

42 Is Sutton Hoo the reality behind the world of *Beowulf*?

Not quite. *Beowulf* is an epic poem about the Germanic heroic age of the fourth to fifth centuries, as written down much later, after the Anglo-Saxons were converted to Christianity. As such, it is full of selected allusions and quotations accrued over four centuries or more, which would be understood and enjoyed by its audience.

A burial is composed of selected objects, and it is likely that the objects, taken individually and together, were also full of allusions to rank, power, ancestry, ideology and allegiance to kin or allies at home and overseas. I therefore regard a ship burial as just as much of a poem as *Beowulf* is, just as difficult to interpret but just as capable of giving us insights into the Anglo-Saxon mind. Burials are poems written with material culture; so that the choice of burial rite and the choice of what is put into the grave are choices referring to what was known or feared or loved by the mourners.

If each burial is a poem, then the cemetery as a whole is a theatre in which the political thinking of the day is reflected as grave succeeds grave. However, as with any text, we must try to distinguish between intended communication and unconscious meaning. This is hard enough for texts. For archaeology, we rely heavily on comparative material, and we have only seen a fraction of it up to now.

With this caveat in mind, we can say that the message of the cemetery, like that of

Beowulf, is heroic and international; in praise of enterprise, achievement and fame, of a life that is memorable even if short, rather than one that is long and virtuous or boring. The allegiance is to Scandinavia and a Germanic pagan brotherhood of the North Sea. The things of Rome and Christianity are brought into service to this end. But Rome and Christianity themselves are not to be served but resisted; and in this perhaps Sutton Hoo differs from *Beowulf*, at least in the form that the latter has come down to us.

Neither Sutton Hoo nor *Beowulf* represents a straight account of reality. Both contain allusions to the real world, but we do not know for certain which they were. From the study of burial we risk at present knowing more about how the Anglo-Saxons thought than about how they lived.[42]

43 How would we discover the reality behind Beowulf and Sutton Hoo?

Material culture is not always and everywhere deposited in an expressive form; on many sites, particularly settlement sites, archaeologists find rubbish pits and midden heaps in which discard is less consciously done. The material culture represented by these deposits has more to say about what resources were available and to which groups in society. This is an argument for investing in more research into settlements, economy and ecology. This research can be achieved by large-scale surveys which discover the settlement patterns, their approximate date and the communication system that joined them; by carefully selective excavation, which can determine the status, function and economy of settlements; and by analysing pollen sequences and animal populations which show what resources were being exploited. This work is more likely to provide us with the evidence needed to understand the Sutton Hoo burials.[43]

ROBBING

44 Why was Sutton Hoo not dug during the Middle Ages?

Preliminary study of this subject suggests that very few burial mounds were robbed during the Middle Ages, but very many were from the Reformation onwards. In Italy a similar surge of tomb-robbing occurred at the Renaissance. This would seem to indicate that the main inhibition to robbing burials was superstition, and people were released from it when there was change in the relationship between God and man.[44]

45 The Sutton Hoo cemetery was excavated at least twice before Basil Brown got to it; Why was Mound 1 not robbed?

We have some indications of robbing attempts at Mound 1; a large pit with a burnt timber in it (a ladder?) was encountered by Basil Brown – in fact it fell in on him. This must have been a robber pit, and the finds of Bellarmine ware suggest it was sixteenth-century. It was offset from the chamber, perhaps because the mound had already been partly ploughed away on its west side. But it was not in any case deep enough to reach the burial, which lay 12 ft (3.6 m) below the old ground surface; this depth, added to the height of the mound, which then could have been at least another 12 feet, would have meant a dangerous and unstable pit.

But Mound 1 was of course unusual in having no central pit for a burial. The ship was sunk in a trench below the old ground surface; so that even an excavator's trench would have passed from west to east without seeing anything. There would be none of the usual guides: no sandy subsoil, no buried soil and no big pit in the middle. The natural conclusion for anyone using this method would be that the mound had been thoroughly dug over already. Basil Brown used the same method himself, and could have easily drawn the same conclusion; the difference was that he found a ship rivet and recognised it, searched for others and then brushed them clean in rows – before realising that the earth actually contained the form of a ship, which went down and down.[45]

DIGGING

46 Was Mrs Pretty psychic?

Like many another, Mrs Pretty sought solace in spiritualism. We cannot say whether she believed she could make contact with the other world. We can, however, be reasonably confident that she did not start digging because of a belief in ley lines, or lines of hidden power or any such nonsense. A feeling of sympathy with the dead is compatible with both a fascination with the spiritual and a spirit of scientific curiosity. Either or both in combination is sufficient to explain her initiation of the Sutton Hoo discoveries.[46]

47 Why wasn't the whole Sutton Hoo site excavated in the latest campaign?

The reason that the whole of Sutton Hoo was not excavated in the latest campaign was that it would have been wrong, both scientifically and ethically. Scientifically, because a 'site' is simply an archaeological concept; the people who built Sutton Hoo walked elsewhere and lived elsewhere. The 'whole of a site' is not a reality, it is simply what archaeologists define as their area of interest. It is therefore impossible to dig 'all' of a site.

It would be possible to find and dig, for example, all the burials (as at Spong Hill). But it would also be ethically wrong to attempt to do so. Archaeological excavation is informative, but destructive. The only digging we are justified in doing is the smallest possible area that makes sense, and even then the research results anticipated have got to be worth the destruction of part of the site. An excavation should always leave something for the future, when we should be able to know more by digging less.[47]

48 Should we dig any more?

One day we could and should, but this is unlikely to be scientifically justifiable for a hundred years or more. The way archaeological research works is slow: it is slow to do, slow to write up for publication and it takes a long time to absorb its meaning. We always rush in too quickly hoping that lucky 'discoveries' will explain everything. But they never do, and they cannot. Explanation can only come as the answer to a question, and the more specific the question, the more chance we have of getting a solid answer.

In 1983 some were against excavation, others encouraged the digging of 'the whole site'. We deliberately slowed up the process, championed the idea of careful evaluation and eventually justified the digging of one quarter, aiming at specific questions. In a hundred years' time that quarter will look very extravagant. Our resources are finite, and the response should be to devise new techniques which will allow more and more of our questions to be answered without the destruction inherent in excavation, especially at a site about which we already know a great deal. The conservation of most of the site for future research was an essential part of the 1986 strategy.

The respite that Sutton Hoo needs is to allow the development not only of new techniques, but also of new ideas. As work progresses on the kingdoms of the North Sea territories, we will understand more about why these kingdoms formed and how burial relates to their origins and development. Then we shall want to return to Sutton Hoo with specific inquiries that we cannot yet foresee; and we shall want it to be there still.[48]

49 What would you do if you could start again now?

On site, the evaluation was probably the best that could be done at the time. But the techniques of non-destructive mapping are much in need of development. An evaluation in the next century should be capable of recognising the thickness and interfaces of strata and the character of buried objects, without having to break the protective seal provided by the surface of the ground. Most urgently needed is a reliable method for locating and mapping graves. That would allow a tighter strategy, with probably less actual digging.

We should also need much better data-handling on site, including analytical programmes that can reveal results from, say, artefact plotting while a dig proceeds. This could then be used to decrease the amount of digging necessary. There is also need for further development of soil stabilising compounds, which hold and improve contrast in strata liable to dry out and collapse quickly in the open air. New easy-to-use consolidants would be valuable for finds, particularly from burials, so that they can be routinely lifted, stored and dug later inside a laboratory.

Off-site, the 'East Anglian Kingdom Survey' made most progress in the Deben Valley, which showed the potential of the work, if it could be energetically prosecuted over the region as a whole. Not only the finding of sites but their non-destructive examination should form part of any future strategy. This is because research will advance most significantly through improvement of the quality of predictive mapping at *undug* sites. These are the cemeteries and settlements contemporary with Sutton Hoo that can answer so many of Sutton Hoo's questions so much better than more digging at Sutton Hoo itself. How special was the Sutton Hoo cemetery? Where did its riches come from? What were ships employed to do? Where were the landing places and what was exchanged there? What were the changes in the seventh-century economy? Where are the early churches of Suffolk and what kind of burial was practised there? What social organisation existed before and after the conversion?

Sutton Hoo has allowed us to ask these more sophisticated questions with greater confidence; but it is not at Sutton Hoo itself that they are likely to be answered.[49]

50 What were the most useful things achieved by the recent campaign?

In prime place, the public trial of a new approach to the problem of where and how to dig, called *Field Research Procedure*.[50] Thanks to an enlightened sponsor, Sutton Hoo was the first British project to have a published, and publicly accountable project design, drawn from an 'evaluation' and 'strategy' phase before any digging began, and it continued to follow a staged sequence of operations, punctuated by reassessments. This did not reduce its attraction for the public, as some had feared. The campaign was presented on television, not as discoveries by the minute, but as an expedition scientifically planned and professionally executed. Thirteen million people watched its programmes and did not seem to find them boring. Feedback suggested that people do relate to scientific archaeology and its aims, as it is and as they are; they do not have to be patronised with mystery, magic and treasure.

It was also very satisfactory to secure the long-term future of the site. After all, for an archaeologist, the presentation of the site itself to the public is part of the publication programme. The acquisition of Sutton Hoo by the National Trust and the creation of a visitor centre there should bring pleasure and interest to millions.

But the principal objective was to throw light upon the past, and to try and write a new 'chapter 1' for English history. The discovery of the Mound 1 ship burial could never be repeated, and even if we had found another intact example, it could no longer have occasioned the same surprise. But a context was provided for the great discovery, by revealing the repertoire of burial rites that had been practised at the cemetery as a whole. The attempt to put the burials in order was less successful, but proved less important, since the cemetery was used for such a short time. Two ship burials, a central group of cremations under mounds, and six ancillary inhumations including women, adolescents and children provided a broader definition of Sutton Hoo's society. Confidence has been greatly increased that this seventh-century site is a special burial ground for the élite, and could be the burial ground of East Anglia's first and pagan kings, and thus the earliest English royal burial ground we have. Two groups of execution burials were also discovered and attributed to gallows first erected during the years of royal burial. Ritual or judicial killing can now be suggested to be an aspect of seventh-century kingship, a practice that was to continue and expand, particularly in the tenth century.

The Deben Valley survey and the excavations at Snape have provided an invaluable contribution to the definition of the role and purpose of Sutton Hoo. The settlement pattern found in the survey has brought the ordinary people into the picture, and showed the great change in the organisation of the landscape that occurred in the early seventh century when Sutton Hoo was being built. Many of the Sutton Hoo burial practices are foreshadowed at Snape, so that it may have been experiments there that acted as a foundation for the extravagance of Sutton Hoo. There were probably other mound-cemeteries along the Deben. We have every reason to believe now that a rich, innovatory pagan élite underpinned and supported the early kingdom of East Anglia.

The roots of the royal burial ground also lay deep in prehistory. Three thousand years of land-use were chronicled, and an agricultural settlement of the early Bronze Age was defined. The land had been cleared, planted, ditched, ploughed, parcelled, exhausted and abandoned in a *longue durée* of agricultural exploitation. After its moment of fame in the seventh century, the long struggle with the land resumed and the cycle of exploitation began again. Now the mounds were a landmark for travellers from across the river into the Suffolk coastlands, and for generations of landowners. Some of these noted the fertile soil of which the mounds were composed and dragged it into cultivation. Others dug into the mounds, for reasons which changed markedly as the times changed. The hero's gold lay in the ground, immutable, but its value – as treasure, as status symbol or as knowledge – varied with the centuries. This variation too is part of Sutton Hoo's story.

APPENDIX I: DIGEST OF EVIDENCE

Abbreviations

SHSB I, II, III: R.L.S. Bruce-Mitford, *The Sutton Hoo
Ship Burial* (British Museum Press, 1975, 1978, 1983)

Longworth & Kinnes 1980: I. Longworth and I.A. Kinnes,
Sutton Hoo Excavations 1966, 1968–70
(British Museum Occasional Papers 23, 1980)

The work of the recent interventions (Int 18–56) is
published in M.O.H. Carver and M.R. Hummler,
*Sutton Hoo: An Early Medieval Cemetery and its
Context* (British Museum Press, forthcoming)

The Field Records of every intervention are to be
deposited in the Sutton Hoo Archive at the British
Museum.

1 List of Interventions at Sutton Hoo

Int 1 1844, 1860: Survey of mounds and later and separate excavation of a mound on land occupied by Mr Barritt. Reported in *Ipswich Journal* for 24 Nov 1860.

Int 2 1938: Excavation of Mound 3 by Basil Brown for Mrs Pretty (landowner). *SHSB* I, 100

Int 3 1938: Excavation of Mound 2 by Basil Brown for Mrs Pretty (landowner). *SHSB* I, 100

Int 4 1938: Excavation of Mound 4 by Basil Brown, instigated by Mrs Pretty (landowner). *SHSB* I, 100

Int 5 1939: Excavation of Mound 1 by (1) Basil Brown (2) Charles Phillips (3) Cdr. Hutchinson, instigated by Mrs Pretty (landowner). *SHSB* I, II, III

Int 6 1965–7: Re-excavation of Mound 1 by R.L.S. Bruce-Mitford for British Museum. *SHSB* I

Int 7 1967–70: Excavations beneath Mound 1 by P. Ashbee for British Museum. *SHSB* I

Int 8 1971: Excavation of a trench in the vicinity of Mound 1 by T. Carney for British Museum. Unpub

Int 9 1971: Excavation of a trench in the vicinity of Mound 1 by T. Carney for British Museum. Unpub

Int 10 1971: Excavation of a trench in the vicinity of Mound 1 by T. Carney for British Museum. Unpub

Int 11 1966: Excavation of an area ('Area A') near Mound 17 by I. Longworth and I. Kinnes for British Museum. Longworth & Kinnes 1980

Int 12 1970: Excavation of an area ('Area C') over Mound 5 by I. Longworth and I. Kinnes for the British Museum. Longworth & Kinnes 1980

Int 13 1968–9: Excavation of a trench ('Area B') east of Int 12 by I. Longworth and I. Kinnes for the British Museum. Longworth & Kinnes 1980

Int 14 1968–9: Excavation of a trench ('Area B') east of Int 13 by I. Longworth and I. Kinnes for British Museum. Longworth & Kinnes 1980

Int 15 1968–9: Excavation of a trench ('Area B') east of Int 14 by I. Longworth and I. Kinnes for British Museum. Longworth & Kinnes 1980

Int 16 1968–9: Excavation of a trench ('Area B') east of Int 15 by I. Longworth and I. Kinnes for British Museum.

Longworth & Kinnes 1980

Int 17 1982: Recording by S. West for Suffolk Archaeological Unit of a robber pit made in centre of Mound 11

Int 18 1983–4: Surface mapping of plants over Zone A by A.J. Copp and J. Rothera for Sutton Hoo Research Trust

Int 19 1983–4: Surface collection of artefacts over Zones D, E and F by A.J. Copp and C. Royle for Sutton Hoo Research Trust

Int 20 1984: Excavation of 100 m long trench to the east of the burial mounds in Zone F by M.O.H. Carver for Sutton Hoo Research Trust

Int 21 1984: Excavation of a trench across a buried anti-glider ditch in Zone F by M.O.H. Carver for Sutton Hoo Research Trust

Int 22 1984: Excavation of a 100 m long trench to the south of the burial mounds in Zone D by M.O.H. Carver for Sutton Hoo Research Trust

Int 23 1984: Re-excavation of a length of anti-glider ditch in Zone A by M.O.H. Carver for Sutton Hoo Research Trust

Int 24 1984: Excavation of a trench in Top Hat Wood, Zone B, by M.O.H. Carver for Sutton Hoo Research Trust

Int 25 1984: An attempt to smother vegetation over the area of Mound 5 preparatory to total excavation, by M.O.H. Carver for Sutton Hoo Research Trust

Int 26 1984–5: Re-excavation of the central point of Basil Brown's trench across Mound 2 by M.O.H. Carver, A.C. Evans and G. Hutchinson for Sutton Hoo Research Trust

Int 27 1983–4: Metal detector survey of Zone A by C.L. Royle for Sutton Hoo Research Trust

Int 28 1984: Magnetometer survey on pilot area in Zone F by M. Gorman for Sutton Hoo Research Trust

Int 29 1984: Soil-sounding radar test on pilot area in Zone F and over Mound 2 and Mound 12 by M. Gorman for Sutton Hoo Research Trust

Int 30 1983–4: Topographic survey of the burial mound (Zone A) by J. Bruce, E. Ingrams and M. Cooper for Sutton Hoo Research Trust

Int 31 1984: Re-excavation of east edge of silage pit, Zone C, by M.O.H. Carver for Sutton Hoo Research Trust

Int 32 1985: Excavation of an area in Zone F by M.O.H. Carver and P. Leach for Sutton Hoo Research Trust

Int 33 1966: Topographic survey of the burial mounds by Hipkin for British Museum.

Int 34 1980: Topographical survey of the burial mounds by Hipkin for British Museum

Int 35 1984: Fluxgate gradiometer survey over a pilot area in Zone F by A. Bartlett for Sutton Hoo Research Trust

Int 36 1985: Resistivity survey over a pilot area in Zone F by R. Walker for Sutton Hoo Research Trust

Int 37 1985: Phosphate survey over Zones D and F by P.A. Gurney for Sutton Hoo Research Trust

Int 38 1986: Stripping and recording of Horizon 1 of an area in Zone F, north of Int 32, by M.O.H. Carver for Sutton Hoo Research Trust

Int 39 1986: Excavation of an area in Zone F east of Int 32

by M.O.H. Carver for Sutton Hoo Research Trust

Int 40 1986: A sieving experiment on the ploughsoil in Zone F by M.O.H. Carver for Sutton Hoo Research Trust

Int 41 1986–8: Excavation of an area in Zone A containing Mounds 2 and 5 by M.O.H. Carver and A.J. Copp, with A.C. Evans (Mound 5) for Sutton Hoo Research Trust

Int 42 1986: Establishment of a permanent loom grid over Zone A by C.L. Royle for Sutton Hoo Research Trust

Int 43 1986: An experiment to determine the inorganic chemical signatures of deteriorated human remains by P. Bethell for Sutton Hoo Research Trust/Leverhulme Trust

Int 44 1988–9: Excavation of an area in Zone A containing Mounds 6 and 7 by M.O.H. Carver and A.J. Copp, with A.C. Evans (Mound 7) for Sutton Hoo Research Trust

Int 45 1988: Magnetic susceptibility survey; pilot studies in Zones A, D and F by C.L. Royle and A. Clark for Sutton Hoo Research Trust

Int 46 1988: Soil-sounding radar survey over Mounds 6 and 7 (Zone A) by Oceanfix Ltd for Sutton Hoo Research Trust

Int 47 1988: Resistivity survey in Zones D and F for Sutton Hoo Research Trust

Int 48 1989–92: Excavation of an area on the west side of Zone A containing Mounds 17 and 18 by M.O.H. Carver and M.R. Hummler, with A. Roe (Mound 17) and A.C. Evans (Mound 18) for Sutton Hoo Research Trust

Int 49 1989: Resistivity survey in Zones D and F by K. Clark for Sutton Hoo Research Trust.

Int 50 1990–1: Excavation of an area between Int 32 and 41 containing Mound 14 by M.O.H. Carver and J. Garner-Lahire, with G. Bruce (Mound 14) for Sutton Hoo Research Trust

Int 51 1991: Resistivity survey of northern half of Int 50 prior to excavation by J. Dunk and I. Lawton for Sutton Hoo Research Trust

Int 52 1991: Excavation of the trench between Int 50 and Int 32 by M.O.H. Carver and A.J. Copp for Sutton Hoo Research Trust

Int 53 1991: Excavation of a trench in the valley below Top Hat Wood (Zone G) to obtain environmental samples by M.O.H. Carver for Sutton Hoo Research Trust

Int 54 1991: Excavation of organic materials buried experimentally in Int 43 to investigate their rate of decay by P. Bethell for Sutton Hoo Research Trust

Int 55 1991–2: Excavation of an area to the south of Mound 7, containing parts of Mound 13, Mound 3 and Mound 4, by M.O.H. Carver and M.R Hummler for Sutton Hoo Research Trust

Int 56 1993: Reconstitution of the areas excavated and reconstruction of the original form of Mound 2 by M.O.H. Carver, A.J. Copp and P. Berry for Sutton Hoo Research Trust

2 Inventory of burials so far encountered at Sutton Hoo

Burial mounds

MOUNDS UNEXPLORED IN MODERN TIMES
Mounds 8, 9, 10 (possibly robbed), 11 (attempted robbing 1982, Int 17), 12, 13 (robbed 19th century, sectioned 1980-91, Int 44/55), 15, 16 (not securely located).

INVESTIGATED MOUND BURIALS

Burial 1, Mound 1: The Mound 1 ship burial. Richly furnished inhumation W–E in a coffin in a chamber in a ship in a trench beneath a mound. Attempted robbing 16th century. Discovered intact and excavated in 1939 (Int 2). Re-excavated 1966–71 (Int 5–10; *SHSB* I, II, III). Dated: after AD 613 (coins). C14: 520-610; 685-765.

Burial 2, Mound 2: The Mound 2 ship burial. Inhumation W–E in a chamber beneath a ship. Robbed in 16th century and in 1860 (Int 1). Re-excavated 1938 (Int 3, *SHSB* I), and 1986–8 (Int 41)

Burial 3, Mound 3: Cremation on a wooden tray or dug-out boat in a pit. Robbed 16th/19th centuries. Re-excavated 1938 (Int 2, *SHSB* I)

Burial 4, Mound 4: Cremation under cloth in a bronze bowl in a pit. Robbed 16th/19th centuries. Re-excavated 1938 (Int 4, *SHSB* I)

Burial 5, Mound 5: Cremation under cloth in a bronze bowl in a pit of a young person with blade injuries to head. Robbed 16th/19th centuries. Re-excavated 1970 (Int 12) and 1988 (Int 41). Surrounded by satellite burials of Group 2

Burial 6, Mound 6: Cremation under cloth in a bronze bowl. Robbed 16th/19th centuries. Re-excavated 1988–9 (Int 44)

Burial 7, Mound 7: Cremation under cloth in a bronze bowl. Robbed 16th/19th century. Re-excavated 1988–9 (Int 44)

Burial 8, Mound 14: Inhumation in chamber, possibly in coffin, possibly of female. Robbed 16th/19th centuries. Re-excavated 1991 (Int 50)

Burial 9, Mound 17: Intact inhumation W–E of young male in coffin; beneath mound with **Burial 10, Mound 17:** Horse in pit without furnishing. Excavated 1991 (Int 48)

Burial 11, Mound 18: Cremation in bronze bowl under cloth. Robbed 16th/19th centuries. Re-excavated 1989 (Int 48)

OTHER POSSIBLE MOUND BURIALS OR FURNISHED GRAVES

Burial 12: Inhumation of a child NW–SE, in a coffin. Originally beneath a mound. Excavated 1987 (Int 41)

Burial 13: Cremation without urn, undated. Excavated 1966 (Int 11, Aiii; Longworth & Kinnes 1980). Perhaps a secondary burial in a mound over Burial 56

Burial 14: Cremation in pottery urn. Excavated 1966 (Int 11, Aiv; Longworth & Kinnes 1980). Perhaps a secondary burial in a mound over Burial 56

Burial 15: Inhumation W–E, extended on back, in coffin. Probably young male (Int 50)

Burial 16: Inhumation W–E, extended on back, in coffin. Probably young female (Int 50)

Burial 56: Pit containing displaced skull. Excavated 1966 (Int 11, pit 1; Longworth & Kinnes 1980). Probably represents an inhumation under a mound, robbed in 16th/19th centuries. C14: AD 680–840

Execution burials

GROUP 1: INHUMATIONS ON THE EASTERN PERIPHERY ASSOCIATED WITH GIBBET
Excavated 1984–91, Int 32, 52

Burial 17: N–S, flexed on back. C14: AD 530–710
Burial 18: W–E, extended, on back, in coffin
Burial 19: E–W, extended, prone, with hands tied behind back
Burial 20: NW–SE, extended, on back, in coffin
Burial 21: W–E, extended, on back, without head
Burial 22: W–E, extended, on back, with head of Burial 21 on lap. C14: AD 690–830
Burial 23: E–W, extended, on back, with broken neck. Probably male
Burial 24: Crouched, in pit beneath Burial 23. Probably male
Burial 25: SE–NW, extended, prone, with wrists and ankles 'tied'. Probable male
Burial 26: W–E, extended, on back, above Burial 25
Burial 27: W–E, on side in 'hurdling' position. With timber pieces. Probably male
Burial 28: W–E, kneeling, top of head missing
Burial 29: W–E, extended, on back, hands 'tied' and stretched above the head
Burial 30: W–E, extended, on back, wrist laid over wrist. C14: AD 970–1220
Burial 31: N–S, extended
Burial 32: W–E, extended, prone
Burial 33: W–E, extended, prone, lying with Burial 32
Burial 34: W–E, flexed, in square coffin, chest or barrel
Burial 35: W–E, extended, on back, head detached and placed over right arm looking north. C14: AD 650–960
Burial 36: NW–SE, tightly crouched, lying on right side, head facing north
Burial 37: NW–SE, flexed at knees, lying on back
Burial 38: NW–SE, lying on back, knees bent back to shoulders
Burial 39: NW–SE, kneeling, face to ground, left arm behind back. C14: AD 880–1030

GROUP 2: INHUMATIONS AROUND MOUND 5
Int 41, 44, 48, 50
Burial 40: W–E, flexed, on side, with head detached and rotated. Probably male. C14: AD 890–1050
Burial 41: S–N, flexed, on side, with additional limbs. Cut into Mound 5 quarry pit
Burial 42A: N–S, prone. Probably young female. On body of Burial 42B
Burial 42B: N–S, extended, on back, with head detached and lying with neck uppermost. Probably mature male. C14: AD 640–780
Burial 43: N–S, prone. Probably young female. On body of Burial 42B
Burial 44: NW–SE, extended, on back.
Burial 45: W–E, posture uncertain. C14: AD 860–1040
Burial 46: NW–SE, flexed, on side. Cut into Mound 5 quarry pit
Burial 47: Suspected body piece, in Mound 5 quarry pit. Probably not a grave
Burial 48: S–N, slightly flexed, on side, head detached and placed over left knee
Burial 49: NW–SE, extended, on back, head wrenched out of alignment, with organic 'rope' around neck. Cut in Mound 5 quarry pit containing bones of large mammal
Burial 50: S–N, flexed, on side
Burial 51: W–E, extended, on back
Burial 52: NW–SE, extended, on back, right arm beneath body. Head detached and replaced at neck end
Burial 53: N–S, extended, prone, right arm beside head. In or cut into Mound 5 quarry pit
Burial 54: S–N, flexed on side, without head. Cut into Mound 6 quarry pit
Burial 55: Dismembered body

Note: all radiocarbon dates are given at 68% probability and calibrated following Clark (Ch. 5, note 14)

3 Inventory of early medieval finds

Finds from the ship-burials

MOUND 1: Assemblage summary for Mound 1 (for descriptions see *SHSB* I, II, III)

No.	Object	Provenance	Date	BM inventory numbers
WEST WALL				
1	iron standard			161
2	support for 1?			210
3	shield	Sweden?	7th c.	94, 206 (ring), 197 (tape), 29 (board)
4	sceptre			160, 205 (stag)
5	bucket 3			119
6	hanging bowl	N. Britain	7th c.	110
7	nail supporting 6			222
8	lyre			203–4, 208, 215(bag)
9	Coptic bowl			109
10	3 angons			99–100
11	5 spears			101–5, 106–8 (ferrules)
ON THE COFFIN LID				
12	helmet	Sweden?		93; 188, 199 (cloth)
13	gaming pieces			172

No.	Object	Provenance	Date	BM inventory numbers
14	bell			212
15	2 silver spoons	Byzantine		88–9
16	10 silver bowls	Byzantine		78–87
17	2 spears			97, 211
18	Great gold buckle	E. Anglia	late 6th/ early 7th c.	1
19	purse, with gold frame and gold and garnet plaques			2, 3
20	shoulder clasps, of gold and garnet			4,5
21	Strap mounts and buckles, of gold and garnet for the suspension systems for sword and purse			6–18
22	coins in purse	France	before 613	34–75
23	sword, with gold and garnet pommel and scabbard studs	France?		19–31, 95, wrapped in cloth 191
24	yellow cloaks	Syria?		SH10
25	wooden bottles		7th c.	122–7, 213
26	Two drinking horns		7th c.	120–1, 218 wrapped in cloth pads A–C
27	[animal] bone			201, cloth SH26
28	silver dish [Anastasius]	Byzantine	491–518AD	76

INSIDE THE COFFIN, HEAP C

No.	Object	Provenance	Date	BM inventory numbers
29	leather bag with studs [?]			209a–f
30	fluted silver bowl			77, containing cowhair, 217
31	otter-fur cap			196, 216
32	silver ladle	Byzantine		90–91
33	7 burrwood bottles			128–34
34	4 knives with horn handles			162–5
35	combs	N. Germany		169–71
36	leather garment with buckles			175, 153 (double buckle), buckles 137–59 [or shoes]

HEAP B

No.	Object	Provenance	Date	BM inventory numbers
37	pillow			207, in pillow-case 186–7
38	shoes			173–4, 181, 198
39	wooden bowl			136
40	2 hanging bowls	N. Britain		111,112
41	horn cup			135
42	leather garment			
44	axe hammer			96

HEAP A

No.	Object	Provenance	Date	BM inventory numbers
45	coils of tape			188
46	mailcoat			92
47	folded twill			
48	wooden pegs			230a–c

BY EAST WALL

No.	Object	Provenance	Date	BM inventory numbers
49	cauldron 1			113
50	cauldron 2			114
51	cauldron 3			115
52	nail supporting 49			223
53	chain			167
54	nail supporting 51			225
55	tub			116
56	bucket 1			117
57	nail			221

ON THE FLOOR

No.	Object	Provenance	Date	BM inventory numbers
58	iron lamp			166, with beeswax 305
59	pottery bottle	? N. France		168
60	bucket 2			118
61	Floor covers			193–4

MOUND 2

The finds recovered in 1938 (SHSB I, 115-23) and in 1983–7 included fragments that suggested the presence in the chamber of the following items

1 An iron-bound tub (1938/17)
2 A cauldron (1987/6)
3 A blue glass jar (1938/2)
4 A sword (1938/8)
5 Parts of a baldric, including a silver buckle (1938/6), buckle fragments (1987/8), and buckle with gilt-bronze bosses (1938/3, 1987/10)
6 A shield with decorated disc mounts (1938/1, 1987/2)
7 Drinking horns with decorated mount (1938/4) and terminal (1987/5), identical to example from Mound 1 (no. 24)
8 A spear (1987/7)
9 Five knives, two in a double sheath (1938/9, 10, 11, 12)
10 Silver-mounted box or cup (1987/1)
11 Bronze bowl(s) (1987/4)
12 Textiles

Finds from cremation burials

MOUND 3 (SHSB I, 100–36)

1 Limestone plaque, 37 × 26 × 3 mm. Possibly from Alexandria. Now lost (SHSB I, 101, 112)
2 Bronze lid of ewer, diam. 45 mm, height 57 mm. Possibly from Nubia (SHSB I, 101, 113)
3 Iron axe head with wooden haft, length 188 mm, width of cutting edge 170 mm
4 Pottery sherd with incised decoration, length 90 mm. Thought to be early medieval in date. Said to be very similar in fabric, and possibly the same shape, as the pot found holding a cremation in Area A (Burial 14)
5 Pottery sherd, undecorated
6 Textile fragment and replaced textiles on iron concretion (9).
7 Six fragments of thin bone sheeting (from a casket, with chi-rho. G. Grainger and M. Henig, 'A bone casket and relief plaque from Mound 3 at Sutton Hoo', *Medieval Archaeology* 27, 1983, 136-41)
8 Fragment of decorated facing of a bone comb
9 Unidentified iron concretion carrying textile
10 Fragments of cremated bone, from an adult male human and a horse (SHSB I, 135–6)

MOUND 4 (SHSB I, 100–36)

1 Sheet bronze from a bowl
1a Textiles
2 Bone or ivory gaming counter
3 Scrap of iron slag
4 Cremated bone from an adult male, an adult female, a horse and possibly a dog (SHSB I, 135–6)

MOUND 5

1 Fragments of copper alloy bowl
2 Fragments of silver rim-binding for a wooden vessel
3 Iron shears
4 Iron knife in leather sheath
5 Fragments of bone gaming pieces (burnt)
6 Fragment of composite bone comb
7 Copper alloy rivet, perhaps from a casket

8 Ivory, perhaps part of the lid of a box for a stylus
9 Fragments of mineralised textile
10 Fragment of fused glass
11 Cremated bone of human with a skull cleft by nine blade cuts
12 Cremated animal bone, possibly of horse and sheep

MOUND 6

1 Fragments of thin-walled copper alloy bowl, with flat out-turned rim
2 Pyramidal strap-mount of copper alloy with garnet and glass inlay (found on the side of the mound)
3 Fragments of mineralised textile
4 Fragments of composite bone comb
5 Fragments of bone gaming pieces
6 Cremated human bone.
7 Cremated animal bone, possibly horse, cattle, sheep and pig.

MOUND 7

1 Fragment of silver foil from a drinking horn or cup
2 Fragments of a copper alloy cauldron
3 Fragments of iron binding from a bucket or similar object
4 Fragments of mineralised textile
5 One half of a biconical reticella glass bead, perhaps part of a sword suspension system (found on the side of the mound)
6 Fragments of bone gaming pieces
7 Fragments of a bone riveted facing, perhaps for a casket
8 Cremated human bone
9 Cremated animal bone, from horse, red deer, cattle, sheep/goat and pig.

MOUND 18

1 Fragments of a copper alloy bowl
2 Fragments of mineralised textiles
3 Fragment of a bone comb
4 Fragments of cremated human bone

Finds from inhumation burials

MOUND 14

1 Fragments of iron rings and rods and copper alloy links and pendant fittings, being the remains of a châtelaine
2 Fragment of a silver bowl
3 Fragments of silver fittings from a wide-mouthed wooden bowl
4 Fragments of silver fittings from a narrow-mouthed wooden drinking vessel
5 Fragment of a silver dress fastener
6 Two crushed beads
7 Iron nails, perhaps from a wooden box
8 Fragments of a copper alloy brooch pin
9 Fragments of copper alloy sheeting, perhaps from a cauldron
10 Fragment of iron, perhaps from an iron-bound wooden bucket
11 Fragments of textile

MOUND 17

1 Human bone from a young male.
2 Animal bone from a male horse, about 5–6 years old, standing 14 hands high
3 Coffin with four iron clamps
4 Fragments of textiles

Within the coffin
5 Sword, with horn pommel, in wooden scabbard, with associated leather, textile, iron buckle, scabbard slide with garnet settings, two pyramidal strap-mounts and silver buckle
6 Copper alloy belt-buckle, with garnet inlay
7 Frame of a leather pouch, containing a beak-shaped garnet, seven other rough-cut garnets, a millefiori fragment and a small copper alloy buckle
8/9 Knife in a leather sheath, with wood/bone/ivory handle
10 Fragment of mineralised leather with copper alloy rivet

Outside the coffin
11 Copper alloy bowl
12 Iron bound tub or bucket
13 Copper alloy cauldron
14 Shield, with central iron boss, two rivets and buckle and fragment of leather strap
15 Two iron spear-heads
16 Bone comb, double-sided
17/18 Ceramic pot
19 'Haversack' (containing ribs of lamb)

Harness at west end, F358
20 Snaffle bit, with ornamental cheek-pieces and two strap connectors attached to each side

Ornamental strap-distributors
21 Gilt-bronze disc with large axe-shaped pendant. Straps 12 mm wide cross the back of the disc at right angles
22 Gilt-bronze disc, with small axe-shaped pendant. Straps crossing back at right angles are 15 mm wide; that connecting to pendant is bifurcated. Association with strap-end 45
23 Gilt-bronze disc, with small axe-shaped pendant. Strap widths not recorded. Strap connecting to pendant is bifurcated. Association with strap-end 42.
24 Gilt-bronze disc, with small axe-shaped pendant. Strap widths not recorded
25 Gilt-bronze disc, with small axe-shaped pendant. Straps crossing back of disc at right angles are 20 mm wide
26 Small gilt-bronze axe-shaped pendant, connected by bifurcated strap 10.7 mm wide. Associated with disc and pendant 25

Strap connectors
27 Two-way strap connector with silver pendant; connecting straps 13 mm wide
28 Two-way strap connector with silver pendant; connecting straps 13 mm wide
29 Figure-of-eight connector joining two strap-mounts. Width of straps joined is 22 mm
30 Two-way strap connector joining straps of 22 mm and 18 mm width

31 Two-way strap connector joining straps of 22 mm and 21 mm
32 Three-way strap connector. Strap width measured at 10 mm
33 Iron, copper alloy and silver ring with strap-mount (strap width 21 mm) and free-running strap through the ring, strap width 21 mm

Buckles
34 Iron and copper alloy buckle fastening 11 mm wide strap
35 Iron and copper alloy buckle fastening 22 mm wide strap
36 Iron and copper alloy buckle fastening 20 mm wide strap
37 Iron buckle with 14 mm strap in the loop
38 Iron and copper alloy buckle connecting a 155 mm wide strap; loop 21.5 mm
39 Iron and copper alloy buckle with strap 20 mm wide fastened.
40 Iron and copper alloy buckle with strap 14 mm wide fastened

Strap-ends
41 Gilt-bronze strap-end with human motif. For a strap 13 mm wide
42 Gilt-bronze strap-end with human motif
43 Gilt-bronze strap-end with human motif
44 Gilt-bronze strap-end with guilloche motif. For a strap c.10 mm wide
45 Gilt-bronze strap-end with guilloche motif. For a strap 12 mm wide
46 Silver axe-shaped pendant
47 Silver axe-shaped pendant

Possibly from a saddle
48 Iron rod and wood
49 Copper nails with domed heads and wood
50 Two iron rectangular strips with wood and leather
51 Tacks associated with a leather strap 19.5 mm wide
52 Large iron buckle with strap 32 mm wide fastened
53 Tacks and leather
54 Iron curved strips on wood (oak)
55 Iron thin curved strips on wood (oak) with nail

Miscellaneous
56 Iron buckle with strap 26 mm wide fastened
57 Decorated nail or rivet
58 Decorated rivet head
59 Strap 15.75 mm wide
60 Strap 20 mm wide

Wooden tub
61 Wooden tub. Survived as stain only.

NEAR MOUND 13
Stray find of gold and garnet cylinder, perhaps from
a purse

BURIAL 56
1 Glass bead
2 Fragments of a decorated copper alloy mount
3 Skull. C14: AD 670–830

BURIAL 12
1 Copper alloy buckle
2 Iron spear-head
3 Pin

BURIAL 15
1 Copper alloy buckle and plate
2 Knife in sheath
3 Copper alloy buckle and plate, with garnet in gold cell

BURIAL 16
1 Iron châtelaine
2 Iron knife
3 Copper alloy pin with white glass bead
4 Fragments of leather purse

APPENDIX II: LOCATION OF SUTTON HOO

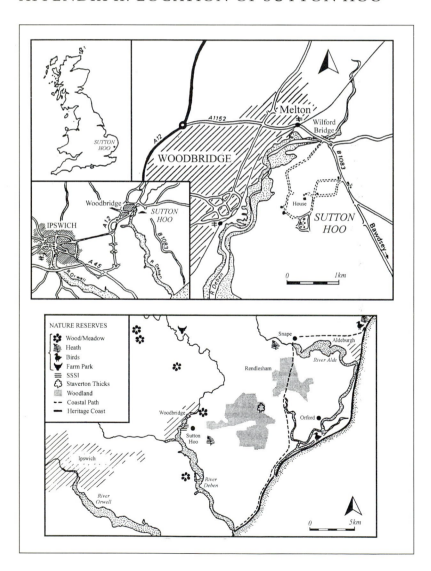

FURTHER READING

The Site

The Mound 1 discovery was published with extraordinary speed in issue 53 of *Antiquity* (1940), with a set of articles on the ship, the objects and Chadwick's identification of the burial as that of Raedwald. After the war, the British Museum published the classic guide by Rupert Bruce-Mitford (*The Sutton Hoo Ship Burial: A Handbook*, 1947, second edn 1972), which sustained Sutton Hoo's many friends and admirers for four decades. The publication of Mound 1 (R.L.S. Bruce-Mitford, *The Sutton Hoo Ship Burial*, 3 vols, British Museum Press, 1975–83; a projected fourth volume never appeared), although now out of print, remains the authoritative source for all material and ideas relating to Mound 1, and the excavations of 1938–9 and 1965–71. The prehistoric discoveries of the latter campaign are described in I. Longworth and I. A. Kinnes, *Sutton Hoo Excavations 1966, 1968–70* (British Museum Occasional Papers 23, 1980). Angela Evans *The Sutton Hoo Ship Burial* (British Museum Press, 1986) is an original account of the Mound 1 ship-burial by a member of the British Museum's Sutton Hoo research team.

Interim reports on the 1983–93 campaign were presented as it went along in the *Bulletin of the Sutton Hoo Research Committee*, published by Boydell and Brewer (omnibus edition 1993). The results of the 1983–93 campaign are to be published in M. O. H. Carver and M. R. Hummler, *Sutton Hoo; An Early Medieval Cemetery and its Context* (Society of Antiquaries Research Report, British Museum Press).

The Sutton Hoo archive is held by the British Museum.

Comparative Studies

The York 50th anniversary seminar was published as *The Age of Sutton Hoo*, edited by M. O. H. Carver (Boydell and Brewer 1992, paperback edn 1994). This contains reviews of East Anglia, England and the North Sea countries in the seventh century. Two other conferences celebrating Sutton Hoo's anniversary in 1989 produced important sets of studies relating to Sutton Hoo and its context: *Voyage to the Other World: The Legacy of Sutton Hoo*, edited by Calvin B. Kendall and Peter S. Wells (University of Minnesota Press 1992) and *Sutton Hoo: Fifty Years on*, edited by Robert Farrell and Carol Neuman de Vegvar (American Early Medieval Studies 2). Two other books which help to describe the context for Sutton Hoo for contemporary students are: *Anglo Saxon Cemeteries 1979*, edited by P. A. Rahtz, T. M. Dickinson and L. Watts (*BAR* 82: Oxford 1980) and *The Use of Grave Goods in England c.600–850* by Helen Geake (*BAR* 261: Oxford 1997). To these we should soon be able to add Stanley West's invaluable *Corpus of Anglo-Saxon Material relating to Suffolk* (East Anglian Archaeology, Gressenhall).

Visiting

At the time of writing, the site is open to the public during the summer months and guided tours for visitors are provided by the Sutton Hoo Society.

A display of the history and significance of the site is to be given at the National Trust Visitor Centre, Sutton Hoo, Woodbridge, Suffolk.

NOTES

The main sources cited are

MPG: BBC TV film *The Million Pound Grave*, directed
by Ray Sutcliffe, 1966–86

SHSB: R.L.S. Bruce-Mitford, *The Sutton Hoo Ship Burial*,
vol. I (1975), vol. II (1978), vol. III (1983),
British Museum Press

C&H: M.O.H. Carver and M.R. Hummler, *Sutton Hoo:
An Early Medieval Cemetery and its Context*,
forthcoming, British Museum Press

Chapter 1

1 Biographical sketch of Mrs Edith May Pretty by Mary
Hopkirk in *SHSB* I, xxxvi–xxxviii, supplemented by
information from relatives David Pretty, Ann Carver
(née Perkins), Andora Carver, Russell Carver and
others. Basil Brown maintained that it was Mrs Pretty's spiritualist interests which had prompted her to
open the mounds (information from Stanley West, a
Suffolk archaeologist who knew Brown well). Another
major source used for this chapter was a memoir by
Charles Phillips which was given to the author on
condition it would not be published until after his
death. It is termed here by the provisional title he gave
it: *Sutton Hoo en Pantoufles*. The full text will be
found in the Sutton Hoo Archive, x2/3.3. Some of
this material appeared in C.W. Phillips *My Life in
Archaeology* (Alan Sutton 1987) ch.7.
2 Source material used for Basil Brown includes his
diary, published by R.L.S. Bruce-Mitford as 'Basil
Brown's Diary of the Excavations at Sutton Hoo in
1938–9' in *Aspects of Anglo-Saxon Archaeology*
(Gollancz 1974), 141–69. Basil Brown's own notebook
with his watercolour paintings was also used (Ipswich
Museum). Brown referred to Mound 1 as 'Tumulus 1',
Mound 3 as 'Tumulus A', Mound 2 as 'Tumulus D',
and Mound 4 as 'Tumulus E'. Another source,
acknowledged with gratitude, was the memoir by
R. Dumbreck cited in note 3
3 Sutton Hoo Archive x2/3.4
4 This film contains classic footage of many of the
characters who appear in this chapter
5 Brown's method, according to his own citation, was
enshrined in R. Rainbird Clarke and H. Apling, 'An
Iron Age tumulus on Warborough Hill, Stiffkey,

Norfolk', *Norfolk Archaeology* 25 (1935), 408–28. This
also recommended use of a cross trench
6 Basil Brown, diary, 19 July 1938. Bruce-Mitford in
SHSB I 108 describes the shape of the Mound 3 wood
lining as 'like a butcher's carrying tray'
7 Found during the 1987 season; *C&H*, ch. 3, pt 3
8 At that date, the only early medieval ship to have been
recognised in England was that at nearby Snape,
unearthed from a mound in 1862. Some rivets from
the excavation were still kept in a little museum in
Aldeburgh, the adjacent town. The following Wednes-
day, Brown went to see them and was able to confirm
his diagnosis
9 Found during the 1987 season; *C&H*, ch. 3, pt 3
10 Phillips, *Sutton Hoo en Pantoufles*. Maynard's role
in the Mound 1 strategy remains unclear. In his letter
to Miss Allen (Archive x2/3.2) he takes the credit for
guiding Brown to a definition of the ship. Phillips,
on the other hand, says that he was away on holiday
in Cornwall during the early part of the Mound 1
excavation
11 Phillips, op. cit. in note 1, 72. Other sources report
J. Reid Moir and B. Reynolds as being present
12 *MPG*
13 *MPG*
14 *MPG*
15 Phillips, *Sutton Hoo en Pantoufles*
16 *MPG*
17 *SHSB* I, 725
18 H.M. Chadwick, 'Who was he?' *Antiquity* 53 (1940);
SHSB I, ch. 10; BL ms Vespasian BVI, f 109v.
written down in the ninth century. *SHSB* I, 693. Bede,
A History of the English Church and People (trans.
L. Sherley-Price (Penguin Books 1968) II, 5
19 *Beowulf*, trans. D. Wright (Panther Books 1957), 27–8

Chapter 2

1 The excavators of the 1965 and 1983 campaigns
discovered slit-trenches and recovered large quantities
of expended shell cases and ammunition clips, as well
as live mortar bombs and grenades. A cap-badge of the
South Wales Borderers was also found. *SHSB* I, 239
and *C&H*, ch. 6
2 Quoted in a memoir by Rupert Bruce-Mitford, entitled
40 Years with Sutton Hoo, deposited in the Sutton
Hoo Archive x2/3.5

3 Bede, *A History of the English Church and People*, trans. L. Sherley-Price (Penguin Books 1968) II, 16. *SHSB* II, 428–9

4 *SHSB* II, 340

5 A. Evans, *The Sutton Hoo Ship Burial* (BMP, 1986), 98

6 *SHSB* II, 146

7 *Beowulf*, trans. D. Wright (Panther Books 1957), 115

8 *SHSB* III, 611 ff

9 *SHSB* III, ch. 4

10 See J.P. Lamm and H.-A. Nordström (eds), *Vendel Period Studies* (National Museum of Antiquities, Stockholm, 1983) for an introduction to the cemeteries at Vendel and Valsgärde

11 T.D. Kendrick (ed.), *Evangeliorum Quattuor Codex Lindisfarnensis* (Lausanne 1960). Equally important was Bruce-Mitford's work on the Codex Amiatinus, a huge seventh-century bible shown to have been made in Northumbria and abandoned on the way to Rome in the early eighth century. R.L.S. Bruce-Mitford, 'The art of the Codex Amiatinus', *Journal of the British Archaeological Association*, Series 3, 32 (1969), 1–25

12 Ch. 1, note 18 above

13 Bede II, 5

14 Bede II, 15; II, 12

15 Bede III, 22

16 R.L.S. Bruce-Mitford, 'The Snape boat-grave', in *Aspects of Anglo-Saxon Archaeology* (Gollancz 1974), ch. 3. See Chapter 3, below, for the recent researches

17 E.g. C. Hawkes, 'Sutton Hoo: twenty-five years after', *Antiquity* 38 (1964), 252–7. J. Werner, 'Das Schiffgrab von Sutton Hoo: Forschungsgeschichte und Informationsstand zwischen 1939 und 1980', *Germania* 60 (1982), 193–209

18 *SHSB* I, II, III; R.L.S. Bruce-Mitford, *The Sutton Hoo Ship Burial: A Handbook* (BMP; edns 1947–1972); C. Green, *Sutton Hoo: The Excavation of a Royal Ship Burial* (Merlin 1988); A.C. Evans, *The Sutton Hoo Ship Burial* (BMP 1986). The British Museum's Sutton Hoo team included: Katherine East, Angela Evans, Valerie Fenwick, Marilyn Luscombe and Susan Youngs

19 *MPG*

20 P.A. Rahtz, T.M. Dickinson and L. Watts (eds), *Anglo-Saxon Cemeteries 1979* (BAR 1980); I. Hodder, *Reading the Past* (Cambridge 1986). See particularly Phillip Rahtz's paper on Sutton Hoo. His proposals to the steering committee anticipated much of what was subsequently done.

21 'We have experienced the thrill of opening a new history book, only to have it slammed shut again … The discoveries of 1939 … have turned upside down our interpretation of seventh-century history, of its cultural and economic history, the status of kings and of East Anglia, their relations to the Continent and to the Baltic, and numerous other topics. But it is also an incomplete document, torn out of the context from which it has been taken.' Christopher Brooke's address to the meeting at University College London on 15 April 1983. Sutton Hoo Archive x1/4

22 For 'total excavation' and its rationale see P.A. Barker, *Techniques of Archaeological Excavation* (Batsford 1977). Challenged in e.g. M.O.H. Carver, 'Digging for

data', in R. Francovich and D. Manacorda (eds), *Lo scavo archeologico: D'alla diagnosi all'analisi* (Siena 1990), 45–120. In essence, the new ethic returned to Sir Mortimer Wheeler's exhortation: 'have a plan'. R.E.M. Wheeler, *Still Digging* (London 1995), 231

Chapter 3

1 M.O.H. Carver, 'Sutton Hoo in context', in *Settimane di studio: Centro Italiano di studi sull'alto medioevo* 32 (Spoleto 1986), 77–123. See also the important work of J. Shephard, 'The social identity of the individual in isolated barrows and barrow cemeteries in Anglo-Saxon England', in B.C. Burnham and J. Kingsbury (eds), *Space, Hierarchy and Society* (BAR Int. Ser. 59, Oxford, 1979), 47–70, a summary of his Cambridge PhD

2 Later published in H.W. Böhme, 'Adelsgraber im Frankenreich archaeologische Zeugnisse zur Herausbildung einer Herrenschicht unter den merowingischen Konigen', *Jahrbuch des Römisch-Germanischen Zentralmuseums Mainz* 40 (1993), 397–534

3 M.O.H. Carver, 'Kingship and material culture in early Anglo-Saxon East Anglia', in S. Bassett (ed.), *The Origins of Anglo-Saxon Kingdoms* (Leicester 1989), 141–58

4 B. Hope-Taylor, *Yeavering: An Anglo-British Centre of Early Northumbria* (HMSO 1977)

5 R. Bradley, 'Time regained: the creation of continuity', *Journal of the British Archaeological Association* 140, 1–17

6 See J.P. Lamm and H.-A. Nordström (eds), *Vendel Period Studies* (National Museum of Antiquities, Stockholm 1983). For Jelling: K.J. Krogh, 'The royal Viking Age monuments at Jelling in the light of recent archaeological excavations', *Acta Archeologica* 53 (1982), 182–216. For Borre: B. Myrhe, 'The royal cemetery at Borre, Vestfold: a Norwegian centre in a European periphery' in M.O.H. Carver (ed.), *The Age of Sutton Hoo* (Boydell Press 1992), 301–314

7 The BBC films produced by Ray Sutcliffe in the Sutton Hoo series for BBC 2 were *New Beginnings*, *The Last of the Pagans and Sea Peoples*. For maritime innocence and experience, see M.O.H. Carver, 'Pre-Viking traffic in the North Sea', in S. MacGrail (ed.), *Maritime Celts, Frisians and Saxons* (Council for British Archaeology Research Report 71, 1990), 117–25, and *idem*, 'On – and off – the Edda', in O. Olsen, J.S. Madsen and F. Riek (eds), *Ship-shape: Essays for Ole Crumlin-Pedersen* (Roskilde 1995), 305–12

8 The 1989 conferences were published as follows:
Kalamazoo: R. Farrell and C. Neuman de Vegvar (eds), *Sutton Hoo: 50 Years On* (American Early Medieval Studies 2, Miami, Ohio 1992)
Minnesota: C.B. Kendall and P.S. Wells (eds), *Voyage to the Other World: The Legacy of Sutton Hoo* (University of Minnesota Press 1992)
York: M.O.H. Carver (ed.), *The Age of Sutton Hoo* (Boydell Press 1992)
The work in progress was published (more or less) annually in the *Bulletin of the Sutton Hoo Research*

Committee (Boydell Press), nos 1 (1983) to 8 (1993). This is the principal source used for this chapter

9 K. Wade, *The Archaeology of Witton* (East Anglian Archaeology 18, 1983)

10 *Bulletin of the Sutton Hoo Research Committee*, no. 4, 1986. The proposed budget was £1.35 million to the end of fieldwork. In the event expenditure was less than £1 million for the complete programme, including post-excavation costs and site management from 1983 up to 1997

11 Horizon mapping was a development of the 'horizontal section' pioneered by Hope-Taylor at Yeavering (see note 4 above). Hope-Taylor was a valued and often inspirational visitor to the site during the latest campaign at Sutton Hoo

12 Especially P. Ramquist, *Hogom I: The Excavations 1949–1984* (University of Umea 1992). Study of the bridle continues at the British Museum under the supervision of Angela Evans

13 A floor of some kind had been accepted or assumed by most commentators (*SHSB* 1, 179, 274; East 1984, 81; Evans 1986, 33). The presence of a coffin was, and remains, much more controversial. Evison (1979, 1980) proposed a large coffin (327 x 121 m) in which the body was placed on its side. Vierck (1980) saw the burial rite as a cremation placed on the Anastasius dish, and explained the clamps as belonging to a podium. The coffin was challenged by East (1984) who argued that the position of the clamps and the traces of wood and textiles they carried precluded their use in a coffin. Evans (1986, 33) preferred a slightly raised dais or bier, and Speake (1989, 11) a wagon-body. See K. East 'The Sutton Hoo Ship-Burial: a case against the coffin', *Anglo-Saxon Studies in Archaeology and History* 3 (1984), 79–84; V.I. Evison 'The body in the ship at Sutton Hoo', ibid. 1 (1979) and 'The Sutton Hoo coffin' in Rahtz *et al* (*op cit* in Ch. 2, note 20) 357–62; H. Vierck 'The cremation in the ship at Sutton Hoo: a postscript' ibid., 343–56; G. Speake *A Saxon Bed-burial on Swallowcliffe Down* (English Heritage, 1989). The coffin proposed here, developed from Evison's, is argued in *C&H* ch. 3.3.

Chapter 4

1 *C&H*, ch. 6

2 Bede, passim. 1, 16 describes the Britons in the late fifth century as trying to avoid complete extermination; at the time Bede was writing in the early eighth century, the Britons were noted as having 'a national hatred for the English', v, 23

3 H.W. Böhme, 'Das Ende der Romerherrschaft in Britanien und die angelsachsische Besiedlungs Englands im 5 Jahrhundert', *Jahrbuch des Römisch-Germanisch Zentralmuseums Mainz* 33.2 (1986), 469–574

4 S.E. West, *West Stow: The Anglo-Saxon Village* (East Anglian Archaeology 24, 1985). K. Wade, *The Archaeology of Witton* (East Anglian Archaeology 18)

5 M.O.H. Carver, *Arguments in Stone: Archaeological*

Research and the European Town in the First Millenium (Oxbow 1993)

6 Ethelbert of Kent had married a member of the Frankish royal house named Bertha (Bede 1, 25). Ian Wood has shown how Frankish pressure was brought to bear on Kent and on the incipient English kingdoms from the mid-sixth century: I.N. Wood, *The Merovingian North Sea* (Occasional Papers on Medieval Topics no. 1, Viktoria Bokforlag, Alsingsås, 1983); *idem* 'Frankish hegemony in England', in M.O.H.Carver (ed.), *The Age of Sutton Hoo* (Boydell Press 1992), 235–42

7 For Spong Hill, see C.M. Hills *et al. The Anglo-Saxon Cemetery at Spong Hill* (East Anglian Archaeology 11, 1981; 21, 1984; 34, 1984, and continuing). For Snape see now W. Filmer-Sankey, 'Snape Anglo-Saxon cemetery: the current state of knowledge,' in M.O.H. Carver (ed.), *The Age of Sutton Hoo*, 39–52

8 M.O.H. Carver, 'Kingship and material culture in early Anglo-Saxon East Anglia', in S. Bassett (ed.), *The Origins of Anglo-Saxon Kingdoms* (Leicester 1989), 141–58. For documentary sources, see Chapter 1, note 17

Chapter 5

1 Information on the settlement pattern comes from John Newman, much of whose work on the Deben Valley survey first appeared in the *Bulletin of the Sutton Hoo Research Committee* (passim). I am also grateful to Stanley West, creator of the Suffolk Archaeological Unit and excavator of West Stow, who allowed me to see his *Survey of Anglo-Saxon Suffolk* while still in preparation. The observation about the stretch of open water at Sutton Hoo was made from a boat. The water-meadows would be well-covered at high tide if it were not for the present flood barrier.

2 *C&H*, ch. 3.1. See Chapter 6 for the execution burials

3 For a list of all the finds from the Anglo-Saxon burials at Sutton Hoo, see the Appendix

4 *C&H*, ch. 3.2. A post-socket was found in the wall of the grave as if from a sloping pole. This might have been a pole-ladder like that in Fig. 90. This suggestion is owed to Rosemary Hoppitt.

5 Only one other example is known of a ship placed over the top of a chamber, and that is a later Viking burial at Hedeby: M. Müller-Wille, *Das Bootkammer-grab von Haithabu* (Berichte über die Ausgrabungen in Haithabu, 8, 1976). Angela Evans sensibly suggests that a roof would have been constructed over the chamber before the ship was dragged into place

6 *C&H*, ch. 3.3

7 See for example the portage experiments, including the use of a wheeled axle, described in E. Nylén, *Vikingaskepp mot Miklagård* (Carlssons, Borås 1987)

8 Longer than Sutton Hoo 1, at 29 m, is the Skudelev longship, radiocarbon dated to AD 810–1010. O. Olsen and O. Crumlin-Pedersen, *Five Viking Ships from Roskilde Fjord* (National Museum, Copenhagen 1985)

9 The arguments for what follows are detailed in *C&H*, ch. 3.3. The form of the chamber is based on parallels

with the Oseberg ship-burial. Phillips supposed that the chamber was constructed in situ, noting traces of 'discarded offcuts' (op. cit in Ch. 1, note 1, p. 77). The existence and form of a coffin is argued from the position of the clamps, the textile traces on the clamps, the form and the position of artefacts in the central area, the position of wood pieces and the orientation of wood grain on the clamps. Decisive was the curvature of the clamps, which also occurred in the Mound 17 burial, and there clearly derived from a burst rectilinear coffin.

10 Evans, *Sutton Hoo*, 77, 78

11 It has been suggested that the gold pieces in the purses represented the pay of the ghostly crew of forty oarsmen: P. Grierson, 'The purpose of the Sutton Hoo coins,' *Antiquity* 44 (1970), 14–18. *C&H*, ch. 3.3 find that the evidence for the number of oars is strongest at ten pairs (twenty oarsmen). Since the purse lay upside down with respect to the gold buckle, it may have been worn at the back (*contra SHSB* II, 579), or even across the back, a position echoed by the ceremonial 'dispatch case' carried on parade by a stick-orderly in the British Army

12 When the 'Honours of Scotland' (the regalia of the Scottish kings) were rediscovered by Sir Walter Scott in a chest in Edinburgh Castle, they were likewise wrapped in cloth to inhibit corrosion (Edinburgh Castle exhibition). The textiles discovered in the Mound 1 burial, and their use, are discussed by Elizabeth Crowfoot in *SHSB* III, ch. 4

13 A.M. Stahl and W.A. Oddy, 'The date of the Sutton Hoo coins', in R. Farrell and C. Neuman de Vegvar (eds), *Sutton Hoo: Fifty Years after* (American Early Medieval Studies 2, 1992), 129–48; Alan Stahl also argues that the Sutton Hoo coins can be a typical commercial assemblage of the early seventh century, rather than a symbolic selection: 'The nature of the Sutton Hoo coin parcel', in C.B. Kendall and P.S Wells (eds), *Voyage to the Other World: The Legacy of Sutton Hoo* (University of Minnesota Press 1992), 3–14. The named rulers are a Frankish monarch, Theodebert II (595–612), and two Byzantine emperors, Justin II (565–78) and Maurice Tiberius (582–602)

14 These dates calibrate to: 520–610 and 685–765 with 68% certainty, using R.M. Clark 'A calibration curve for radiocarbon dates', *Antiquity* 49 (1975), 251–66.

15 See Chapter 6

16 We do not know who was buried at Sutton Hoo; they may have been the named kings of East Anglia, although this would not of itself provide an explanation for the cemetery; see Chapter 7, questions 37, 38

Chapter 6

1 For an inventory of the burials, see the Appendix. All radiocarbon dates were provided by the British Museum laboratory, with the exception of Burial 17 (Harwell) and Burial 22 (Oxford). All dates are calibrated and at 68% confidence intervals

2 PhD thesis in preparation by Andrew Reynolds at University College London. I am most grateful to

Andrew Reynolds for discussions of his work and mine. See his 'Sutton Hoo and the archaeology of execution', *Saxon* 27 (1997) 1–3.

3 A. Young *Agriculture of the County of Suffolk* (3rd edn, 1804)

4 W.G. Arnott, *Suffolk Estuary* (Ipswich 1950), 169

5 M.O.H. Carver, 'Burial as Poetry', in E. Tyler (ed.), *Anglo-Saxon Treasure* (forthcoming, University of York)

6 The survey had been carried out sixteen years previously in 1844. This reference was rediscovered by Hugh Moffat and published in R. Hoppitt, 'Sutton Hoo 1860', *Proc Suffolk Inst. of Archaeology* 36.1 (1985), 41–2. Also R. Serjeant in *Saxon* 23 (1995), 4 for Mr Barritt.

7 *Gentleman's Magazine* 130.2 (1860), 634; *Proceedings of the Suffolk Institute for Archaeology and Natural History* 3 (1863), 410; *Journal of the British Archaeological Association* 21 (1865), 343; *Archaeological Journal* 9 (1852), 115

Chapter 7

1 For the legal status of burial mounds in England, see M.O.H. Carver, 'Burials as poetry', in E. Tyler (ed.), *Anglo-Saxon Treasure* (University of York, forthcoming)

2 I would like to record my gratitude to Mac Miles and his successors in the chair of the Society's executive committee, Robert Simper and Rosemary Hoppitt, and all the guides, especially Andrew Lovejoy, for their service to the site and its public

3 It should be gratefully acknowledged that whatever the official policy, English Heritage officers were consistently vigilant and supportive, and were instrumental in providing financial assistance to the Sutton Hoo Research Trust for the maintenance of the site through a management agreement

4 The announcement of 12 August 1997 stated: 'The National Trust has been offered the 96 hectare (232 acre) Sutton Hoo Estate, which includes the Anglo-Saxon burial site and Sutton Hoo House and stables, as a gift by the owners, the Trustees of the Annie Tranmer Charitable Trust. The grant from the Heritage Lottery Fund means that the National Trust can now accept the gift of the Estate, increase public access and adapt existing buildings to provide visitor reception and explanatory exhibitions. The exhibitions will tell the story of the Sutton Hoo burials, and the programme of excavations from the original discovery of the Sutton Hoo treasure in 1939 to more recent work carried out by Professor Martin Carver of the University of York and the Sutton Hoo Research Trust.

'As well as the exhibitions, the visitor reception area will include facilities for school and family visits, a tearoom and shop.

'A footpath network will be developed on the whole estate to increase opportunities for informal access, and views will be opened up to the River Deben which will help visitors to understand the relationship between the river and the burial site. Grazing will be re-introduced on the acid grassland to help enhance the diversity of the vegetation and the introduction of heather will be considered.

'It is hoped that the exhibitions and the footpath network will be enjoyed by over 50,000 visitors annually.'

Chapter 8

1 See P.A. Rahtz, T.M. Dickinson and L. Watts (eds), *Anglo-Saxon Cemeteries 1979* (BAR 1980), ch. 2, n. 17.

2 See, e.g., M.O.H. Carver, 'Sutton Hoo in context', in *Settimane di studio: Centro Italiano di studi sull'alto medioevo* 32 (Spoleto 1986), 77–123; M. Müller-Wille, 'Burial mounds and burial practices', in P. Pulsiano (ed.), *Medieval Scandinavia: An Encyclopaedia* (Garland 1993), 58–60; M.O.H. Carver, 'The meaning of mound-burial in Anglo-Saxon England', Festschrift for Michael Müller-Wille, forthcoming

3 For Frankish attitudes to England, see I. Wood, *The Merovingian North Sea* (Alsingås 1983); 'The Franks and Sutton Hoo', in I. Wood and N. Lund (eds), *People and Places in Northern Europe 500–1600: Essays in Honour of Peter Hayes Sawyer* (Boydell Press 1991), 1–14

4 For Childeric, see M. Müller-Wille, 'Konigtum und Adel im Spiegel der Grabfunde', in *Die Franken: Wegbereiter Europas* (Reiss-Museum Mannheim 1996), 206–21

5 M.O.H. Carver, 'Boat burial in Britain: ancient custom or political signal?', in O. Crumlin-Pedersen (ed.), *The Ship as Symbol in Prehistoric and Medieval Scandinavia* (National Museum Copenhagen 1995), 111–24

6 Bruce-Mitford believed there was a strong link with Sweden. David Wilson, 'Sweden-England', in J.P. Lamm and H.-A. Nordström (eds), *Vendel Period Studies* (National Museum, Stockholm 1983), 163–6, thought the link had been overstressed

7 *SHSB* I, 693. See also M.O.H. Carver, 'Pre-Viking traffic in the North Sea', in S. Macgrail (ed.), *Maritime Celts, Frisians and Saxons* (Council for British Archaeology Research Report 71, 1990), 117–25

8 For the dating of Mound 1 see *SHSB* I, ch. IX. *C&H*, ch. 3 for a summary of all dates

9 For a view that burial rite represents a personal religious choice, see W. Filmer-Sankey, 'Snape Anglo-Saxon cemetery: the curent state of knowledge', in M.O.H. Carver (ed.), *The Age of Sutton Hoo* (Boydell Press 1992), 39–52

10 A.J. Lawson, E.A. Martin and D. Priddy provide a survey in *The Barrows of East Anglia* (East Anglian Archaeology, 12)

11 *C&H*, ch. 5

12 *C&H*, ch. 5, 7. B. Hope-Taylor, *Yeavering: An Anglo-British Centre of Early Northumbria* (HMSO 1977), suggested that Yeavering was a long-lived 'folk-centre'; R. Bradley, 'Time regained: the creation of continuity', *Journal of the British Archaeological Association* 140, 1–17, showed that prehistoric sites could be recognised and adopted by later peoples

13 *C&H*, ch. 6; and see p. 107 for the seventh-century 'marina'

14 M. Gelling, 'A chronology for Suffolk place-names', in Carver (ed.), *The Age of Sutton Hoo*, 53–64

15 Carver, 'Sutton Hoo in context', op.cit. in Chapter 3 note 1

16 M. Mundell-Mango, C. Mango, A.C. Evans and M. Hughes, 'A 6th century Mediterranean bucket from Bromeswell Parish, Suffolk', *Antiquity* 63 (1989), 295–311. The fieldwork information is from J. Newman and J Garner-Lahire

17 See Fig. 85

18 *C&H*, ch. 3, Table 3

19 For Spong Hill, see C.M. Hills *et al.*, *The Anglo-Saxon Cemetery at Spong Hill* (East Anglian Archaeology 11, 1981; 21, 1984; 34, 1984; and continuing). For other rich burials, see J. Shephard, 'The social identity of the individual in isolated barrows and barrow cemeteries in Anglo-Saxon England', in B.C. Burnham and J. Kingsbury (eds), *Space, Hierarchy and Society* (BAR Int. Ser. 59, Oxford 1979), 47–70. L. Webster 'Death's diplomacy: Sutton Hoo in the light of other male princely burials', in R. Farrell and C. Neuman de Vegvar, *Sutton Hoo: Fifty Years On* (American Early Medieval Studies 2, 1992), 75–81. Helen Geake in her *The Use of Grave-Goods in Conversion Period England c. 600–c. 850* (BAR 261, 1997) now offers us a review of burials of all classes in the period of and following Sutton Hoo and an explanation of the use of grave goods. They are seen as refering to political leanings rather than being used to distinguish rank

20 *C&H*, ch. 7. Studies by Stanley West over many years have shown that a number of rich mounds can be suspected along the banks of the Deben and elsewhere in Suffolk, and still await full discovery. See also Question 37

21 M. Müller-Wille, 'Pferdegrab und Pferdeopfer im frühemmittelalter' *Berichten van de Rijksdienst voor het Oudheidkundig Bodemonderzoek* 20–21: 119–248; idem: 'Boat graves in Northern Europe', *International Journal of Nautical Archaeology* 3 (1974): 187–204. idem. 'Burial mounds and burial practices' in P. Pulsiano *Medieval Scandinavia. An Encyclopaedia* (Garland: New York and London), 58–60

22 Carver, 'Boat burial in Britain',

23 For Snape see Filmer-Sankey in note 9

24 H.R. Ellis-Davidson, 'Human sacrifice in the late pagan period in north-west Europe', in Carver (ed.), *The Age of Sutton Hoo*, 331–42; idem, *The Lost Beliefs of Northern Europe* (Routledge 1993), esp. ch. 1. For execution in Anglo-Saxon England, see the work of Andrew Reynolds, forthcoming and *op. cit.* in Ch. 6, note 2.

25 *C&H*, ch. 7

26 Ellis-Davidson, 'Human sacrifice'

27 The Oseberg ship-burial is published in A.W. Brogger, H.J. Falk and H. Shetilig, *Osebergfundet: Utgit av den norske stat* (Kristiana 1917)

28 P. Grierson, 'The purpose of the Sutton Hoo coins', *Antiquity* 44 (1970), 14–18; A. Stahl, 'The nature of the Sutton Hoo coin parcel', in C.B. Kendall and P.S. Wells (eds) *Voyage to the Other World: The Legacy of Sutton Hoo* (University of Minnesota Press 1992), 3–14; N. Scarfe, *Suffolk in the Middle Ages* (1986), ch. 2

29 *SHSB* 11, 428; Carver, 'Sutton Hoo in context', op.cit. in Chapter 3, note 1 for Zuran; Bede 11, 16

30 *SHSB* 11, ch. 7; G.-P. Brogiolo and L. Castelletti, *Archeologia a Monte Barro I* (Lecco 1991), pl. 59

31 See Chapter 5 above, p. 122

32 *SHSB* 1, ch. 5

33 Evans (*SHSB* 1, ch. 5) concludes that this could be a sailing ship. E. and J. Gifford, 'The sailing performance of Anglo-Saxon ships as derived from the building and trials of half-scale models of the Sutton Hoo and Graveney ship finds', *Mariner's Mirror* (1996), 131–53; *C&H*, ch. 3.3 for the structure of the chamber

34 *C&H*, ch. 3.3

35 Evans in *SHSB* 1, ch. 5. See also Carver, 'Pre-Viking traffic'

36 Charles Phillips thought the question of the presence of a body was unsolved (*op. cit* Ch. 1 note 1, 79). For chemical mapping, see P. Bethell and J.U. Smith, 'Trace element analysis of an inhumation at Sutton Hoo, using Inductively Coupled Plasma Emission Spectrometry: an evaluation of the technique applied to organic residues', *Journal of Archaeological Science* 16 (1989), 47–55; *Bulletin of the Sutton Hoo Research Committee* 6 (1989), 22. 'Forensic archaeology' has been notably developed at Bradford University, especially by Professor John Hunter

37 D. Whitelock, *The Beginnings of English Society* (Penguin Books 1952)

38 As proposed by H.M. Chadwick in 1940 and Bruce-Mitford in *SHSB* 1, ch. 10; *C&H*, ch. 7, n. 40 for the citations of all the other candidates

39 M. Parker-Pearson, R. van de Noort and A. Woolf, 'Three men and a boat: Sutton Hoo and the East Anglian kingdom', *Anglo-Saxon England* 22 (1993), 27–50, suggested that Sutton Hoo was the burial ground of the kings of Essex. In addition to the reasons against this notion already given, the conjecture has little support from the character of fifth–seventh century artefacts distributed in Essex and Suffolk. Information from S. West and J. Newman of the Suffolk Archaeological Unit

40 Carver, 'Pre-Viking traffic'

41 Carver (ed.), *The Age of Sutton Hoo*; P. Ramquist, *Hogom I: The Excavations 1949–1984* (University of Umeå 1992)

42 M.O.H. Carver, 'Burial as poetry', in E. Tyler (ed.), *Anglo-Saxon Treasure* (University of York, forthcoming). I. Hodder, *Reading the Past* (Cambridge 1986), enjoined archaeologists to read their findings as a text, rather than as a fact. His ideas have proved to have their most useful application in cemetery studies. R. Frank, 'Sutton Hoo and Beowulf: the odd couple', in Kendall and Wells (eds), *Voyage to the Other World*, 47–64 shows how the interpretations of Sutton Hoo and *Beowulf* have exploited each other. Sam Newton has made a case for placing the composition of *Beowulf* in eighth-century East Anglia: *The Origins of Beowulf and the Kingdom of East Anglia* (Boydells 1993).

43 The East Anglian Kingdom Survey, initiated by the Sutton Hoo project, was a project designed to discover the settlement and economy of early Anglo-Saxon East Anglia

44 See B. Marsden, *The Early Barrow Diggers* (London 1974)

45 See SHSB 1, 155 for the removal of soil at the west end. *C&H*, ch. 6 interpret this as due to sixteenth-century ploughing.

46 *op cit* in Chapter 1, note 1

47 M.O.H. Carver, 'Digging for data', in R. Francovich and D. Manacorda, *Lo scavo archeologico: D'alla diagnosi all'analisi* (Siena 1990), 45–120

48 *Bulletin of the Sutton Hoo Research Committee* 4.

49 A record of the techniques that were tried out during the project will be found in the *Bulletins*

50 For Field Research Procedure see Carver, 'Digging for data' and M.O.H. Carver and N. Rothschild, *Field Archaeology*, forthcoming.

INDEX